EAST ASIAN HISTORICAL MONOGRAPHS

General Editor: WANG GUNGWU

ADAT LAW IN
MODERN INDONESIA

ADAT LAW IN MODERN INDONESIA

M. B. HOOKER

KUALA LUMPUR
OXFORD UNIVERSITY PRESS
OXFORD NEW YORK JAKARTA
1978

Oxford University Press
OXFORD LONDON GLASGOW
NEW YORK TORONTO MELBOURNE WELLINGTON
KUALA LUMPUR SINGAPORE JAKARTA HONG KONG TOKYO
DELHI BOMBAY CALCUTTA MADRAS KARACHI
IBADAN NAIROBI DAR ES SALAAM CAPE TOWN

● *Oxford University Press 1978*

All rights reserved. No part of this publication may be reproduced, stored in a retrieval system, or transmitted, in any form or by any means, electronic, mechanical, photocopying, recording or otherwise, without the prior permission of Oxford University Press

ISBN 0 19 580394 9

*Printed by Charles Grenier Sdn. Bhd., Petaling Jaya
Bound by Art Printing Works Sdn. Bhd., Kuala Lumpur
Published by Oxford University Press, 3, Jalan 13/3,
Petaling Jaya, Selangor, Malaysia*

PREFACE

THIS book is concerned with the place of adat in modern Indonesia. Adat no longer constitutes the only law for the autochthonous Indonesian, it is now one of a number of sources of law. The organs and institutions of the state are predicated upon the legal equality of all citizens of Indonesia and these institutions are directing the state toward an economic and social system which is not in accord with the traditional principles of adat. In this context, it is the whole sphere of adat which is in question; we speak, therefore, of adat *law* and not of adat *laws*. Our concern is not with the study of the particular adat systems which the earlier generations of Dutch scholars did so much to establish, but with the present status of adat in the modern Indonesian legal system. Although adat remains an important manifestation of the Indonesian cultures, its present status is uncertain. It undoubtedly has a part to play in modern Indonesia but what this will be depends very much upon how adat is defined for purposes of the Indonesian legal system. The chapters in this book are all, in their own individual ways, attempts at such a definition. They can be only a summary in the space available; a number of volumes could and should be written on the topics treated in this book. I feel, however, that the most important task is to isolate the issues involving adat and, in so doing, to contribute to the further development of Indonesian law.

It is customary in lawbooks to give a date up to which the contents are accurate. I am unable to do this here because not all legislation and regulations on the topics covered were published when this book went to press. I do claim a relative degree of completeness up to about the middle of 1974. The addition of some legislation and regulations of 1975–6 is not a complete treatment for those years and later material has not yet become available.

Research in Indonesia was supported by a grant made available by the Faculty of Social Sciences, University of Kent at Canterbury, to which I am very grateful. I should also like to acknowledge the hospitality and help of Professor and Mrs. Moh Koesnoe of Surabaya and Judge and Mrs. Ali Boediarto of Malang. I was fortunate enough to know the late Raden Mas M. M. Djojodigoeno to whose memory all adat scholars owe a considerable debt.

PREFACE

I am especially indebted to Puan Shaikha Zakaria who provided some of the material on which Chapter 7 is based, and to Professor Geert van den Steenhoven who read an early draft and made many useful corrections and suggestions. However, any mistakes or omissions lie wholly with me.

Eliot College, M. B. HOOKER
University of Kent at Canterbury,
April 1977

CONTENTS

Preface	v
INTRODUCTION: ADAT AND INDONESIAN LAW	1
1. THE STATE AND ADAT	9
Introduction	9
The Colonial State and Adat	11
Adat in the Republik Indonesia	20
Summary	29
2. THE SOCIAL CONSTRUCTION OF ADAT	33
Introduction	33
The Definition of Adat Systems	34
The Definition of Adat as Law	41
Summary	48
3. ADAT IN LEGAL THOUGHT	50
Introduction	50
Adat Thought in Indigenous Culture	51
Dutch Legal Thought on the Adats	56
Contemporary Legal Thought on Adat	62
4. ADAT AND INDONESIAN LEGAL PLURALISM	70
Introduction	70
Adat in the Plural Law System	72
Adat Law in the Context of Pluralism	79
Summary	87
5. ADAT AND ISLAM	91
Introduction	91
Adat and Islam in the State—Colonial Period	93
Adat and Islam in Legal Pluralism—Contemporary Indonesia	98

Summary: Islam and Adat in Contemporary Legal
    Thought   106

6. ADAT AND THE LEGISLATURE   111
    Introduction   111
    Adat, Law Reform, and the Basic Agrarian Law   112
    Adat Rights and Statutory Rights in Land   118
    Summary   123

7. ADAT AND THE COURTS   127
    Introduction   127
    Stability and Change in Adat   129
    Judicial Innovation   134

8. ADAT AND VILLAGE JUSTICE: AN
    ISSUE IN THE ETHNOGRAPHY OF LAW   140
    Introduction   140
    The Ontology of Village Justice   141
    The Structure of Village Justice   145
    Summary   151

Bibliography   154
Index   167

INTRODUCTION: ADAT AND INDONESIAN LAW

THE peoples of Indonesia include a variety of cultural and linguistic groups each with its own adat (law). The present state is characterized by a pluralism of language, culture and law, and so it has been throughout Indonesian history. Legal pluralism was formalized by the Dutch colonial authorities on the basis of race, giving rise to a system under which each racial group was governed by its own laws. For the autochthonous Indonesian this meant adat, and just as there was a diversity of cultures so there was a diversity of adats—seventeen in all—in Indonesia. The Dutch created 'adat law areas' (*adatrechtskring*) so as to organize the plurality of adats, and these divisions remain, with some change, as provinces in the independent Republik Indonesia.

Since the formation of the Republik at the close of the Second World War, legal policy has been directed toward eliminating the racial divisions upon which the colonial legal system was based. The administration of the law has been unified and the distinction between Native land and European land has been swept away. In other areas, notably family law, progress has been much slower. The goal of a national unified legal system has not been achieved and debate has revolved around such issues as pluralism versus unity and tradition versus modernity as suitable bases for a national law. The place of the adats has been of central concern in these debates and, so far as adat is concerned, the discussion has been distinguished more for its eclecticism than for its coherence. Discussion has often been carried out on an insufficient knowledge of adat. This is largely a consequence of the debate being 'city-centred'; the proponents of the modernizing Western-based law are, in the main, practitioners and professional men whose knowledge of law and life outside the cities tends to be somewhat limited. This was well expressed two decades ago by a noted scholar as follows:[1]

It was quickly evident that information regarding the status of adat law was indeed limited from the date of outbreak of the war. Many were prepared, however, to speculate on the future of adat law. On this topic opinions ranged from the one extreme to the other....

Arriving at Djakarta the situation was found to be little different. There had long been no sign of adat law in this urban centre. There was little knowledge in Djakarta of the present scope of adat throughout the archipelago. The old guard confidently believed that adat law would continue, certainly among the masses in rural areas. In spite of the introduction of western codes they held that adat would remain the basis of village administration of justice. A leading Indonesian authority of adat law anticipated that it would remain supreme in the fields of family law and succession, but he foresaw the fashioning of a new agrarian (property) law and he felt that the law of obligations and labor would be legislated, that is, westernized. The younger group of Indonesian Republicans on the other hand saw no place whatsoever for adat law. To these young men adat was age-old tradition imposed upon the people. In the future Indonesia the individual would come to the fore, he himself would determine what was to be the law rather than follow what had been prescribed by ancestors.

It was apparent that there was no predictability about the future of adat law. Neither was there extensive knowledge of the scope of adat in the present. As a matter of fact at the moment little interest was evidenced in this subject.

The present position is little different from that described in this passage.

Second, it is now commonly accepted that, in some fields of law, particularly those related to economic development, a divorce can properly be maintained between the sphere of adat, *i.e.* rural Indonesia, and the sphere of modern economic law which is largely city based. For example, in a recent study of the legal issues arising out of development finance in Indonesia, one reads that:[2]

Securities under *adat* law have little relevance as securities for modern development finance because they are limited to transactions between autochthonous Indonesians.

However true this might be in strictly technical terms, it implies that adat has no place in the economic development of Indonesia. This is an implication which must be firmly rejected. Firstly, there is no evidence for it; secondly, if it is believed, it will result in the sort of short-term entrepreneurial type of development which is largely exploitative and for the benefit of the foreign multi-national corporation. There is evidence that this is taking place at the moment.[3] Thirdly, it ignores the fact that economic and financial development, to be of true benefit, must extend to the rural areas. Adat is, therefore, involved and there must be at least some accommodation with adat. Bland statements that adat is 'not necessary' or 'is not relevant' can do nothing but lead to immense difficulty in the future.

This introduces us to the issues of the definitions of law and of adat; in Indonesia the situation is one in which some sort of definition is required as a matter of practical legal necessity. Despite the post-war surge of adat literature[4] this is a question which, with the odd exception,[5] has never been squarely faced. Given the complexity of the legal situation in Indonesia it is essential that some attempt be made although, as with so much else in Indonesia, any answers can only be tentative.

Most of the present definitions of law or projections of what legal policy should be in Indonesia are unsatisfactory because the general issue of what a definition is and what it is supposed to accomplish has never been properly explained. To a large extent this accounts for the divergencies and difficulties which are encountered in contemporary adat thought, particularly when one bears in mind that the preservation of adat was a plank of colonial legal policy but it is such no longer in the Republik Indonesia, although *as a fact* the majority of the population is subject to adat. Such an ambiguous situation makes it all the more urgent and necessary that attention be given to definition while keeping in mind the peculiar nature of the Indonesian situation. There are three questions which must be answered:

(i) What is the law which constitutes the effective system of obligation for the bulk of the Indonesian people? What is the legal system in reality? The answer is adat in one of its several forms. If one wishes to confine the definition of adat to the formal legal process, that is, to judicial determination, this answer is still descriptive of reality. The law governing the incidents of peasant life in the courts is still adat law.

(ii) Given the foregoing, is it true to say that adat is prescriptively valid and is the only system of obligation in Indonesia with this characteristic? The answer here is much less clear; adat is prescriptively valid in so far as it forms the basis of judicial decision and is contained in legislation. On the other hand, there is legislation which limits adat rights (e.g. the Basic Agrarian Law of 1960) but that legislation itself is not fully operable for administrative reasons. Consequently, the adat persists, that is, it is *descriptively* valid although formally limited.

(iii) Finally are the answers indicated to the two foregoing questions consistent with the theories of justice and social purpose[6] adopted as proper in Indonesia? Again, the answer is unclear. The political history of Indonesia since independence has been confused; not only have the interpretations of social and political purpose varied widely but the politics of legal development likewise have not been consistent.[7]

These issues are all raised in acute form in attempted modernizations of law, as for example in land law.[8] Herein lies the problem; what in the light of (i)—(iii) above is to be the status and definition of adat?

This issue is not of interest to jurists alone but has a very real relevance to actual legal practice both for the courts and for the legislature as well as for the executive administration in the state. The essential question is obviously whether or not lapses from the official law and its rejection in favour of adat forms part of the state legal system. Even where this system includes within itself principles from adat systems the question of precise scope remains a continuing problem. The solution is not wholly a matter of law nor wholly a matter of fact. In some fields it is possible to specify that one or the other applies but no general specification over the whole range of the legal system is possible. Even where a legislative or judicial statement on this point is found as a matter of law, this does not mean that the problem is always decided on the court's conception of the legal system. Other legal considerations may be involved, but whether this is so or not cannot be gathered from a decision as such, though it may be obtained from the arguments used to justify the decision.[9] For example, is the fact that adat must be proved by expert witnesses an indication that it is not part of the legal system under which the courts operate? A question such as this cannot be answered on a general basis because each solution may bear different legal consequences and might well be guided by different considerations.

It is possible, however, to isolate three main issues which bear upon the question of definition in the adat context.

(a) *The relation between the existence of a law and its efficacy.* There are two extreme positions on this question: first, there is the claim that a law created in the appropriate manner exists and is valid. Its efficacy or inefficacy does not affect its existence or validity. The opposing position is that laws exist because and to the extent that they are socially accepted and followed. Social customs are laws even if not enacted whereas enacted law has no validity if it is not part of social practice.[10] In addition, there have been and are compromise positions of which Kelsen's is perhaps the best known. He says:[11]

A general legal norm is regarded as valid only if the human behaviour that is regulated by it actually conforms with it, at least to some degree. A norm that is not obeyed by anybody anywhere, in other words a norm that is not effective at least to some degree, is not regarded as a valid legal norm. A minimum of effectiveness is a condition of validity.

Each of these positions has an important element of truth in it; laws guide behaviour and also provide standards for the evaluation of action. A lack of knowledge of law obviously precludes the law from acting as a guide to behaviour. At the same time there are social practices which also guide behaviour but which are not laws in the sense of statute, but they may affect the decisions of the court sometimes even without the judges even being aware of this.

Against these arguments is the view that although both law and social practice guide behaviour, the two should not be coalesced. Social practice differs from law because it is not institutionalized and practice is not law until recognized by the courts. This is an important argument in the plural law field. Its importance lies in the fact that the national legal system is dominant and therefore exclusive; it cannot admit social practice as valid law except upon its own premises, for to admit the validity of social practice without more is tantamount to discarding the dominant-servient division. Whatever may be the case in unified legal systems, the issue in the plural law field is one of *legal politics*. It seems fairly clear from the data adduced in this book that the relevant factors in deciding the issue are not solely to be derived from the characteristics of law as described in legal theory alone. On the contrary, the primary factor which will determine the issue must be located in the particular reason for the lack of implementation of the institutional law. It may be because the legal administration is inefficient either at the national or the local level. It may be because the institutional laws of the national system are epistemologically meaningless to the intended recipients. In both these cases, the intention of the institutional system is clearly not to admit social practice. On the other hand, the lack of application may be the result of a positive policy to limit the application of institutional law and so admit social practice. In all of these situations the deciding factor is a matter of legal politics. This brings us to the second main issue—the relation of law and state.

(b) *The relation of law and state.*[12] The relation between the law and the state raises in its most immediate form the question of the scope of the national legal system. Every state has one legal system which constitutes the law of that state. At the same time the state is a political system which is part of a comprehensive social system. The legal system is only part of the norms constituting the political system and the latter includes numerous non-legal norms. It is a characteristic of the state system that it provides a backing or support for its own system of institutionalized law. But the state system also has a further function and this is to maintain and support the norms of other forms of social groupings. In a municipal Western law system this includes supporting the agreements and customs of private persons and associations. In the Indonesian situation this function of the state is also present and it may give positive support to such norms. It may also allow, either expressly or implicitly, the continuance of a normative system contrary to its own institutional law not for the sake of the normative system as such, but because an attack on that system would result in an attack on a social grouping which it is the state's duty to support. The precise degree of support varies from time to time and from place to place and is conditioned by such factors as the efficiency of the state system as a whole, the needs for reform or social change and the role which the state sees the institutions of law as having in relation to political power.

(c) *The courts and plural law*.[13] In any legal system the courts have a duty to apply the laws of the system when they are applicable but there may be and are cases in which there is no clear solution as to application. In the plural law context this typically arises when norms, such as adat, are sources of law for portions of the population, but there is no valid law recognizing this. In this case there is a duty upon the court to resolve such a conflict; the exercise of this duty may be guided by some procedural or constitutional provision such as the 'justice, equity and good conscience' provision or by the civil law provision that the judge is to consider himself a legislator. On the other hand instructions such as these may exist in the practice of the courts alone. In either situation the relevance of distinction between the institutional law and some other law is minimal. It is a matter of evidence in each particular case whether one can say that a norm is enforced because it is part of 'the law' or because of the duty of the court to support other social norms in the solution of conflict.

It is therefore crucial in understanding the plural law situation that we understand the function of the law-applying institution rather than the law-creating institution. There are several reasons for this:

First, although law-creating institutions are of the greatest importance in modern society this is only partially true in Indonesia. This relative lack of importance is due to many factors of which the most important seems to be that there is little in the way of an effective communication and administration of institutional law.

Second, since the Indonesian legal system is a system of diverse *sources* of law, the only way to determine which are the relevant sources or proper sources or even institutional sources is a resort to the law-applying organ, that is, the court. It is in the court that these questions are answered and it is here that fact and law meet.

Third, if we admit that law guides behaviour by stipulating consequences, then it is clear that the law-applying organ must be a focus because this is the institution which ultimately enforces such consequences. This point also returns us to our earlier description of efficacy, and according to this approach the existence of a law is logically related to the practice of the law-applying organ.

Finally, we should not forget that laws, from whatever sources, are normative and guide the actions of the courts as much as they guide the actions of ordinary people. Their existence is therefore based in social practice and this is common to all positive norms.

These comments raise the question of identifying the law-applying organ. In our own societies we are accustomed to a variety of such organs—the courts, tribunals of various sorts, and so on. These bodies, however, all have one thing in common, and this is that they are part of an institutionalized hierarchy. Such exist in Indonesia but in addition there are other forums of justice such as the village and kinship administration of justice.[14] These tribunals administer the adat rules of a locality.

The trend of the foregoing tends to the view that law may usefully be considered not as an ultimate value in itself but as a means of realizing other values, including a variety of social and political goals. The law may be regarded as a medium or instrument of social and political worth which need not necessarily have an intrinsic value. It should be obvious that this view clearly distinguishes the instrumental value of law, on the one hand, from the value intrinsic goals that law is used to serve on the other. This is not always as easy to accomplish in practice as it is to put on paper for the reason that the law's value as a medium is often transposed to become an ultimate value. Very often this is a consequence of the conviction or experience that it is better to have some law rather than no law at all.

The proper utilization of law as an instrument depends primarily upon two factors. First, the prescriptive and descriptive roles of law must correspond to a satisfactory degree. That is to say, the methods of thought and conceptions of reality of the population must be adequately represented in the principles and procedures of the legal system. The bodies of native law and custom in the colonial system represented this factor even though in many cases distortion did arise. This distortion was partially the result of the autonomous character of law, even as an instrumen.. The second major factor in the proper utilization of law is that it must fit in with the complex of external conditions, economic, technical, ecological and so on, within which its subjects find their existence. The initial problem is to establish what the goals of the social and political development are to be and this is a matter of (value) choice which must be exercised by the government concerned. It seems now fairly well established that the more or less consistent goal is 'development', by which is meant the attainment of some degree of economic sufficiency and social egalitarianism. The precise nature of these varies from one society to another and within the same society over a period of time. Having established as exactly as possible what it is that these terms mean, the second problem is to decide how the law is to be properly utilized in this aim. The alternatives are (a) the continuation of the plural systems or (b) the abolition of the plural system in favour of some model, either Western or Socialist, of a unified law. The actual choices made in the contemporary world vary from state to state and, in some cases, include a compromise between the two major alternatives.

It is clear from the data in this book that complete change has not been demanded in all aspects of life. Even so far as status, legal personality, obligation and so on are concerned, the state system has not in general demanded total change. On the contrary, it has applied or allowed selected parts of the adat systems to continue. The chapters of this book each deal with a different aspect of adat in modern Indonesia in which the issues just indicated are dealt with in detail.

1. Schiller, 1955: 2–3.
2. Gautama et al., 1973: 104.
3. Mostly through the so-called 'Contract of Work' which is an agreement between the Indonesian Government and a foreign corporation for the exploitation of Indonesian resources, particularly mineral resources.
4. See Chapter 3.
5. See, for example, Djojodigoeno (1971).
6. See, for example, Tasrif (1971) on the rule of law in the 'New Order' Indonesia.
7. See Chapter 7.
8. See Chapter 6.
9. See Chapter 7.
10. See Chapter 8 where this question is discussed.
11. Cited in Raz, 1971: 801–2.
12. See Chapter 1.
13. See Chapter 7.
14. See Chapter 8.

1

THE STATE AND ADAT

Introduction

WHEN one speaks of the 'state' in Indonesia one is referring to at least three distinct entities—the pre-colonial, the colonial and the modern states. Each of these systems of government is quite distinct from the others and even within them a variety of important sub-categories exists. For example, in the pre-colonial period one must distinguish between the forms of government characteristic of Majapahit and the later developments in Muslim Mataram and in the Islamic sultanates of North Sumatra. Similarly, during the period of Dutch rule important constitutional distinctions existed between the directly governed and indirectly governed territories. In the independent Republik Indonesia the new idea of the 'nation state' based upon a constitutional form of government was introduced. These distinctions must be kept in mind so far as adat is concerned, particularly as it is true that it is only in the colonial and contemporary periods that political boundaries have determined both the scope and nature of adat. This of course is not to deny that the adat systems had a relationship with the institutions of the princely powers before the Dutch period; as Pigeaud illustrates in his discussion of the Jaya Song Decree,[1] the system of justice in Majapahit did take account of and affirm adat rules. However, the royal groups in Java, Acheh, Palembang, Jambi, in the Malay lands of Sumatra and Borneo and in the Celebes, Ternate, Tidore, the Timors and Bali and Lombok governed their internal conduct by their own special sets of rules. They were, to a large degree, legally divorced from the populations amongst whom they existed. At the same time there were important points of contact between them as in taxation and local levies.[2] A more important factor was that the royal ruler, whether indigenous or alien, was a religious and ritual figure whose existence and well-being was vital to the welfare of 'his' people who owed him a loyalty and submission the extent of which should not be underestimated.[3] The honorifics commonly borne by the rulers of all the princedoms bear witness to their ritual and cosmic significance. Their actual influence on the adat rules by which the great mass of their populations lived was, however, quite slight. This was so even in those kingdoms which produced complex and lengthy legal texts. One needs only to read the texts of Majapahit[4] and Mataram[5] to realize why this was so. In all cases, and not excluding the later Islamic sultanates,[6] the point of such texts was not properly to provide a workable code of laws but to present a view of sovereignty which was an explanation for the existence of a royal group and a justification of its rule for subject and ruler alike. They also served a subsidiary purpose of legitimizing the status and position of the text patron. The idea of the nation state as such was conspicuously absent; the issue was the nature of the relationship between the people, the ruler and the cosmos. The introduction of Islam did little to change this function, at least insofar as the texts were concerned.

It was not until the full establishment of the Dutch as a colonial power in the bulk of the Indonesian territories (excluding the self-governing territories) that this notion became obsolete. The new situation introduced the government of the whole Indonesian territory on a unitary basis. This of course did not occur overnight—indeed it was not until well into this century that this rule was fully established. Its consequences were enormous for adat; for the first time there was a direct and immediate connection between each adat and the legislative, judicial and executive arms of government.

In the post-war period the relationship between adat and the state has become more complex. Many of the Dutch colonial administrative mechanics have been dismantled, most notably the law area (*rechtskringen*) and the native court (*landraad*). Adat as such is not administered by the Republic of Indonesia government but, on the other hand, many of the contemporary economic and social policies (such as land reform) have had an immediate impact in the adat world. In addition, the Indonesian is now a citizen in the Republic, he is subject to its laws and may, as through the franchise, affect the composition of government (at least in theory). His adat may also be limited by legislation and may be declared invalid if it runs contrary to the Republic's Constitution.

For about the last century or so, therefore, adat and the state have been intimately connected, and this connection is likely to persist in the future. The aim of this chapter is to describe the main features of this connection in both colonial and contemporary Indonesia.

The Colonial State and Adat

During the first century of the (Netherlands) East India Company's rule in Java, control over the native inhabitants was partially exercised through Dutch rule and partially by an indigenous élite supported by the Company, and generally known as 'Regents'. The judicial administration even in these early days was a plural system, with law courts for the Europeans and indigenous tribunals for the natives. The former administered Dutch law with local modifications, but in the Ommelanden of Batavia a 'Commissioner for Native Affairs' came to exercise extensive judicial power as did a Landraad for the north-east coast set up in 1747 which applied native law so far as consonant with European ideas. This, however, was an exception to the general rule of non-interference in native legal affairs except insofar as the Company used the Regents and so, by its support, allowed them a much greater freedom of action than would otherwise have been possible. This, as we shall see below, had important consequences.

The transition of government from Company to State[7] at the end of the eighteenth century was accompanied by several administrative reforms, notably those initiated by Governor-General Daendels who took office in 1808. He divided the colonial territory into Praefectures for whom the Regents, as 'officers of the King', were to accept instructions although they were to derive their emoluments from the land and the native population and not by way of salary. He also set up a *landgerichte* or native court for each Praefecture with a Bench of Regents and the Praefect as their Chairman. In addition there was a Supreme Court and a Court of Aldermen applying Dutch law for the Europeans. The system was thus dual with different courts and separate law and procedure for Europeans and Javanese.

Java came under British control in 1811 as a consequence of the Napoleonic wars, and Raffles, the founder of Singapore, was appointed Lieutenant-Governor. The British interregnum is important because Raffles not only carried on Daendel's reforms but built upon them and, in the land question, provided a new departure for later Dutch administration. Raffles took over the Praefectures but substituted the term 'Residency'; he re-named the Regencies 'Districts' and the Regent now became a mere District Officer who no longer sat on the Bench in native cases although he might be present in an advisory capacity. The District Officer had jurisdiction in petty matters in his district but no criminal powers. In fact, Raffles took great care to deprive the Regent of all political or other influence. Important as this reform was, Raffles is mainly remembered for his land policy in Java. The object of this was to confer upon the inhabitants a private property in land and to take from this, in the form of a 'land rent', an increased state revenue. To accomplish this Raffles undertook an enquiry into land tenure and 'discovered' that all land was the property of the (indigenous) state. In addition, the village was considered the basic unit of administration because from time immemorial the headman had charge of all matters concerning its members including land, taxation and the services required from a Javanese village. He also found that the village headman was at once the representative of the village and could be made the agent of government. The village and land systems then formed the basis of his judicial system in respect of the natives. Raffles aimed at taking in 'rent' the value in cash of two-fifths of the gross produce. Irrespective of whether or not this actually increased the revenues of the government, and there is evidence that the system did not do for the Javanese economy what Raffles had planned,[8] the important thing was the subsequent classification of land as *state property*, something quite foreign to Indonesian legal thought.

On the cessation of the Napoleonic wars in Europe, a new Constitution had been drafted for the Netherlands in 1814, and this provided that the colonies, which had been returned to the Dutch, were to be governed by the Crown. Three High Commissioners were appointed and provided with a Constitutional Regulation (*Regeringsreglement*) by the home government in 1815. This was drafted in liberal terms and looked to the preservation of native welfare as well as to the introduction of a land revenue system. The High Commissioners decided to continue Raffles's land scheme, though with various improvements, and in 1818 published the important Regeringsreglement of that year, the general effect of which was to adopt parts of Raffles's land system but which also re-introduced the earlier Dutch principle of the separation of the races. This was emphasized by the creation of Landraad, native courts, in the reconstituted Regency (i.e. Raffles's 'Districts') and the Regents now became salaried employees of the government. Police matters relating to the natives were delegated to the Regents: in fact, as Furnivall says,[9] the rule was that 'like over like is welcome' (*soort over soort genade is*). Under Raffles, the Regent was subordinate to the Resident and although this was continued, the Resident was now directed to treat the Regent as a 'younger brother' and not just as a mere subordinate; however, in fact, the Regent was all but excluded from administrative routine. This continued to be the situation up until the middle of the 1830s, but by then economic conditions had forced upon the colonial government a series of restrictive measures to combat poverty, unrest and increasing crime.[10] This was dealt with in a new Regeringsreglement of 1836, Art. 80 of which provided that the native population should be left under the government of their own headmen. This was reinforced by further regulations for police and judicial matters, and in 1848 a new Code of Police and Criminal Procedure for the natives appeared. Consonant with past Dutch practice, this was a matter for the executive, not the judiciary, and placed extensive police power in the hands of the Regent. Subordinate native officers, such as Village Heads and District Officers, came directly under the Regent instead of, as in 1819, directly under the Resident, and the Regent was given criminal jurisdiction. It was followed by the recognition of the hereditary claims of the Regents and the granting to them of lands. All this tended toward the restoration of their prestige so sadly dented from the time of Raffles onward. By 1848, the pattern of administration for the colony was set for the rest of the colonial period. The definition of land classification and the village system was settled, a dual administration in laws had been set up and the position of the Regent consolidated.

The next development of note took place in 1848 when the Netherlands received a new constitution drafted on liberal lines. This resulted in a new Regeringsreglement for the Indies promulgated in 1854. In this, the by now traditional plural organization was again affirmed with the natives being left under their own appointed or recognized heads. This was, however, the first constitutional recognition of the position of the natives in a dual organization in which they were subjected only to laws drafted in accordance with that constitution. The Regulation, however, left much to be legislated for by subsequent acts or decrees. It did not, for example, settle the status of the Regent nor did it deal in detail with land matters. This had to await the Agrarian law of 1870 which amended and added to Art. 62 of the Regulation of 1854. Although it guaranteed existing customary rights over land, it affirmed, for the first time in legal form, Raffles's principle that all land was state land (*domein van den staat*) including land held by natives. It thus became necessary to distinguish between Free land, that is, State land free of native rights, and Unfree land, which was State land subject to native rights. This was followed by a Crown Ordinance in 1875[11] prohibiting the alienation of native land to foreigners, although by a later Crown Ordinance in 1885 it became possible to convert native tenure into private ownership under Dutch civil law. A new Penal Code for natives came into force in 1872 so that there was now a complete dualism of legal organization. In addition, the bureaucracy continued to grow and included, amongst others, a Department of Education, Religion and Industry in 1866, and a Department of Justice in 1870. New regulations were given out on the duties of Resident and Regent in 1867[12] which in the main were a re-arrangement of earlier instructions.[13] A new provision of note for the Regent was the instruction to maintain a register of native 'priests' so that no one should assume the title without the Regent's authority. Further regulations laid the foundation of a Native Civil Service[14] but the Regent still represented government to the natives and still remained the 'younger brother' of the Resident. However, in 1867, he was deprived of the lands he held as part of his office and in 1882 he lost the right to claim personal services (*pantjendiensten*) of his people.

The position described so far pertained almost entirely to Java, but by the turn of the century internal Netherlands political and economic factors[15] were forcing attention to the Outer Provinces while at the same time requiring that in the government of such lands the colony rely more upon its own resources. This meant decentralization of control from the Netherlands to Batavia, but at the same time account had to be taken of the new socialist impulses influential in the Netherlands. In addition, a new Islamic policy had succeeded in putting an end to the wars in Sumatra in 1908 and the by now generally peaceful situation made possible a formula by which the various native states in the Outer Provinces regulated their relationships with the colonial government. This was governed by a document known as the Short Contract, and by 1927 out of 282 states, 267 were parties to such a contract.

The stable conditions to which these provisions of government had given rise allowed the introduction and development of a new colonial policy, the so-called 'Ethical Policy'. This originated in the then new socialist impulses in the Netherlands itself and saw the colonial situation as being one wherein the colonial power held a position of trust for the betterment of the indigenous conditions of life. At the same time, that is at about the turn of the century, the Ethical Policy coincided with the rise of nationalist sentiment in Indonesia, much of which was Muslim inspired. These twin influences had important repercussions on legal organization. The most interesting was the formation of the *Volksraad* in 1916. This included native members although these were mostly at least indirect nominees. As a body it had no formal law-making powers but as a forum for debates it provided such criticism of the colonial government that a Revisional Commission on the question of the relation between Indonesia and the Netherlands was set up with the cooperation of the *Volksraad*. The reforms eventually proposed resulted in a reconstituted *Volksraad* in 1927, and the most important powers of this body were that its assent was necessary for the budget and for legislation in internal affairs. It could also amend draft ordinances and initiate legislation.[16]

So far as purely legal reforms are concerned, a common police court (*landgeracht*) for all classes was established in 1914, and in 1918 a common Penal Code was introduced. This was the furthest extent to which the plural system was broken down, but in the same period the status of the plural system in non-criminal matters was reinforced, in accordance with the increased emphasis placed upon the welfare of village cultivation. It was in this sphere that the separate 'native' legal system—the adat—was primarily based and it was this system whose separateness was emphasized in the early decades of the twentieth century. A scholarly basis was provided for this separation by the activities of the 'Adat Law School' based in Leiden University. The *doyen* was the great adat law scholar, van Vollenhoven,[17] whose activities and those of his followers soon overshadowed any policy of Westernization. Van Vollenhoven represented a group of scholars who, from the late nineteenth century onwards, collected and compiled the adat of the various groups in the Indonesian archipelago. However, the basic assumptions of the 'Adat Law School' far exceeded this work in influence. Members of the school disapproved strongly of the rapid Westernization of Indonesia, especially where this was to be accompanied by the introduction of a codified Western legal system. They warned against a forced pace of Westernization and advocated a gradual social evolution through the growth of stable adat communities especially in the Outer Provinces.[18] This resulted in the formation of a school of jurisprudence whose whole philosophy came to rest upon positing a distinction between the laws of various races and with elaborating a methodology for the inevitable cases of conflicts of 'racial law' (*intergentiel-recht*) and the principles upon which these laws should be dealt with inside the boundaries of one territorial state.

The preservation of and administrative support for the adats[19] of the East Indies was a continuing feature of Dutch administration, especially from the late nineteenth century onwards. In part this support was founded in the desire of the colonial government to minimize the scope and influence of Islam, although at the same time the preservation of adat was also dictated by a conscious policy of preserving indigenous laws. The motives for this included the view that such a policy was not only ethically desirable but also inevitable, given the wide variety of peoples and cultures in the Indies. The rest of this section will be confined to summarizing the place of adat in the colony of the Indies by setting out the salient features of its organization.

First, as to methodology, the Dutch divided the Netherlands East Indies into adat law areas or law circles (*Rechtskring*)[20] based on a classification of adat systems as cultural and geographic units. Nineteen such areas were distinguished and each was delimited on a general internal similarity of adat systems. While the dangers of such generalizations were well realized by scholars, it was nevertheless felt that the concept of the law area was essential in dealing with highly differentiated adat systems. While adat studies of the nineteenth and twentieth centuries were almost invariably put into the context of one law area, it was also common for such studies to draw attention to comparative material on the 'nature of adat' from other law areas.

So far as the administration of the law was concerned there was a conscious policy of pluralism adopted by the colonial authorities. In general such a policy did not favour a general law for the whole population, although in some areas provisions for a unitary law did apply. There was the Police and Procedure Code for Natives and Foreign Orientals of Java and Madura in 1848 which was drafted along European lines. The latest pre-war revision of these rules was the Revised Native Regulations of 1941.[21] In 1872 a Criminal Code for Natives[22] was produced and, for other oriental groups of the population, notably the Chinese, the Civil and Commercial laws of the Europeans were extended in 1919 and 1925. Adat law in civil matters, notably family and property matters, remained separate though in 1920 a Draft Civil Code for all elements of the population was promulgated. This was not accepted largely as a result of criticism by van Vollenhoven, but at the same time there were areas in which a policy of unification was applied. An example is Book II of the Commercial Code which was completely revised by the laws of 1938, but this process was confined to areas in which the demands of modern economic conditions were held to require uniformity.

The overriding pluralism, however, was largely maintained[23] in adat civil matters and is well exemplified in judicial administration. This had two aspects: 'government justice' (*inlandse rechtspraak*) administered chiefly in directly governed territory and 'non-government justice' (*inheemse rechtspraak*) administered in self-governing territory. The former was administered in the name of the Netherlands sovereign. These distinctions are significant not only in respect of the organization of the courts but also as they dictated the scope of the adat law. So far as the former was concerned, in the directly governed territory there were three types of tribunal: European courts, native courts and courts for all classes of the population. These divisions were founded not upon racial class but upon the types of private law administered in each tribunal. The European courts comprised the Residency Courts, Superior Courts and the Supreme Court. The Native Courts in Java and Madura were those of the District judge, the Regency judge and the Superior Native Court. The latter had competence in all civil and criminal cases, and appeals from this court were heard by a special chamber of the Batavia Superior Court which was composed of specially named jurists trained in adat law. This court was the chief source for adat law decisions in Java and Madura. The procedure for the native courts, although modelled on that of the European courts, was established by its own Codes of Procedure, the Revised Native Regulation of 1941.[24] In the Outer Territories, the structure of Native Courts varied somewhat from this organization but, in common with Java and Madura, appeals from the Superior Native Courts in the Outer Territories were to Superior Courts of Law either in Padang, Macassar, Medan or to the third chamber at Batavia. Further, the organization and procedure of both European and Native Courts in the Outer Territories were provided for in a single enactment, the Law Regulation for the Outer Territories of 1927.

In a dozen districts of the directly governed territories general principles for the administration of native justice assuring its continuance and applying it to all natives in the area were provided for by legislation enacted in 1932.[25] This provided for judges of the native communities who applied adat where this was not in conflict either with other legislation, for example the criminal codes, or with certain sections of the European codes. In the self-governing lands, that is those areas which had retained some autonomy, the administration of justice was a matter for native courts who applied the adats of the area. However, the constitutions of the native states were circumscribed by a variety of regulations, the latest of which, the Self Government Regulations of 1938, Arts. 12 and 13, provided for the administration of justice. These recognized the extraterritoriality of Europeans and foreign orientals and also limited the criminal and some civil jurisdiction.

The result of the differing political statuses of territory and of the various administrations of European and adat law[26] was to limit the competence of adat very largely to what we should describe as civil matters. In both directly and indirectly governed territories, village justice,[27] that is, local processes, to which the villagers submitted their disputes, was also recognized.[28] This recognition probably came too late to counteract to any extent the spread of Western legal concepts. Indeed, the general competence of adat as a viable system of law in any area was defined on the basis of constitutional provisions. The important linking mechanism between law and area was whether or not the colonial government was the judicial administrator. The following summary taken from the introduction to Ter Haar[29] illustrates this:

I. In the area of direct government judicial administration:

i. The general rule was that (substantive) adat law remained valid for natives insofar as it was not replaced by statute or by European law. Art. 131(2)(b), 131(6) Constitution of 1925.

ii. Ordinances regulating adat enacted prior to 1 January 1920, must be declared applicable to natives, if necessary by amendment.

iii. Ordinances made after 1 January 1920, might depart from adat law if the public interest or social needs of the natives so required. Art. 131(2)(b) Constitution of 1925.

iv. The adat rule might be applied even if in conflict with a generally recognized rule of equity or justice. Art. 75 of Constitution of 1854 omitted from Constitution of 1925.

II. In the area of native administration of justice in directly governed territory.

i. Adat civil and procedural rules applied insofar as they had not been replaced by general ordinances. Arts. 130, 131(5) Constitution of 1925.

ii. The ordinance on native justice in directly governed lands determined the extent of the validity of adat law. Staatsblad 1932. No. 80.

iii. Adat law alone applied in the village administration of justice in directly governed territory.

III. In the area of native administration of justice in self-governing lands.

i. Adat civil and procedural law applied insofar as it was not replaced by ordinances rendered effective by treaty or agreement. Art. 21(2) Constitution of 1925.

From this summary it is clear that the maintenance of adat and the continuance of a plural legal policy were prerogatives of the constitutional authority and the scope of adat had in fact been reduced. In addition to legislation under the Civil and Commercial Codes relating to contracts of service,[30] certain forms of leasing, for example, were governed by European law.[31] Further, legislation based on European models and directly applicable to the native had not only limited the scope of adat but imported European legal concepts in the guise of regulatory statutes. For example, an enactment of 1874[32] allowed the imprisonment of natives for debt under certain circumstances, something totally alien to adat in general.

A further limitation on the scope of adat is to be found in the right, provided in the 1925 Constitution (Art. 131(4)), and regulated by an ordinance of 1917,[33] to voluntarily accept European law. This is a topic on which a large literature exists, and it is usual to classify acceptance into (a) complete, (b) partial, (c) for a particular transaction and (d) implied acceptance. These various forms of acceptance allowed the native to adopt European law for particular reasons and in specific circumstances but with the proviso that partial, particular, or implied acceptances could not override the adat law in family matters or in inheritance. Only in the case of complete acceptance, where an administrative declaration before the local authorities must take place, could the adat of the family be overridden. On the other hand it was open to the native to change his ethnic group affiliation permanently by becoming a member of the European law group. This occurred upon naturalization or, in the case of females, marriage where the male partner was European.

Adat was again limited by the old rule contained in Art. 75(3) of the Constitution of 1854 which provided that adat was not to be applied where it offended recognized principles of (Western) justice and equity. This was analogous to the repugnancy clause in English colonial law or the civilization clause in French law. In the great debates at the turn of the century, scholars and administrators such as de la Porte and Nederburgh proposed that a judge should be free to override those rules of adat which he thought violated European ideas of justice. Nederburgh even proposed that the future policy on legislation be such as to draw the native towards the 'higher' European law. As we saw earlier, this point of view succumbed to that represented by van Vollenhoven;[34] the Constitution of 1925 does not repeat the earlier article of 1854, but it does, however, provide that legislation—not the judge—may depart from adat where 'the public interest or the social needs of the native so require' (Art. 121(2b)). This seems to have been interpreted by the courts as a standard for the applicability of an adat rule.[35]

Dutch policy was clear and unambiguous: adat was administered as a suitable law for the bulk of the indigenous population.

Adat in the Republik Indonesia

With the cessation of the Japanese occupation in 1945 the colony of the Netherlands East Indies was unilaterally proclaimed a republic by nationalists. This was followed by a series of 'police actions' by the Dutch and by United Nations intervention. When the dust began to settle and organs of government began to be established,[36] a major new policy orientation appeared in respect of judicial organization. This was that the administration of the law and the substantive body of the law itself were to be placed on a unitary basis. An early attempt was made in January 1947 when the Supreme Court (*Hooggerechtshof*) was reconstituted[37] for what was planned to be the Federal Republic of Indonesia. The court was given cassation powers not only in regard to statute but also in respect of any laws, written or unwritten, and so including adat. It was hoped thus to bring about uniformity in the administration of law. In the period 1945–9 when it was planned that a federal structure be implemented for Indonesia, state courts were accepted in various territories, either as functioning bodies or, in cases such as Java and Timor, for future establishment. Their competence within the state area was similar to that of the Supreme Court. The general result was that native justice in all territories, whether directly governed or self-governing, was replaced by government administration except that at the level of the village, local laws such as village adats were specifically allowed to continue. Islamic law administration was reorganized in Java and Madura where *penghulu* courts were set up. In the other areas, the position of Islamic law was unchanged from pre-war days.[38]

In addition there was a unification of judicial administration in areas controlled by the Dutch authorities and achieved by military ordinance in the early post-war period.[39] The federal state of Republik Indonesia Serikat specifically recognized 'adat judges and religious judges',[40] but in January 1951 the establishment of the unitary state, in which particular attention was paid to the administration of law, came to fruition. Police courts, regency courts and their equivalent in the former self-governing territories were abolished. Village justice, however, was left undisturbed, but under the control of the official government courts. With all this, however, the problems which had faced the colonial government remained to plague the now independent state. These were (a) the issue of legal pluralism as against unification, (b) the place of codified law as against judge-made law and finally (c) the position of the adat. The simplification and unification of the judicial administration did not of itself make for radical change in the civil law immediately. On the one hand, adat, for example, was felt to be primitive and somehow not suitable for a revolutionary situation, but on the other, a contrary view that adat was distinctly Indonesian and thus of great importance for the new nationalist era, was also current. An Indonesian voice on this latter viewpoint from the period is Djojodigoeno,[41] who not only approved of the work of Ter Haar and van Vollenhoven but came down against codification of the law although, rather paradoxically, he would accept a unification based on a 'national law'. This was the crux of the revolutionary problem: what was such a law to consist of? It was a matter for public policy discussion but the various constitutions of the period, those of 1945, 1949 and 1950, provided for the continuation in force of all existing laws though apparently recommending codification of some sort.[42] The laws in force consisted of both books of the Civil Code, Books I and II of which applied mainly to European law institutions; in addition, adat remained the civil law of the Indonesians. Furthermore, the courts themselves tended to elaborate the old conflicts disputes much beloved of the Dutch jurist. One author[43] reports a judicial decision from Djakarta where it was held that a contract for the purchase of trucks between two Indonesians from different law areas must be subject to the civil code. The grounds for this were that the trucks were to be used for public transport and thus for the benefit of all population groups; second, that the contract was concluded in Djakarta where the civil code was assumed normally to apply. The choice of proper law was thus founded in the object of contract and the place where it was made although this has obvious drawbacks in a multi-ethnic community, especially in that the particular law chosen may not lead to the desired unity. Apart from examples of this sort of situation nothing much was done in the way of law reform, although it is interesting to note that the Chinese community favoured an extension of the European civil code rather than a unification based on adat, and insofar as Chinese jurists favoured unification at all, this was in commercial law where they advocated a Western-style code.

The fact remained, however, as Lev points out,[44] that the Indonesians themselves saw codification and unification of the law as necessary (a) to reform a humiliating (colonial) discrimination against Indonesians and (b) to achieve a national unified population. The first reason had a largely anti-colonial appeal to emotion, but it became of fundamental importance from the mid-1950s onwards. In 1957 parliamentary democracy, as this is understood in the West, gave way to President Soekarno's guided democracy, and in 1958 Dutch-owned enterprises were nationalized. It became fashionable to speak of *hukum revolusi* ('revolutionary law') rather than *hukum regina* ('state law') in what became the focus of reform efforts, an attack on the colonial legal system. The so-called 'Eight Year Plan' of 1959–60 drafted by the National Planning Council, in addition to calling for the codification of commercial law, also called for the elimination of plural law groups based on race or law areas, and demanded that a national law to replace colonial laws should be immediately developed. The new Agrarian Act of 1960 was perhaps an attempt at this. This legislation[45] abolished Book II of the Civil Code and its European-inspired land systems and replaced them with rights to property based in 'social function', 'national interest and national unity'. In fact, although said to be based on adat principles, it ignores specific adat rights[46] and, indeed, tends to obliterate adat property rights in providing for a modified form of the European individual right to ownership and disposal. The intention was clearly to create a common land law, and although concerned with specific land reform, the act has had as yet little effect in the village lands of Indonesia; it is, however, serving to destroy a pervasive assumption from colonial days that each population group requires its own law.

The pace of the ideological revolution, however, overtook the working of these reforms and in the light of the revolutionary ideology, a proposal was made by the then Minister of Justice, Suhardjo, that the civil and commercial codes be directly abolished. This is less radical than it seems at first sight. Book II of the civil code had already been eliminated by the Agrarian Act of 1960 and all that remained were Book I on personal law and Book III on contracts. The latter was to be replaced by a short contracts code. Book I, however, was to be not so much abolished as declared applicable, as a customary law, to those to whom the code had formerly applied. In practice this meant the Eurasian and Chinese communities and not the mass of the people who continued to be governed by the adat. However, both the 'code personal law' and the adat were to find their level of applicability in the light of the conditions of independent Indonesia, specifically in the light of *Pantjasila*, the five-point ideological statement of Soekarno, made in 1945: Belief in One God, Nationalism, Internationalism, Social Justice and Government of the People.[47] In the event, the Civil Code was declared no longer in force by a Supreme Court Circular dated 5 September 1963. The reasoning behind the declaration was set out in an accompanying statement:[48]

> From the beginning it has been felt strange that in Indonesia, even though now independent, many laws still apply which in character and object ... cannot be freed from the thinking of the colonialists ... who sought mainly to satisfy Dutch interests.... In view of the fact that the Dutch colonialists drafted the civil code wholly in imitation of the Dutch civil code, and, moreover, that it was applied only to Dutchmen (and those assimilated to them) in Indonesia, therefore the question arose whether in independent Indonesia ... it was proper to regard the civil code as formally valid.... Thus the idea occurred to consider the civil code not as a law, but rather only as a document describing a part of the unwritten law ... (on the basis of this view) the authorities, particularly judges, are freer to disregard various articles that are no longer in harmony with this period of Indonesian independence.

One may ask how effective such a programme is likely to be in practice where the judges, as during the period of the Japanese occupation, continue to rely upon the colonial legislation.[49] The reform is applicable mainly to Chinese family law, this being the legal system assimilated to Book I of the civil code, but this is only a part of the general legal and political pressure which is being imposed upon the Chinese. For the rest, the high-flown sentiments appear to have had little effect, with one exception. This is that the idea of separate legal systems, as in pre-war days, is no longer accepted but that codification and unification are now seen as matters of state policy. The old Indonesian conflicts law has lost most of its importance and, as unification proceeds, at least on paper, it will eventually disappear. However, the situation is still one of flux with no drastic moves being taken on codification and new law is being laid down only on an *ad hoc* basis.[50] Typical of this, and of the eclecticism of the sources for new law is Wirjono Prodjodikoro's *Draft Law on Contract*[51] which first appeared in 1961. A first source of contract is said to be adat though this is more a passing comment than anything else. A second source is the national or local consciousness and the sense of justice of the people. It seems that these two so-called sources are in reality little more than standards by which one may judge what would be ethically right in particular circumstances. Alternatively but connectedly, a rule accepted as a usage (i.e. an adat) may be taken as a source. But the fact remains that the substantive principles which appear in the draft legislation come from the third source of modern law—that is, the European civil code, either by resurrecting old principles and justifying them on the two bases put forward earlier or by importing from abroad new principles of law—especially commercial law—which have the justification of international practice behind them. The question is primarily one of legitimacy, in the context of having law on paper and law in fact, the latter being actual living practice and including even such things as corruption. However, this is not to say that the formal organs of the court and the prolific new legislation have had no effect on the civil law—they have, as we now go on to describe.

Before commencing a description proper, two points must be emphasized which are important in post-independence legal developments. First, it is not really possible to consider such developments under the same neat headings of 'adat' and 'inter-personal law' which were the colonial currency if we keep in mind the possible distortion which can occur. The second point is that the sources from which the new laws flow and the new ways of thinking about law have a number of origins, in sharp distinction to the colonial situation where the source was primarily the dominant legal system.[52] Most important here is the fact that in the colonial situation any change in law was put forward (or rejected) on the assumptions and in the terms of that system. This is in contrast to the present position where the sources of change include not only the courts and the legislature but also the demands of political ideology and the theories about the nature of law in general, especially adat law, in its relationship to the 'new' Indonesia.[53] These two factors do not mean that one can no longer discuss law in terms such as 'adat' and so on, but they do mean that one must provide a framework within which these strands can be considered together. The point is that the various categories of law extruded by the colonial situation were developed within a legal system characterized by a relationship of dominance and servience, and this characterization now no longer exists. However, the legal classifications established in that period do persist to a large extent and are moreover related to each other. That is to say, a mention of any one of adat, interracial law or Islamic law, necessitates a consideration of the others, even if this is merely to exclude its relevance in any particular case. At the same time, Indonesia now possesses a legal and constitutional system in which the characterization dominant-servient no longer remains valid, its place having been taken by the ascription of a common status—'citizens of Indonesia'—for the total population. Such an ascription implies at least the development of a national law and it is within this context that the early (colonial) classifications now find a common meeting point.

At the same time, however, adat was and remains the law primarily applicable to something like 85 per cent of the population, but it is now increasingly subject to pressure for modernization. This takes a number of forms, and it is apposite that these be sketched here because they represent new initiatives in the adat/state relationship.

In an early study one author[54] considers the question of the position of the widow in inheritance under adat as administered in the courts. Data are drawn from bilateral and patrilineal-based societies, and the cases are discussed so as to show that there has been an increasing tendency to recognize the widow as an heir of her husband. This is a considerable advance on the older adat position where, in general, a widow has a right only to property which she brought to the marriage plus a share in any property jointly acquired during coverture. Two interesting points arise out of this process of change in the adat. First, the reasons found to justify the departure from adat; the following passage[55] effectively exemplifies the justifications put forward:

... One of these [a condition requiring 'new' adat inheritance law] is the present 'transitional period' of Indonesian history, a process of transformation from the attributes of colonialism to those of freedom and independence. This process presents judges with many novel problems of conflict and law, which they must evaluate according to society's sense of justice. The implication is that judges must help guide the nation through the transition. But Wirjono's[56] use of 'society's sense of justice' leads one to conclude that he actually means the sense of justice implicit in the ideals of independent Indonesia, as they are expressed by national leaders. A related consideration is the egalitarianism of the revolution, and the equal rights of women which their role in society and the independence movement justifies.

The reasoning apparent in this passage has been repeated in a number of other cases and, as one commentator[57] describes, gives rise to fears that the detailed adat rules of particular groups may eventually have no legal standing at all. It is conceded, however, that this might be necessary in the interests of a unification of the legal system despite the disruption of the social system to which this will give rise. On the other hand it is recognized that although detailed adat rules may no longer be admitted, the foundation of such a right as that of a widow's inheritance is *an adat law concept*. We return to this point later.

The second feature which arises out of this description of legal change is the gap which some observers have noted between the activities of the Supreme Court and the following of its decisions in the lower courts. In one case it has been said[58] that at first instance level it is not possible to give effect to the new departures in adat law at local level. The population is not prepared for them and will refuse to countenance them. Another observer[59] has noted that many people are reluctant to carry suits to the official courts for, amongst other reasons, the unwillingness of such courts to give effect to traditional adat principles. In yet a further case,[60] we are given information as to the cooperation of an adat and state tribunal in giving effect to an adat process of dispute settlement.

With the replacement of the Constitution of 1950 by the re-introduction of the 1945 Constitution and the introduction of 'guided democracy' in 1959, the position of adats in Indonesia underwent a further change. The Agrarian Act of 1960 was the first indication of this change in that it attempted to create new land rights applicable to all population groups, although these were subject to restrictions imposed by 'social function' (Art. 6). The drafters of the Act asserted that it was based on adat law (Art. 5)[61] although this is severely qualified in that such adat must be free from 'feudal and capitalistic principles'. The key to understanding this reference to adat is to be found in the fact that although specific and local adat rules as to land rights have been ignored, some of the general principles common to all adat areas may have been specifically recognized. The Act may be seen therefore as both a limitation on specific adat property rights and as an affirmation of adat general principles relating to land. The following provisions of Art. 3 illustrate this dual reference:

... The *hak ulajat*[62] [the village *adat* 'right of disposition over land cultivated or claimed as waste by its members'] and similar rights of *adat* law communities, so far as they still exist in fact, must be exercised in such a way as to accord with national and state interests, based on national unity, and so as not to contradict laws and other regulations which are of higher order.

It can easily be seen, therefore, that much depends upon what one means by 'adat', especially in its second, broader, sense. Implicit here is a view of adat law as a law in accordance with the principles of the state and, as such, a law which is dependent upon political ideology.[63] The importance of this factor is attested to by various pronouncements of the 'Provisional People's Congress'[64] where in its decision MPRS No. 11/1960, adat was said to be the basis for an Indonesian national law:[65]

... That the principles for developing the national law have to correspond with the political direction of the state and must be based on adat law which does not hamper the promotion of a just and prosperous society.

Interesting though these statements are, one must look also to the work of the courts and the jurists to obtain some idea of the present adat position in the development of Indonesia's national law. We have already seen clearly that the focus of interest has shifted away from the colonial-inspired primary points of contact toward an attempt to find the underlying adat bases of a unitary legal system. Naturally enough, this attempt is by no means complete as yet, especially as it only seriously commenced in the early 1960s, particularly under the impulse of *Pantjasila*. Having said this, it must not, however, be supposed that the *development* of a national law is a wholly political matter. The process of development is carried on in the courts and in the writings of jurists who proceed upon the assumptions and methodologies of law, although avowedly for goals set by national ideologies.[66]

The issue of unification was of course important in the colonial period and this must be kept in mind in what follows if only because the contemporary debate on this question commences from its colonial exposition, either as a development of this or in opposition to it. Both van Vollenhoven and Ter Haar consistently opposed any unification of adat law, especially in the proposed form of codification. To a large extent this may be attributed to the definition of adat law adopted by van Vollenhoven which, as one author has noted,[67] owes much to the influence of Malinowski, namely:

[Adat is] the mutual interaction between a normal custom and the other normal customs on one side and between normal customs and disturbing divergencies on the other side.... Even recommendation and disapproval ... are law and not just morals if they are indissolubly connected with command and prohibition in collective consciousness and behaviour.

Ter Haar's approach was similar in that he fundamentally regarded as law any adat which occurs in a decision of a judge, either a community 'judge' or a legal functionary *in or outside of dispute*. Such decisions are related to and are part of general principles of structure and values of the community (... '*van de structureele bindingen en de waarden in de gemeenschap*'). In other words, the understanding of adat as a concept by these authorities precluded any unification in code form in favour of a reliance upon the 'organic authority' inherent in the adat system of a particular area. The influence of these views continued into the post-independence period although in a number of variant versions. Kusumadi Pudjosewojo, for example, while holding, as does Ter Haar, that adat is that which is enforced in decision, tends also to see adat ('*hukum adat*') as the unwritten rules still extant in independent Indonesia.[68] Supomo, on the other hand, sees adat as the expression of the 'idea of justice' of the Indonesian people.[69] Both these viewpoints assume the adoption of Western law categories and the view that the primary referent for any law or legal system is the individual person. This is a view which later Indonesian writers have tended to reject. One of the foremost proponents of rejection is Djojodigoeno who says:[70]

> Individualistic and liberalistic views do not live in the minds of Indonesians. We are socio- and traditio-bound people: everyone of us has to act and to behave as all others do; one has to be common, *biasa* (Javanese *lumrah*). Being different from others is being strange, astonishing, wicked, condemnable. In this course of ideas an individualistic state of mind and an individualistic pattern of behaviour and action will arouse opposition, disapproval and condemnation. Freedom of contracting and competition is out of place, as are definite actions in law, containing definite claims.

The same author goes on to assert that the use of precedent tends to produce a situation of 'static' law and so to lead to a situation where the law is out of phase with the needs and desires of the people. His view of adat law is that in any case one can distinguish a formal and a material definition. Adat, in its formal sense, is all law which is not derived from written law but which has as its source the authority of government. This is reminiscent of the colonial definition of *adatrecht*. In its material sense adat consists of norms which emerge directly from the general Indonesian culture, particularly in social relationships including not only such matters as family arrangements but also activities such as 'contract' between individuals. It is, as another commentator says,[71] an expression of the sense of justice (*keadilan*) and propriety (*kepatutan*) of the people. In any discussion, therefore, one must establish the content of adat in both senses and in all its manifestations and relate these to the total social relationships in the state. This leads jurists such as Djojodigoeno to distinguish judicial procedures as 'static', i.e., the fact of being bound by statute or precedent, and 'dynamic', i.e., taking into account existing social conditions and needs. The former is castigated as an indulgence in 'subtlety and chicanery' which should have no place in an Indonesian court. The court should instead give effect to the material sense of justice but this does not necessarily involve codification which is only suitable to the static situation of the West.[72] Such jurists, however, propose a *unity of treatment* in an emphasis upon the obligation of the court towards the allowing of the people's sense of justice.[73]

Summary

This outline of the contemporary relationship between adat and the state must end in an inconclusive way. The constitutional problems which have beset Indonesia since independence have had their effect on legal development most notably in that they have tended to create an excessive degree of uncertainty in the law. As a result legal policy has not been clear, although it is probably correct to say that the development of a unified legal system has now become firmly established as the major goal for the contemporary period and into the foreseeable future.[74] However, a great degree of uncertainty remains as to what the proper basis of this unified law is to be; this issue is a continuing feature of Indonesian legal life and it reappears in later chapters insofar as it concerns adat.[75]

1. Given about 1350 A.D. cf. Pigeaud, 1962: (iv) 391–8 especially at 396.
2. cf. Moertono, 1963: 134–51 on taxation and local levies in later Mataram.
3. cf. Moertono, 1963: 14–82 for an account, based on older authors, of the position of the King in sixteenth-century Mataram.
4. cf. Pigeaud, 1962: (iv), Slametmuljana (1967).
5. Moertono, 1963: 14–82 and the sources there cited.
6. Except possibly Acheh. See Snouck Hurgronje (1893).
7. cf. van der Kroef (1951) for an account of the transfer.
8. cf. Bastin (1960). See also van Niel (1964).
9. cf. Furnivall, 1944: 89.
10. ibid: 115–23.
11. 1875. S, 179.
12. I.S.B. No. 114.
13. 1819. I.S.B. No. 16. 1820. I.S.B. No. 22.
14. cf. Furnivall, 1944: 191–2.
15. ibid: 225–8.
16. See also Benda (1965–6).
17. Author of the monumental three-volume classic *Het Adatrecht van NederlandschIndie* published in Leiden in 1906–1933. See also van Vollenhoven (1919) (1921).

18. For a short account of the methods and procedures of the school cf. Bisschop (1934). See also Ter Haar, 1948: 234–7.

19. Adat is used here throughout in its Dutch legal usage (*adatrecht*) as native law having legal effect. For a full range of various specific usages from different parts of Indonesia cf. Hinloopen Labberton, 1933: 4–10. For an outline of the difficulties of such terms as 'customary law' and the translation of adat concepts into European concepts, see J.P.B. de Josselin de Jong (1948) and Vandenbosch (1932). For outline sources of the vast adat literature, see Bisschop (1934) and Ter Haar, 1948: 234–8.

20. These are as follows:

i	Acheh	x	Toraja Territory
ii	Gayo, Alas and Batak lands	xi	South Celebes
iii	Minangkabau	xii	Ternate Archipelago
iv	South Sumatra	xiii	Ambon Moluccas
v	East Sumatra, Malaya and West Borneo	xiv	New Guinea
		xv	Timor Archipelago
vi	Bangka and Billiton	xvi	Bali and Lombok
vii	Borneo (except Malayan West Borneo)	xvii	Central and East Java
		xviii	Principalities of Jogjakarta and Surakarta
viii	Minahasa		
ix	Gorontalo	xix	West Java

21. Staatsblad, 1941, No. 44.

22. Replaced by the Criminal Code of 1918 applicable to all elements of the population.

23. See below Art. 131(4) of the 1925 Constitution providing for the acceptance of European law.

24. Staatsblad, 1941, No. 44.

25. Regulation of Native Justice in Directly Governed Territory, 1932.

26. The description given here is a very brief summary. Fuller details can be got from Ter Haar, 1948: 14–31 including a diagrammatic representation drawn by Schiller at pp. 20–1.

27. '*Dorprechtspraak*'.

28. Staatsblad, 1935, No. 102 and Arts. 12 and 13, Native States Regulation, 1938.

29. Ter Haar, 1948: 32.

30. cf. Ter Haar, 1948: 33–34.

31. Staatsblad, 1918, No. 88.

32. Staatsblad, 1874, No. 94.

33. Staatsblad, 1917, No. 12 'Regulation governing the Voluntary Acceptance of European Private Law'.

34. See further Chapter 3 below.

35. cf. Ter Haar, 1948: 40.

36. For accounts of the constitutional questions of the early independence period see Schiller (1955) and Krishnamurthy (1960–1).

37. Staatsblad, 1947, No. 20.

38. For a full summary cf. Schiller, 1955: 322–32. See also Chapter 5 below.

39. cf. Han Bing Siong, 1961: 2–16 for a summary. Dual prosecution under the colonial system disappeared though the Japanese maintained most colonial legislation in force. A revised Regulation for Indonesians (H.I.R.) was adopted for procedural purposes.

40. Art. 144(1) provisional Constitution, Republik Indonesia Serikat.

41. cf. Djojodigoeno (1952) 1953: 38, 45. For sociological data see van der Kroef (1952) (1958), Weatherbee (1966).

THE STATE AND ADAT

42. cf. Lev, 1965: 286 n.7 and the discussion as to whether, in the absence of express stipulation, the constitutions did recommend codification. In the event, nothing has yet been codified. For the structure of the formal legal system and its present characteristics, cf. Damian & Hornick (1972).
43. cf. Lev, 1965: 287.
44. ibid: 289.
45. Undang2 tentang Peraturan Dasar Pokok2 Agraria No. 5/1960, No. 104/1960. cf. Soemardjan (1962). See below Chapter 6.
46. See, for example, Gautama & Harsono, 1972: 25–9. See below Chapter 6.
47. See Soeripto (n.d.) and (1973) on adat and the idea of Pantjasila.
48. cf. Lev, 1965: 293n.
49. On this point cf. the present writer's review of van den Steenhoven (1970) in (1972) *Berita Kadjian Sumatera* 1: (2) 48. The point here is that a State Court in North Sumatra cited a pre-independence Dutch law, the 'Regulation for the Administration of Justice in the Outer Territories', in proceedings carried out in 1969. See also Damian & Hornick (1972) on the formal continuance of Dutch-made legislation.
50. But see below on the development of a 'Hukum Nasional'. See also Koesnoe (1970) and the cases there cited.
51. *Rantjangan Undang2 Hukum Perjandjian*. Discussed in Lev, 1965: 301–3.
52. Earlier in this section we mentioned the changes made in the effects at law of the colonial laws. These changes may be summarized here as follows:
   (a) The Codes left by the Dutch East Indies administration do not have the same legal value as the laws of the sovereign state of Indonesia.
   (b) The rules of the (Dutch) Civil Code remain valid if not considered contrary to the principles of the 1945 Constitution.
   (c) The judge determines validity in the case above.
   (d) The (Dutch) Commercial Code remains generally valid. See the following authorities: Gouwgioksiong (1962), Gautama (1970), Schiller (1956).
53. See, for example, Djojodigoeno (1961) on the 'reorientation' of law and adat law. See also Supomo (1953).
54. cf. Lev (1962).
55. ibid: 216–17.
56. Wirjono, then Chief Justice of the Supreme Court and one of the most influential jurists in Indonesia. Lev (1962) attributes the 'new' adat inheritance law largely to his influence.
57. Jaspan, 1964–5: 262–3.
58. Lev, 1962: 222–3.
59. Jaspan, 1964–5: 261–2. See also below Chapter 7 where this question is discussed in detail.
60. van den Steenhoven (1970). Further examples of traditional adat procedures can be found in Jaspan (1971).
61. See Koesnoe (1971a).
62. cf. van den Steenhoven (1970) for an account of an adat proceeding on this topic in which the adat authorities and the State Court cooperated.
63. See also Stirling, 1965–6: 54 who, in commenting upon Jaspan (1964–5) makes the same point.
64. *Madjelis Permusjawaratan Rakjat Sementara*—MPRS.
65. See also the decision MPRS xx/1966 where a similar point was made.
66. See the following sources: Koesnoe (1970), Soebekti (1970), Kartohadiprodjo (1969) (1971).
67. cf. Jaspan, 1964–5: 254.
68. cf. Koesnoe, 1971: B9 (para. 8).
69. ibid: see also Supomo (1958).
70. Djojodigoeno, 1952: 13.
71. cf. Koesnoe, 1971: B 13 ff.

72. Djojodigoeno, 1952: 17.

73. See, for example, the following: Farid (1969), Adiwinata (1972) and Notopuro (1969).

74. Attention is increasingly coming to be concentrated upon the role of law in the process of national development. cf. Gautama (1972).

75. We should note here that apologists for Islamic law, specifically in its relation to adat and the problem of the national law, see Islam as being more in phase with modernization primarily because, unlike adat, it does not found itself in social groupings of the patrilineal or matrilineal type. That is to say, in developments such as the modernization of the law of inheritance, the Islamic emphasis upon the nuclear family as the prime social unit corresponds more exactly to modern social legislation. See generally Hazairin (1961). See also Chapter 5. It is notable that the Agrarian Act of 1960 assumes a nuclear family consisting of seven persons. See further Chapter 6.

2

THE SOCIAL CONSTRUCTION OF ADAT

Introduction

THE title of this chapter indicates a complex of difficulties. If the definition of adat is confined to 'rules and principles of law' then the following questions immediately arise. Are we speaking about the social structure of 'rules of law' or are we discussing the nature and function of law in society? More generally, is the social construction of adat a reference to the relationship between law and society? These questions are not made any easier to answer by the variety of legal and sociological usage of the terms 'law' and 'social structure'. The range of meaning which the term 'adat' itself has is an additional complication.

The aim of this chapter is to try and provide some answers to these difficulties. In essence it is an attempt to describe the referents of the term 'adat' in the context of societies based upon what Sir Henry Maine described as the principle of status.[1] In a negative sense this means that the relationship between individuals or groups is not determined by a (voluntary) submission to predetermined rules of universal application within territorial limits. There is, in effect, no system of internally self-justifying norms, which exist independent of society and require no specific validation from society. On the contrary, and so far as jurisprudence is concerned, status societies are those in which legal rules and principles cannot be distinguished from the social structure itself.[2] The law is not a distinct and special sub-culture; the individual in a status society exists both as an existential and as a 'legal' object, a proposition which is by no means always true in Western jurisprudence.[3] The problem facing the student of adat is, therefore, to describe those features of society which are necessary to identify the adat systems as legal systems, that is as normative systems which guide human behaviour.[4] So far as adat in Indonesia is concerned this is an issue which must be tackled in two stages. First, one must describe the ways in which an adat system is defined, and second, one must look at the implications of this description for jurisprudence.

The Definition of Adat Systems

The Dutch authorities traditionally defined the adat laws in terms of two factors—kinship relationships and the 'territorial factor', that is, the common concern of a group of people with a defined area of land.[5] It is these factors which, either separately or, more commonly, taken together, define or distinguish an adat system as a system distinct from other systems. Kinship relations are usually discussed in terms of standard anthropological classifications such as the matrilineal, patrilineal and bilateral systems. The territorial factor concentrates attention upon a number of forms of territorial organization such as the village community, the regional community and the union of villages. The basic structure of any adat system is, therefore, determined by the nature of the individual's kinship relationships with his fellows—as in a clan structure—or his relationship in respect of a defined area of land where questions of occupation, possession or ownership are primary—as in the Javanese village. On the other hand it was and it is not unusual for one of these two factors to be absent. Ter Haar instances the Gayo whose adat was based exclusively in clan membership. Communities in which the kinship factor (in the sense described above) has little or no significance are common in Indonesia; examples include the Javanese, Sundanese and Balinese *desa*, the *gampong* of Aceh and the villages of the Malay regions. Furthermore, both factors are sufficient and necessary in the definition of the *uma* of Mentawei, the *huta* and *kuria* of the Batak and the *nagari* of Minangkabau, amongst others. Adat law scholarship and, it might be added, the administration of adat by state organs, proceeded upon a series of elaborations of this sort. Ter Haar, for example, lists units such as the 'non-localized clan', 'regional communities of mixed clans' and many others.[6] The result was the establishment of the 'adat law areas' (*adat rechtskringen*) which consisted of a series of boundaries between different systems. The legal relevance of such groupings was thus established on the basis of a differentiation of social structures.

Now on this view of social structures it is clear that adat is not, as such, being used as a technical legal term. It does not have the character of such terms as '*milik*', '*pencharian*', and so on, although it can, like them, be used in legal argument or figure in court decisions. The concept is not even primary in day-to-day legal administration as are the concepts of property or ownership. Its use in the present circumstance is primarily in thinking about the law and not in the actual use and application of the law. In its relation to social structure, therefore, the aim was and is to forge a useful conceptual tool, the *primary* aim of which is to provide a means of differentiating different types of adat systems.[7] Its basic referent in this context is to a grouping within which there is a common system of obligation. Such a system implies a society-wide consensus although this need not depend upon the existence of fixed political boundaries. Indeed, although the princely states of Indonesia issued *undang-undang* (Malay lands) or *nawala* (Java), the ordinary legal life of the community continued unaffected.

This use of the concept denotes a certain view of law or rather a range of views which have two related ideas in common. The first is that law is pre-eminently normative, the law represents the articulated 'ought' propositions of a society grounded in widely accepted values. This view is common both to colonial and modern adat scholarship although there is dispute as to whether the element of sanction is a necessary condition. The latter was certainly the view of van Vollenhoven[8] although there are contemporary objections to it.[9] Leaving aside the question of sanction, the normative quality of the concept was, and to a large extent still is, seen as being culturally confined. In other words, the notion of obligation has a confined and specific existence relative to a particular culture. The relationship between the notion of obligation and the facts of a specific culture was thought of as existing on two levels or in two ways which must be distinguished. First, there was the relationship conceived as a general relationship referring to all the facts of the foreign culture, for example, to its kinship, religion, economic features and so on.[10] Second, there was the sort of relationship which was primarily of interest to jurists or to legal administrators; in this case the adat obligations of a particular culture were conceived and formulated on the basis of *selected* features of the culture in question.[11] These were the kinship and territorial factors which were taken as constituting indigenous obligation systems. In addition, and perhaps more important, they were able to be described in terms cognizable to a Western system of law. They were, of course, distorted in being treated in this way, but perhaps less than might have been expected in that native terminologies were retained so far as was possible. This did not amount to a complete retention, but the Dutch terms[12] used were employed for the purpose of referring directly to indigenous groups as these were found to be established as existing units.[13]

In its relation to social structure adat may be said to be a complex whole made up of indigenous units acceptable to (Dutch civil) law. The essential element fixed upon by the jurists of all periods was the method of control over the individual. This was described in two main ways: first as a 'kinship' matter as exemplified in the various clan systems and, second, as a control exercised through the allocation of land resources—the so-called 'territorial' factor. Colonial legal thought was interested only in those *forms* of social structure which were seen to have a direct relevance to the distribution of power. This point must be borne in mind because it explains the apparent inconsistencies of the so-called 'special forms' of social structure and the sometimes obsessive attention paid by the Dutch to the divisions and sub-divisions of these forms. This is a matter which, in contemporary Indonesia, receives rather less attention than formerly because the focus of attention has shifted to trying to discover principles of social and political unity for the Indonesian peoples as a whole. At the same time, however, the major forms established in colonial scholarship persist, at least in broad outline, and condition much contemporary thought on adat matters. It is also worth mentioning, particularly for the benefit of sociologists, that the use of sociological terminology may not be as exact as they would wish. Finer elaborations within the social structure of a particular people are often not made and there is commonly a blurring of the distinctions between different types of social structures. The definition of adat systems does tend to be rather crude in some cases[14] because the aim was not sociological exactitude but a broad differentiation sufficient for legal administration. The major adat systems identified on the basis just outlined are as follows:[15]

(i) *Non-localized clans.* This category refers to the patrilineal clan system which is exogamous. The example most commonly cited is the Gayo of northern Sumatra. The basic adat law unit was (and is) taken to be the sub-clan on the ground that the only traditional political authority is that of the sub-clan headman (*reujeu*) over the members (*saudeureu*) of the sub-clan. In the traditional system territorial issues were thought not to be decisive; however, under Acinese influence certain headmen were appointed as chiefs over regional areas. In some parts of Gayo territory these chiefs (*kejuron*) were backed by the authority of the Netherlands Indies administration.

A further example is the Pubian clans of the Lampong area of south-eastern Sumatra whose basic unit was the sub-clan (*kabiun*). Members of various sub-clans may live intermingled in the same village but authority lies in the headman (*paksi*) of the sub-clan even if they live out of the village in which he himself resides. From 1928, with the setting up of regional communities (*marga*), a regional authority was developed and lay in the '*marga*' chief. However, the sub-clans still function as autonomous adat communities although the authority of the head does not now extend to sub-clan members residing in other villages. This of course is an important qualification because it gives rise to disputes about sub-clan membership and leads to practical difficulties in deciding to what adat system an individual might belong. Although contemporary data are lacking it seems probable that village attachment rather than sub-clan membership will become the decisive criteria in locating the adat of an individual. This is true also for the Gayo.

(ii) *Localized clans*. This term refers to complexes of sub-clans which occupy a defined area of land and reside in a village under the authority of a village chief. The authority of the chief does not, however, extend far, if at all, over persons outside his clan. Examples of this category were typically found in the smaller islands, Enggano, Buru, Ceram, Flores, and in the New Guinea interior. Ideally, a village is occupied by one clan but at the present time resettlement in coastal areas has tended to result in mixed villages populated by emigrants from the interior and by overseas aliens.

(iii) *Regional communities of mixed clans*. The common example of this form is the Minangkabau of central Sumatra. This area is made up of regional communities (*nagari*) inhabited by named lineages (*sa buah peruiq*) of the same or different clans. Authority over lineage members is exercised by the lineage head (*mamaq kepala waris*) and membership of a lineage is reckoned by matrilineal descent. A *nagari* is defined as being in existence when it has a council house (*balai*), a bathing place (*tapian*), a cock fighting space (*galengang*) and a mosque (*mesjid*), and at least four kin groups not belonging to the same clan are in residence. The *nagari* controls the allocation of land resources[16] and this of course is the basic reason for the reference to 'regional communities'. The structure of the *nagari* falls into two main types which are especially distinguished on an adat basis. There is, first, the Bodi-Chaniago adat system found predominantly in Agam in which the *nagari* is ruled jointly by a council of kinship group (called *suku*) headmen (*kerapatan negari*). The adat rules relating to this form of *nagari* organization are collectively known as the adat Parapatih. The second system, found in Tanah Datar and Limapuloh Kota, is the Kota-Piliang adat system where the resident sub-clans (called *kampuang*) are combined into unions of four, five, six or nine unrelated *kampuang* from as many different clans. The unions of such *kampuang* are known as *suku*. There is a hierarchy of officials engaged in government, and the detailed rules regulating the system are known as the adat Katumanggungan. In both systems, however, the *nagari* is the central organizing principle for the definition of the 'Minangkabau adat' which is, incidentally, complex and variable in important details throughout the Minangkabau areas.[17]

In addition to Minangkabau, the regional community form is also characteristic of the Korinchi, amongst whom matrilineal kinship groups (*lurah, relebu, perut*) whether related or not form a village (*dusun*) above which stands a regional community (*mendapo*). The same pattern is found also among the Batin of Jambi. The inhabitants of Nias island may also be included in this adat system where the population of villages are the members of unrelated patrilineal sub-clans organized into a form of regional community (*euri*). In all cases, however, there is a good deal of local variation which tends to complicate matters, although the structural principles are well recognized. For the purposes of defining an adat system the structural features were and are taken as the norm.

(iv) *Patrilocal clans.* This class is confined to the special case of the Batak whose adat system is organized on the basis of localized, exogamous patrilocal clans, each inhabiting its own territory. Village populations are composed of the members of one clan or sub-clan although non-members may also be resident; they cannot, however, claim proprietary rights in agricultural or house lands, nor are they eligible to provide the community chief. They may and commonly do have some representation in the affairs of the whole area. There is usually a complex set of rules governing the relationships between such people and the members of the dominant resident group. In addition, each clan is a partner in a fixed relation to another clan for the purpose of marriage by which one clan ('*hula hula*' among the Toba or '*mora*' in the south) supplies women to another ('*boru*' or '*beru*'). The relationship is not mutual and results in asymmetrical marriage. The woman-receiving clan must therefore have some other clan as its *boru* for which it in turn plays the part of *hula hula*. Two clans in this relationship may be found in the same village. If this is the case, the *hula hula* (the woman provider) enjoys a certain dominance. There are many complex features in this arrangement,[18] but the general principle is that clan membership and residence in the clan area are the basis of the adat system.

(v) *The localized tribe.* This term refers to the bilateral kinship group which inhabits its own specific territory. This class includes the bulk of the Dayak peoples of the Borneo (Kalimantan) interior. In the coastal areas on the other hand this form of organization tends to be replaced by a territorial village organization. The localized tribe also occurs in the central Celebes among the To Mori and the Sadan Toraja, although the latter is not exclusively a community of tribal members because outsiders may attain equal rights to residence and land use.

(vi) *Territorially-based tribes.* With this class there is a shift from kinship factors to an emphasis upon groups who find their primary form of identity in a relationship based upon territorial boundaries. The basis of the adat system is the occupation and utilization (in some cases amounting to ownership) of a defined area of land. The meaning of 'tribe' is taken to indicate the existence of kinship factors which are not, however, decisive. The example most commonly cited is the patrilineal lineage of Minahasa who live together and cultivate an undivided estate on a partnership basis. This area, the *negori*, is defined as a geographically based community for adat purposes.

(vii) *Territorialized kinship-based communities.* This refers to territories inhabited by clan members but territories in which clan membership does not (at present and in the recent past) give any special privileges. The south Sumatra *marga* is the example commonly given. Any person who occupies and cultivates land can become a member of the *marga* although as a practical proposition some kinship links within the area are necessary. At the same time it should be remembered that kinship factors as a basis for adat systems are still probably important in the more remote regions of the area.

(viii) *Kinship-based communities transformed by alien power.* This is typical of Ambon and the Uliasers, the *negorys* of which were formed of small family groups (often unrelated) under the influence of the Netherlands East Indies government. This replaced an earlier localized patrilineal clan organization, the land-owning functions of which have now largely disappeared although there are examples of lineages which maintain possession of tree groves.

(ix) *The Gaukang.*[19] This is confined to the south Celebes and is a representation or symbol of the vital spirit or soul of a regional community which is defined by its relationship to the symbol. The object which represents the vital spirit is believed to have supernatural qualities; it may be a stone, a branch, a weapon or some other object.[20] This institution has been much influenced by the

Dutch administration, but the basic principle of social structure in this area remains the territorial community.

(x) *The Balinese desa.* The village (*desa*) in Bali is a community which depends upon a common duty to participate in religious ceremonies for its existence as an adat form. There are two basic varieties, the old style and the new style *desa*. In the former a special group of married citizens fulfil the requirements of worship, and these people are the holders of particular lands. There is a social stratification in such villages where the possession of ancestral land and participation in worship constitute the first rank. The second rank is made up of a larger group who have some share in land and a less important religious role. The lowest class is made up of immigrants and lodgers (*sampingan*) who have none of these responsibilities. In addition, in the territories outside the former principalities there are various societies, subordinate to the village authority, such as the young men's society, drama and music societies and so on. In the appanage territory these societies exist as autonomous communities.

The new style village is less complex; its membership is made up of all adult married males who possess a residential compound and who have resided in the village for one year. In addition to these two types of Balinese community there are important irrigation associations (*subak*), a union of *sawah* owners organized in a number of ways under a headman and variously linked to the villages.

In Lombok the *desa* is a territorially-based community possessing an area of land and governed by a *kepala desa*.

(xi) *The Javanese desa.* This also is a purely territorial grouping made up of unrelated individuals and families. There are several sub-divisions of members, first the nuclear villagers (*pribumi* and other terms) who own agricultural land and agricultural compounds. Second, those persons (*indung* and other terms) who own land or compounds and finally those (*nusup* and other terms) who own a house in another person's compound or who work for another person and reside in his house. There are regional variations on this pattern in Bantam, Preanger, central and east Java and Madura.

(xii) *The territorially-based community in Acheh.* Prior to independence Acheh was divided into a hundred or more regional communities under autocratic hereditary governors. The smaller village communities within these divisions are exclusively territorial and so far as adat systems in Acheh are concerned the basis is territorial.

(xiii) Finally, there are scattered territorially-based adat systems in

Bangka, Billiton, in the Malay lands of Borneo and East Sumatra and in Gorontalo.

It is apparent from this summary that the concept of adat as a definer of a legal system is not a unitary structure. It is located in two different criteria—kinship and territorial organization—in defining the boundaries of its own system. This cannot imply a degree of logical unity but such is not in itself a fault or invalidation; the point was made at the beginning of this chapter that an adat law system could not be other than culturally confined. Further, and perhaps more important for the present subject matter, the notion of adat in its relation to social structure has been used in a consistent way. That is to say, it has been defined by a direct reference to the cultures of the Indonesian peoples. There were and are no exceptions to this standard approach which was one of absolute consistency. One can ask little more in respect of a teleological concept. There is yet a further aspect of consistency, the implications of which it is essential to consider. This arises out of the common concepts through which the rule contents of all systems, widely varying though they are, were and are discussed and administered. The issue, in other words, is the definition of adat as 'law'.

The Definition of Adat as Law

The legal implications of this sub-heading revolve around the practice of discussing different adat rules within a common set of European law-inspired legal categories. Adat rules were discussed in terms of 'marriage', 'inheritance', 'legal personality', 'delicts', and so on;[21] in this discussion the definition of law adopted was and remains that the principles of social structure constitute the principles of (adat) 'law'. There is no question that adat was to be defined in terms of justice, nor was it to be defined as the carrying out of a sovereign imperative, although the movement to codify adat principles in the early part of this century may be interpreted as an attempt to impose this view. The criterion for determining what were the proper principles for admission as law became settled in the pre-war period as those principles admitted by judicial or quasi-judicial authorities. Authors such as Ter Haar drew attention to the dangers of importing Western concepts inherent in this criterion, but attempted use to avoid these by encouraging the judicial authorities to use traditional Indonesian methods in the solution of disputes. He instances for example the use of *rukunan* (mutual arrangement or compromise),[22] and it is worth pointing out that this is still an important element in contemporary judicial dispute settlement.[23] Indeed the procedure code governing the judicial process in the District Court[24] specifically enjoins the judge(s) to make attempts at conciliation, and in adat cases this is done on the basis of local adat rules.[25]

The topic for discussion here, however, is the general issue of the fact-dependence of adat. The source of its internal validity is clearly in social structure but its external or continued validity insofar as the organs of state were and are concerned lies in the policy of the state, first in colonial policy and now in the policies of the Republik Indonesia. There are two aspects of external validity: first, the administration of adat by the organs of state (which was discussed in the last chapter), and second, there is a complex of legal issues which arise out of the fact-dependence of adat within a colonial or national legal administration.[26] The main features of these are as follows:

(i) THE ISSUE OF LEGAL CONCEPTUALIZATION

The language of the law was both Indonesian and Dutch and, moreover, in both cases it was a confined and special sort of language —the language of lawyers. It consisted of a vocabulary of terms used by specialists but not generally understood by non-specialists, although this is only partially true in the Indonesian case. The situation is more complex and had perhaps better be set out in some form of schematic arrangement.

(a) *Indonesian terms of legal relevance—colonial period.* Such terms fall into two classes. (1) Those in general use amongst the people but having also a significance in adat. Examples include the major kinship and territorial terms such as *suku, kuria, marga*, and so on. They tend to give rise to two sorts of complication. First, such terms may receive a defined content in administrative terms which is a variation on its common or loose usage. Second, there may be difficulties in distinguishing its significant referents as between sociologists and jurists and/or legal administrators. (2) Indonesian terms which have a specific 'legal' meaning within the terms of a particular adat system. Again, this raises a number of problems.

First, there are classes of terms, especially those referring to ownership or transfer (*jual*) of property which are assumed to 'be legal' but at the same time these are also terms for which an assumption of legal reference is necessary. This is very much a matter for the individual, whether judge, administrator or scholar of adat. Ter

Haar himself refers to this problem,[27] citing particularly a number of words, even including '*jual*' which is normally taken to have a self-evident reference.

Second, there is the difficulty of translating these into the framework of the judicial administration of adat. This was not really a serious issue at the low level judicial proceedings because every effort was made to utilize adat institutions, but it became and remains a serious problem at the level of legal description. Could one, for example, properly describe and analyse adat rules as to sale and purchase and conclude that, according to adat, a contract of purchase 'is not a consensual but a real contract'? At first sight there would appear to be little point to such a question, especially when one remembers that it seems to be an attempt to force a set of cultural facts into the technical categories of another legal system. But such questions do have a relevance, unfortunate although this might be. In contemporary Indonesia land transactions and commercial transactions of all types involve elements of contract which may refer to the rules of more than one legal system, and technical questions can and do arise in this situation. This is what is meant by 'legal pluralism' (see Chapter 4) and the implication of this is that one must come to some opinion on the propriety of such questions at the conceptual level. Given that questions of pluralism and technical conflict do arise as a matter of practice, then the jurist has little choice but to take account of this in formulating primary concepts. This does not mean that one must necessarily talk about an 'adat real contract'; it does mean that in describing the form of contract under some adat system the jurist must, in all honesty, justify the basis upon which he uses a set of terms and explain how his description is related at the conceptual level to the concepts of any other relevant legal system. A failure to do this can result in nothing but confusion.

(b) *Indonesian terms of legal relevance—contemporary period.* There are also the same two classes in this category. The problems indicated above in respect of the first have not changed, that is, terms in general use amongst the people, the issues on which remain the same. However, in respect of the second class, the terms which have a specifically 'legal' meaning, a new complication has arisen. This is the introduction of legislation which has as its motive the development of Indonesia in the social and economic spheres. In this exercise a large number of the older terms which had a settled meaning have now received a whole new set of referents. The outstanding example is the effect which the Basic Agrarian Law[28] has had. Section 5 of this law states that 'adat' is to be the basis of new rights in land but that the adat must also not be contrary to the interests of the state in national unity, to Indonesian socialism, to the regulations of the new law, or to other state regulations. This means, for example, that the adat community right of disposal (*hak ulajat*) is subject to state regulation. In addition, various terms used in land matters generally have either received new meanings or have had their old meanings substantially varied.[29] Further, a new language problem has arisen in which indigenous terms have received a new 'revolutionary' meaning. For example, the term '*musjawarah*', which means the search for a communal decision in resolving a conflict, came to have a political content in that it was said to be the appropriate method for state organs to use in coming to a decision.[30]

(c) *Dutch terms of legal relevance.* This was a subject of major concern during the colonial period; van Vollenhoven paid it a good deal of attention as did Ter Haar.[31] Put shortly, a case was made out for the necessity of using Dutch as the language of government and legal administration but with a constant safeguard in its use by reference to local languages in which the adat rules were and are expressed.

In the case of both Indonesian and Dutch the legal language was accepted as providing a set of categories under which fact situations can be more or less automatically subsumed. Its most obvious function is in dividing facts into relevant (with legal effect) and irrelevant (with no legal effect).

The use of language, whether 'ordinary', 'correct', or otherwise, is regarded by the law as being susceptible to confinement and specialization within the orbit of the court. This poses several difficulties in the field of adat laws. First, on the general question of the relation of languages and concepts of law, the formulation of concepts for whatever purpose is based upon features of language which may or may not be universal. It assumes the possibility of an adequate characterization of the uses of language, a position which is denied by some authorities. The particular concepts which flow from these views of language are limited to those linguistic usages upon which they are based and do not necessarily extend to data from outside that system. Therefore, any cross cultural application is not possible except if it be shown that the foreign data supports this particular view of language use.

Second, because adat law appears in the form of positive law (judgments) it would, therefore, seem that the analyses used in the original municipal systems could be applied *mutatis mutandis* to analyse such judgments. The objection to this, however, is that in many cases the mixing of concepts from a number of obligation systems is not possible. The language theory of Western law assumes that, as a matter of fact, the usage established by the court can and will be translated into action in the application and enforcement of any judgment. This is a reasonable assumption in European jurisprudence not just because of the efficiency of legal machinery but also because, on the question of usage, the pronouncements of the court are more or less cognizable to the individual concerned. Neither of these features is necessarily present in the adat situation; in particular the mode of procedure is often based on concepts which are wholly alien to the bulk of the recipient population. This also results in considerable difficulty in ascertaining usage in a specific instance, extending also to the non-possibility of ascribing a particular (legal) consequence to any usage.

The implication of this description and also of the foregoing examination of the language issue in the formation of legal concepts may be summarized as follows:

1. There is a clear distinction between lawyer's usage and the understanding of this usage on the part of persons subject to the law.

2. So far as the *practice* of positive law is concerned, reference to the rules of the particular system involved is sufficient. For example, the administration of adats on marriage or any other topic is a practice carried out in terms of stated rules and not in terms of defining the characteristics of 'law'.

3. For an adequate description of *how* adat law works at all levels, a reliance upon the concepts of some particular positive system is not sufficient. This is simply because, in the question of usage, the particular system does not of itself admit the relevance of usages outside its own conceptional boundaries.

4. Finally, and as a result of these points, it is necessary to develop a method of adequately representing the reality of a number of laws in interaction. This is primarily a question of language—of ascertaining upon what basis the verbal symbols of various interacting systems are built up. At a superficial level this is merely a question of translating words and phrases from one language to another. But as any comparative lawyer will know, and as the adats fully illustrate, grasping a foreign reality, and this is what is implicit, is much more complex.[32] The reason for this is not difficult to see; language is not just a medium for the transmission of ideas but is an important factor in the formation of ideas. Our concept of what the world is, is related to the language in which we express our experience, because this experience is organized and interpreted in terms of

language structure. This was stated clearly by Edward Sapir who said:[33]

> Language is a guide to 'social reality'. Though language is not ordinarily thought of as of essential interest to the students of social science, it powerfully conditions all our thinking about social problems and processes. Human beings do not live in the objective world alone, nor alone in the world of social activity as ordinarily understood, but are very much at the mercy of the particular language which has become the medium of expression for their society. It is quite an illusion to imagine that one adjusts to reality essentially without the use of language and that language is merely an incidental means of solving specific problems of communication or reflection. The fact of the matter is that the 'real world' is to a large extent unconsciously built up on the language habits of the group. No two languages are ever sufficiently similar to be considered as representing the same social reality. The worlds in which different societies live are distinct worlds, not merely the same world with different labels attached.

Although not all jurists accept this statement without qualification, a close inter-relationship between language and culture is accepted. The importance of this is particularly marked in studies of comparative law and in the adats.

(ii) CULTURAL FACTS

The facts of the adat systems described earlier in this chapter were not all admitted as legally relevant but were limited in various ways to what was felt to be acceptable to state authority. Only *some* facts of morality and culture were and are permitted to determine the grounds for dealings between individuals. Article 75, para. 3 of the Constitution of 1854 forbade the application of adat rules which were in conflict with generally recognized principles of justice. The latter, needless to say, was the concept of justice as defined in European terms.[34] On the other hand, this provision has been interpreted as a direction to the judge to test a given adat rule in the light of social reality and in connection with the demands of humanity.[35] A contemporary provision also exists in the constitutions of the Republik Indonesia,[36] which provide that the validity of *any* law may be tested against the provisions of the constitution. In essence what is involved in both cases is an assessment of cultural fact in terms of some standard which is both outside and independent of the indigenous *milieu*. Further, this is not just some theoretical assessment; on the contrary, it is made for a purpose and it directly affects the application of adat rules. This process is comparatively easy to understand in the colonial period because the standard remained fairly constant for most of the twentieth century. Under the influence of van Vollenhoven and later of Ter Haar, it became settled as the preservation of indigenous cultural principles subject of course to a correspondence between these and the practicalities of day-to-day administration.

However, the issue is more difficult in contemporary Indonesia for two reasons. First, the systems of adat are systems of diverse *sources* of law, and the only way to determine which are the relevant sources or proper sources or even institutional sources is a resort to the law-applying organ, that is, the court. It is in the court that these questions are answered and it is here that fact and law meet.[37] If we admit that law guides behaviour by stipulating consequences, then it is clear that the law-applying organ must be a focus because this is the institution which ultimately enforces such consequences. We should not forget that laws, from whatever source, are normative and guide the actions of the courts as much as they guide the actions of ordinary people. Their existence is therefore based in social practice and this is common to all positive norms.

These comments raise the question of identifying the law-applying organ. In our own societies we are accustomed to a variety of such organs: the courts, tribunals of various sorts, and so on. These bodies, however, all have one thing in common and this is that they are part of an institutionalized hierarchy. However, in the adat situation it is not uncommon to find other forms or modes which, although outside the ambit of the courts, are yet part of the cultural *milieu* in which such laws exist. The example of *rukunan* which has already been referred to indicates the scope of this problem.[38] The practice of the courts is by no means easy to understand at the moment. It is not sufficient to say that the Supreme Court initiates change while the lower courts in applying or giving effect to local rules of adat aim to preserve or insulate cultural features from change or development. The real situation is far more complex than this,[39] but it is undeniable that in the various indigenous processes of dispute settlement the only standards applied are those peculiar to the adat cultures themselves. The Indonesianization of the judicial process has itself probably contributed in no little way to the encouragement of a turning inwards to indigenous values.

The second difficulty in contemporary Indonesia is to know exactly what the standards are in the assessment of adat systems. Since independence there have been a number of politically imposed standards, all of which are traceable, at least to some extent, in judicial activity. One may cite, for example, the principle of 'revolutionary independence'[40] and the principle of 'revolutionary socialism' in legal development.[41] In addition there are the more mundane legal principles of certainty in the law and the issues of adapting or translating a colonially defined adat into a system suitable for independent Indonesia. These concepts have all been or are standards for the assessment of adat; the only constants in the shifting kaleidoscope of standards have been the cultural facts of the Indonesian social systems themselves. They, at least, are relatively certain in this uncertain legal world and for this reason alone it is as true to say now, as it was a century ago, that adat law is socially constructed.

Summary

In looking at the Indonesian adats one is obliged to admit the primacy of sociological factors in both their substance and in their form. The problems in comparative jurisprudence to which this fact gives rise have been indicated in the last section, and it is also clear that in modern Indonesia the political pyrotechnics of the past quarter century have had little effect on the basic concepts of adat. This is not to deny any or all influence of a movement toward change; on the contrary, as the following chapters of this book illustrate, significant change has occurred. But whatever the nature of this has been, it is still true that the principles of adat laws in Indonesia remain culturally defined and the judicial process in modern Indonesia has accommodated itself to this fact and will continue to do so in the foreseeable future. Indeed, a quarter century of jurisprudence (legal decision) which has consistently given effect to adat can hardly be said to have advanced the breakdown of culture-specific definitions of adat. This issue is dealt with further in Chapter 7.

1. Maine (1861).
2. cf. Sally F. Moore (1969) on a description of descent as a legal category.
3. For example, an infant exists as a fact, but this existence is denied for some legal purposes in many Western laws.
4. For recent jurisprudence on this topic cf. Raz, 1970: 1–3.
5. cf. Ter Haar, 1948: 50 ff.
6. ibid: 60–74.
7. This of course is not to deny that the term has other uses. See the following chapter.
8. van Vollenhoven, 1918: (i) 14.

THE SOCIAL CONSTRUCTION OF ADAT 49

9. Koesnoe, 1971: 9–10. See further Chapter 3 on Indigenous and European thought about the concept of adat.

10. This is dealt with in more detail in the next chapter.

11. The selective use of some features was often criticized as unjustifiable, most notably by Vergouwen (1964). See also van Vollenhoven (1921) on the wider issues involved.

12. For example, 'clan' for the *nagari* of the Minangkabau; 'familie' for the extended family; 'gezin' for the nuclear family.

13. It is worth noting that the units established by the Dutch are retained in adat law discussions in contemporary Indonesia. See Soekanto (1969) and (1972). There are of course new legislative and judicial initiatives which affect the adat systems, but a discussion of these is put off to a later part of this book. See Chapters 6 and 7.

14. This is very apparent in the system of *rechtskringen* (law circles). See also Koentjaraningrat (1967) for examples of the complexity of village organization in Indonesia.

15. Taken from Ter Haar, 1948: 60–74.

16. cf. Willinck, 1909: 635.

17. cf. Josselin de Jong (1951) for a comparative description. See also Nasrun (1957), Nagari Basa (1966), Mochtar Naim (1968).

18. See generally Vergouwen (1964).

19. Also *kalompoan* and *arajang*.

20. This social complex was called '*het ornamentschap*' by the Dutch administration.

21. cf. Ter Haar (1948).

22. ibid: 231.

23. cf. van den Steenhoven (1970).

24. Pengadelan Negri.

25. See further Chapters 7 and 8 below.

26. cf. Ter Haar (1929) for an introductory summary.

27. Ter Haar, 1948: 226–7.

28. No. 5/1960. See further Chapter 6.

29. cf. Gautama & Harsono (1972) for examples. See also Chapter 6.

30. Decision of the Provisional People's Congress (MPRS) No. XX/1966.

31. Ter Haar, 1948: 224–5 for a brief summary.

32. See the discussion in Nader, 1969: 337–48.

33. Cited in J. C. Smith, 1968: 194.

34. cf. de la Porte, 1933: 46 ff.

35. cf. Ter Haar, 1948: 40 and the authorities there cited including Carpentier Alting, van Vollenhoven, Soepomo and Wertheim, and decisions from a number of courts. Art. 75(3) was repealed by Art. 131(2b) of the ISR. 1925.

36. Constitutions of 1945, 1950.

37. See below Chapter 7.

38. See also below Chapter 8.

39. See below Chapter 7.

40. cf. Lev (1964–5) for a description from the cases heard in the Supreme Court.

41. As summarized in Pantjasila—cf. Soeripto (1973).

3

ADAT IN LEGAL THOUGHT

Introduction

ADAT is generally translated as 'custom' and, specifically in its legal reference, as 'customary law'.[1] This apparently simple usage tends to disguise or obscure the complex nature of the term which seems to resolve itself into three major aspects. The first is the variety of reference which the term bears; it can mean any one of the following: law, rule, precept, morality, usage, custom, agreements, conventions, principles, the act of conforming to the usages of society, decent behaviour, ceremonial, the practice of magic, sorcery, ritual. The precise meaning of the term depends upon the context but an important underlying sense seems to be the idea of proper behaviour in one's relations both with other people and with natural phenomena.

The second aspect is an extension of the first. Upon the basic reference just outlined there are more specific uses of adat which are peculiar to a locality or to a people in the adat world. This world stretches from southern Thailand, through Malaysia and the Indonesian archipelago to the southern Philippines. It encompasses a variety of linguistic and cultural groups each with their 'own' adat. Throughout Indonesia this is indicated by specific terms which refer either to an area (e.g. adat Minangkabau) or to an institution (e.g. *adat rasan, adat 'anggaw'*).[2] This aspect was dealt with more fully in Chapter 2.

The final aspect which the student of Indonesian adat has to contend with is the great number and variety of theories of and about adat produced by scholars, administrators and jurists. The adat literature is vast and new work is constantly being added. It is written both by social scientists and by jurists, and this is probably one reason for the diversity of adat studies and for the lack of agreement within them. On the other hand all studies of adat are based in a long tradition of fieldwork; it is thus not the data as such which are in question but rather the explanations offered for different adat institutions. Debate arises not from adat so much as from different conceptions of law—of what it is, how it is to be described, and what use to make of the idea of law in the study of peasant cultures. This question is treated in more detail in the following sections of this chapter.

A word also needs to be said in this introduction about the diversity of adat data in Indonesia. The quantity is immense and the quality is generally very high. As already indicated, it appears both in legal studies and in works written by social scientists. It is therefore impossible in a book of this size to deal with all manifestations of the adat cultures; on the other hand adat study raises a number of general questions and it is with these that we shall be concerned. In this chapter two in particular are primary: first, the nature of adat in indigenous culture, and second, the referents attributed to the term in legal theory. These questions are of course closely related and are usually considered together, particularly in law. However, it is useful to separate them here because, though connected, they are separate aspects of the relationship between cultural traditions and the administration of law.

Adat Thought in Indigenous Culture

As already pointed out in the early part of this chapter, the range of meaning which can be attributed to adat is wide and tends also to be somewhat vague. However, there is clearly a core meaning which we can generally describe as involving an element of obligation. The precise meaning of obligation is a function of particular social structures[3] which, as they vary, also give a variety of elaborations on the idea of adat. It may be useful to indicate some of these here concentrating not so much on principles of social structure but on indigenous elaborations on the idea of obligation. It is of course difficult to separate these, and this is acknowledged, but it should be attempted for the light it throws on the concept of adat.

It is essential, first, to stress that there is practically no sphere of life to which the term 'adat' is not somehow apposite. This is a consistent feature in all accounts of adat, and elements which are thought of as disparate in European legal thought are commonly referred to in the same usage. For example, one finds accounts of magic, religion, ethics and land holding, amongst others, discussed in the same framework. A further difficulty is that the terms used are sometimes interchangeable. For example, behaviour which is described as '*adat istiadat*' (custom in general) may also be described as '*adat kebiasaan*' (habitual behaviour). A further distinction between these terms is also sometimes made; the former may refer to norms *for* behaviour and the latter to norms *of* behaviour. The point of this example is that the classification of obligation is, in general, fluid, and this is reflected in the accounts of specific adats. Some writers on the subject may choose to define obligation rather narrowly whilst others are prepared to include elements of religion, in other words, to construe 'law' in a much wider sense. However, it must be emphasized that no general rule of construction can be laid down unless it is qualified in two ways: first, by reference to the facts of a particular society, and second, with reference to the aim or purpose for which the account is written. Much will depend, in the second case, upon whether the account is a general description of a culture in which adat is but a part, or whether the account is specifically on adat as a legal institution. Further, if it is on adat then for what purpose and in what framework is it being written? Is it for purposes of law reform, a theoretical investigation into obligation systems or an exercise in comparative law? All of these will materially affect the description and the view of adat subsequently arrived at.

From the point of view of comparative law, where the comparison is conducted by European scholars[4] into the laws of largely preliterate communities, two major classifications may generally be distinguished. These are claimed to be direct representations of adat reality:[5]

(i) Adat comprises the forms of all social institutions, and the behaviour expected of the individual in terms of these institutions.

(ii) Adat refers to the regulations and directives which are specific according to time, place and circumstance and bind the individual or groups. Although comparisons are dangerous, the nearest analogy in our own societies is with prescriptions.

Such a classification is proper to jurists who operate within the bounds of European systems of municipal law and its transference to the investigation of adat is only natural when, as is the case, adat is a subordinate body of law in a state system based upon Dutch civil law. It is oriented toward isolating the analytical features of adat within the state legal system, and for this reason it tends to ignore or diminish important epistemological and ontological factors. The latter must be taken into account so as to truly reflect the reality of adat and it is to these that we now turn.

It is clear first of all that in its traditional formulation adat is largely unwritten in form. One is inclined to say 'largely' because some of the adats do appear, at least to some extent, in written texts, most though not all of which post-date the Islamic era. Such texts are characteristically either Sumatran, containing large elements of *fikh* or else are texts from the Islamic sultanates of Java also with the same Islamic content. With the possible exception of the Minangkabau texts[6] and the Balinese *awig-awig*,[7] such documents had little relation to the real life of the adats. The typical form of the adat is in oral traditions such as the *umpama* of the Toba-Batak, the *perbilangan* of the Minangkabau and in the proverbs of the Javanese and other peoples of Indonesia. Form was and is important in oral traditions of the adats because by its very nature it acts as an important link with the past. In addition, the use of the correct form is itself an adat, a usage, which can have the effect of validating certain courses of action. Traditionally there was little in the way of a written codification of adat; of those which are known, some, for example the Minangkabau and Balinese books, are important because they state prescriptions. These, however, are the exception rather than the rule; most adat texts are important for stating a view of law and do not concern themselves except in the most general way with prescriptive statements. The oral forms of adat are, however, prescriptive as well as classificatory, and the important reference in both cases was to previous practice, or ancestral practice as set out in this tradition. This was recognized by European commentators,[8] but the problem so far as the colonial administration was concerned was the adaptation of oral tradition to the demands of the state. This is dealt with more fully in a later section.

The second feature is that the oral adat admonitions tend to be vague in character and often elusive in meaning. This is partly a consequence of the oral form which demands a striking phrase for ease of retention. Not uncommonly the demands of the linguistic form give rise to an ambiguity which is not without its advantages. The *asas-asas* (principles) in oral tradition allow a wide latitude in interpretation and this permits a variety of accommodations in dispute settlement. It cannot be emphasized too strongly that a knowledge of oral tradition needs to be complemented by a knowledge of the principles of social structure for proper interpretations to be given; this, of course, is self-evident to the Indonesian populations. The characteristic latitude is sometimes indicated by the use of the term '*luwes*', variously translated as 'plastic'[9] or 'simple and supple'.[10] But the principles remain immutable not least because they are connected with past tradition and possibly involve also elements of the supernatural: the latter need not necessarily involve sanction as such. It is worth pointing out that such latitude does not always accord with some aspects of adat. In many fields, especially property, the adat rules are minutely defined and rigidly followed.

A third characteristic form of adat is found in the typical hierarchical arrangements which describe the relationships between man and nature (including non-empirical natural forces) and between man and man. Emphasis is commonly laid upon the duties of individuals involved in the scheme toward nature and toward each other. Various individuals have specific duties attached to them, most particularly those who hold positions of power or authority. The interesting feature of this, however, is that power does not necessarily imply the inevitability of sanction nor does the process of adjusting conflicting interests result in the imposition of a unilateral decision. Most often a process of mediation is gone through with the purpose of arriving at some compromise solution. Rights and duties are not absolute or fixed principles but are relative according to the proper behaviour adat requires from specific individuals. There is no conception of the individual as a fixed point of normative reference which is absolute and independent of circumstance. Obligation varies depending upon circumstance and upon an individual's position (in status, or kinship relationship) within or without the adat universe. This is not a process of arbitration, properly speaking, and nor is it thought of as such. The essential of arbitration is the decision by the middleman, but the adat situation may more properly be described as mediation. A dispute is not settled until both parties become so sensitive to each other's feelings, circumstances, and standpoint on the matter that they agree upon a mutual adjustment which meets the *esse est percipi*, the special particularity of the situation. There is little scope here for physical sanction which is replaced to a large extent by an emphasis upon internal and external harmony, the reverse image of which is shame (*malu*).[11] Each moral choice, each judgment, and each individual is regarded in its normative nature as unique rather than as an instance of a determinate general rule. The key to morality and law is to be found not in the constancy and absoluteness of a universal code (except to the extent that social structure itself is such) but in an intuitive sensitivity to unique and particular situations.

This view is often objected to or felt to be open to the criticism that it leaves morality and law excessively relative, without any absolute criterion of the moral good and the legally just. Such a charge rests upon the assumption that for ethics or law to possess an absolute standard requires a constant codified or codifiable universal rule.[12] This assumption would form the basis of a valid criticism if such a code or universal rule could be said to be the only source of an absolute criterion. But as the data on adat thought so clearly demonstrate, such a criterion may be found in reactions to the special particularities of successive unique problems rather than in determinate universal propositions. Given this factual situation there is no good reason for the outside observer to deny the suitability of concrete moral choice in favour of some codified solution as an absolute criterion. This might be described, somewhat disparagingly, as an exercise in nominalistic epistemology, but for all that, it is a true and accurate description of a working system which gives satisfaction to the participants. After all, each fact in experience and each adat process is at least partially unique and deserves to be looked at in terms of its own ontology. The European observer has no right at all to deny this or to deny its implications.

Having said this it still remains to be demonstrated that there are constant characteristics in the world(s) of adat which, although they do not amount to the existence of a constant codifiable universal criterion, do indicate the existence of some common analytical features. The following are put forward as possible candidates which might fulfil this function. Firstly, the distribution of obligation is often a function of an actual or putative genealogical relationship. Secondly, the community, whether defined on a genealogical or a territorial basis, almost always has a greater right over land distribution than the individual possessor or occupier.[13] Thirdly, the institutions of *tolong menolong* (mutual help) and *gotong-rojong* (communal duties) exemplify the individual's subjection to a common set of obligations. These institutions have important implications in the field of economics as referring to a technique of teamwork,[14] but in neither case is it possible to distinguish between individual obligation and group interest (*gujub*).[15] Fourthly, all the adats posit the preservation of harmony between the community and nature.

These features may be described as the 'proper' relations which constitute the requirements for a good and just society. While not implying that this is an exhaustive account it is clear that they indicate a view of law which is radically at variance with European systems. The most striking factor is probably that the adats do not generally see relationships of obligation as being bilateral and, as a consequence, the individual is not taken as the point of normative reference. So far as individual systems are concerned *qua* system, the idea of sovereignty is not formulated in terms of exclusive adherence; the idea is replaced by a conception of the real world as one in which man and nature are indistinguishable parts of a unitary whole.

It was with this situation that the Dutch colonial administrators had to deal.

Dutch Legal Thought on the Adats

In the last two chapters a description was offered of the methods adopted by the colonial power for the administration of adat. Briefly, this took the form of basing legal administration upon indigenous adat units and of defining the adat system in terms of Indonesian social structures. Both of these approaches have been continued or at least have not been formally abolished in the Republik Indonesia, though some of the recent legislative and judicial development has taken the Indonesian people as a whole as its primary point of concern. This is dealt with in a later section of this chapter and throughout subsequent parts of this book. This section is concerned to describe the conceptions of adat as a system of law in Dutch legal thought.

Dutch legal theory had to take account of two facts of adat legal life. First, the many different systems of adat which existed and their arrangement into law circles as has already been described. Second, the complex systems of different laws for different racial groups in the Netherlands East Indies which gave rise to the interracial conflicts of laws. This is the subject of the next chapter, but it should be emphasized here that although discussed in separate chapters, the issues raised in legal theory are connected.

If we turn now directly to the adat systems we find that there were basically two questions of theory which engaged the attention of Dutch jurists from the closing years of the last century until the establishment of the Republik Indonesia. These were (a) the relationship between adat and state sovereignty and (b) the definition of adat.

(a) *Adat and state sovereignty*. The issue here revolved around arguments put forward in the four decades from the turn of the century for the codification of all existing civil law in Indonesia along European lines. The necessity for this was justified on the grounds that because of the changes occurring in the native community the adats were, as they stood, not suitable for modern conditions. Behind this motive there lay a view of the law as deriving its ultimate validity from the will and acts of the legislator. This was a common standpoint at the time, especially as there was already legislation in force providing for a unified Criminal Code (1918) and rules of criminal and civil procedure. The arguments in support of the codification (later unification) of the civil law were put forward most forcibly by Nederburgh over a period stretching from 1896 to 1933.[16] Apart from the practical issues of adapting adat to modern conditions of life (mainly economic) in the Netherlands East Indies the basic premise, repeated at length, is that a law derives its validity from the authority of the state. The opposite view was put most strongly by van Vollenhoven,[17] whose theoretical argument was that validity is primarily a matter of sociological existence and not necessarily existence within the conceptual state structure. Much of van Vollenhoven's writing is concerned with this question, particularly in papers arguing for the limitation of Western law concepts in adat and for the recognition of adat law decisions as valid propositions of law.[18] This is primarily a dispute as to the *source* of law and to the mechanism of validity, both of which hinge to a large extent upon the view of law adopted.

We may take each of these ideas separately. First, the nature of law or the view of law adopted will determine that in which one locates its source or sources. For Nederburgh the law is clearly a complex of rules arranged in a hierarchy and validated by the sovereignty of the state. The location of a valid rule is therefore to be found in the organs of the state. This, of course, was always a factor in Dutch colonial policy, and the adat systems identified on the basis of social structure were consistently validated in that the legislation of the Netherlands East Indies accepted their existence for many purposes. Nederburgh, however, would go further and argue that the rule content of such systems had necessarily to be conceptually related to the norms upon which the sovereignty of the state itself rested. The Netherlands East Indies was, in essence, a territorial sovereign and not a personal sovereign (as were the pre-Dutch Indonesian rulers) and the law, therefore, could not be any other than territorial or, more exactly, common to all the inhabitants. The logical answer was a codification which would, of itself and in terms of territorial sovereignty, define what was and what was not law properly so called. Validity, therefore, depended upon the *form* of prescription.

Van Vollenhoven's argument in answer to this position was essentially constructed around a distinction between prescriptive and descriptive validity, although he does not use this terminology. For a law to be properly called such van Vollenhoven claimed, rightly, that it must be both prescriptively and descriptively valid and that the mechanism by which this was accomplished was its proper and only source. He saw that the institutions of the dominant colonial system must, by their very existence, effect some sort of social change in the Indonesian population. He recognized also that this must be inevitable, given the emphasis upon the prescriptive element in law in its task of defining and securing a certain social order, that is, of creating social conditions, patterns of behaviour and modes of organization felt to be suitable. The major effort was in the creation of a legal apparatus to carry out these tasks. This has comprised the identification of one source of authority and the establishment of institutions under that authority. Positive law was seen as a tool to accomplish a desired purpose in the same way that the prescriptive role of law accomplishes desired purposes in our own societies.

The fact that this prescriptive function of law was seen as strictly analogous is of particular importance here. In the municipal states of the West there is a close co-ordination between law acting in its prescriptive role and the actual order within which it functions. The legal order, substantively and procedurally, reflects the circumstances that gave rise to it; but in fact the prescriptive role of law, although important, is only one amongst a number of other factors which operate the legal order. In most cases, legal prescription is already the subject of a normative acceptance amongst the population at large so that law is both the creator and servant of social facts and values. But if the prescriptive role of law is insisted upon and emphasized for purposes of social change its function is to re-define and re-structure social fact and social values. In other words, it must change social fact by destroying the close and harmonious co-ordination between prescription and the actual social order. In this situation the only source of its ontology now lies in the exertion of prescription through the legal apparatus. The effectiveness of law is thus severely limited for it is not possible merely by putting out a prescription effectively to change a social order. It may of course be possible to amend parts of it, but in extreme cases the result of a too heavy reliance upon law in its prescriptive role alone will be either the rejection of a programme of social reform or the dismissal of the legal apparatus as a whole by the population. Both of these reactions were and are endemic in the Indonesian adats. From the viewpoint of the national legal system, however, such rejection is 'illegal' because the prescriptions involved 'are valid law'. On the other hand, the outside observer clearly sees that the changes prescriptively ordered 'are not valid', that is, are not found to occur in practice: the particular propositions of law do not have a descriptive validity.

These were the arguments which were fundamental to van Vollenhoven and later to his followers. The distinction which they saw between the prescriptive and descriptive modes of law was essentially based upon a recognition of the facts of Indonesian culture, as they understood it, and a recognition that the concept of law may properly be defined in sociological terms. This seems to be reasonably clear, although there may well be argument over the motive of the colonial administration for accepting the views of van Vollenhoven in preference to those of Nederburgh and his like-minded colleagues. It is quite common, for example, to see it argued that this acceptance was a cynical move to divide and rule the Indonesian people. The contrary argument is that the recognition of a legal pluralism was in accordance with the facts of Indonesian life and it protected and retained the basic features of Indonesian culture. It is unnecessary here to pass an opinion on the question of motive although it may be observed that, in common with all political polemics, there is a grain of truth on both sides. In any case, legal pluralism was accepted as the norm in the Netherlands East Indies, and this fact both explains and is an explanation for the definition of adat 'as law' which became established in the early decades of this century.

(b) *The definition of adat.* Given the acceptance of legal pluralism as a constant feature of colonial administration, especially after 1927,[19] it became necessary to decide upon some definitive meaning for adat as 'law'. What was the legal content of adat to be and how was it to be established? These questions were of course important in the nineteenth century, particularly in distinguishing between Islam and adat,[20] but their importance was enhanced with the increasing amount of legislation affecting adat particularly in jurisdictional matters, although it was not until just prior to the Japanese occupation that this issue was fully worked out.[21] At the turn of the century, however, the position was still unclear although Snouck Hurgronje had pointed out in 1893 that it would be fruitful to speak of 'adat that has legal consequences',[22] or '*adatrecht*'. This was a reference to legal consequences within the framework of colonial administration and it is important that this fact be remembered. Dutch legal scholarship at that time was not really interested in the definition problem for its own sake, or as a basis for some ethnography of law; they saw their task as defining a concept for use in a legal administration which was concerned with the administration of native custom. This is especially true of van Vollenhoven[23] for whom a minimal definition was sufficient. He saw his task as emphasizing the legal character of a large body of uncodified oral traditions with a view toward dispelling contemporary misconceptions as to their legal nature. It was important to him to make clear the distinction between Islam and adat on the one hand, and to establish the positive law aspect of adat on the other. His early definition of adat, therefore, was that it 'is a body of uncodified rules enforced by sanction'.[24] Sanction meant organized sanction involving the existence of some institution, either an individual or a group, which had authority to punish or reward. This was a perfectly acceptable definition at the time and within the context for which it was meant. However, in 1931, his thought on this subject developed further, and to a large extent he got away from a reliance on sanction as a necessary criterion. It may be supposed that the less positive position adopted in 1931 was a consequence of the fact that the *adatrecht* was now formally accepted as a constant part of the Netherlands East Indies' legal system. The new definition was:[25]

[Adat is] the mutual interaction between a normal custom and other normal customs on one side and between normal customs and disturbing divergencies on the other side....

Within these terms he saw even recommendation and disapproval as legal and not moral elements if they are clearly linked to command and prohibition in collective consciousness and behaviour. It is only when somebody tries to violate such elements that formal judgment becomes necessary. Sanction is not abandoned altogether but a new element is introduced—the mutual interaction of normal custom enforced by recommendation and disapproval. Some commentators[26] have seen here the influence of Malinowski and Radcliffe-Brown, but however this may be, it is at least as likely that this definition owed much to van Vollenhoven's method of adat law study. This consisted of describing in detail the institutions of adat as these were observed in the daily conduct of the Indonesian peoples. The intention was to arrive at a plain and fixed formulation of the principles of adat. The formal descriptive process was intended to provide certainty of content and to be of assistance to the professional judge in adat suits. This later definition is quite different in kind from the earlier one. It is a definition in terms of both sociological and legal *process* rather than in terms of static characteristics or essentials. It is also a definition which attempts to comprehend the facts of Indonesian life and not, as in the earlier one, a view resting upon an ethnocentric concept of law. It is also a view of law which fitted the administration of adat as this was established in Indonesia.[27] This is an important consideration; indeed it might be said, as indicated a little earlier above, that the administrative system itself determined the extent of *adatrecht*.

ADAT IN LEGAL THOUGHT

This interpretation appears even more clearly in Ter Haar, who concentrates upon the idea of judicial process. He defines adat law as the decision given by some functionary in an adat community who is acting in a judicial capacity.[28] This is some way from the later van Vollenhoven view which, although it does include an element of sanction, does not specify judicial function. The distinction between these authorities can quite reasonably be explained by the different contexts within which the definitions are given. Van Vollenhoven is discussing the institutions of adat as observed in the daily conduct of the Indonesian people. The intention was to provide a certainty of content. Ter Haar on the other hand is looking to the formulation of principle which can, because of its mode of formulation, be subsumed within the mainstream of state jurisprudence. The common factor, which Ter Haar saw as fulfilling this function, was a decision given by some judicial functionary either 'native', i.e. within an adat system, or official. It is a definition in other words which rests upon the same criterion of validity as the rational written state system. This is a long way from the indigenous concepts of adat discussed in the last section; the clear implication in Ter Haar's view is that the adats were capable of constituting a series of fixed universal principles within the wider Netherlands East Indies jurisprudence. The emphasis upon judicial function also represents a break with tradition in that mediation is, in theory at least, subordinate to decision. This was rather mitigated in that the judicial procedure in the courts did and still does require efforts toward mediation on the part of the judicial authority.[29] But the institution of law reporting[30] and the definition of adat in terms of reported decisions represents a new view of the Indonesian as an individual in law. The individual is now a point of normative reference and obligation is defined in terms of the individual.

Further support can be got for these comments in the later development of Ter Haar's thought. This is contained in his discussion of 'precedent and the judge'[31] where the following proposition occurs:[32]

> The decisions rendered by officials, chiefs, and judges can and should always be regarded not only as applying concretely in a given case but also as setting precedents for 'similar' cases—cases, that is, which in whole or in part are relevant as to the facts and in this sense similar and subject to precedents. Such decisions indicate the legal principles which are valid in the community; their concise legal forms are drawn from a multitude of less precise living patterns, from conceptions and values cherished in the community.

This proposition must be read in the light of the fact that the legal system of the Netherlands East Indies had no rule as to the binding power of precedent as has the common law. All the same it is a somewhat startling proposition for a civil lawyer although less so for an adat scholar searching for a criterion. It may be perhaps that this quotation taken alone is a somewhat unfair exposition of Ter Haar's views because he does go on in the following pages to limit somewhat the scope and role of precedent. At the same time, however, he does cite an Anglo-American jurist[33] in support of his proposition that precedent, or some sort of precedent system, is primary. The point is that this uncertainty demonstrates an inherent contradiction in Dutch legal thought on adat. There was a conscious policy and effort to preserve traditional institutions and to identify obligation in terms of indigenous systems. At the same time the organization and administration of the state institutions could not treat the adat institutions and obligation systems on its own terms. As Nederburgh saw so clearly this was primarily the question of the sovereignty of one normative system over another. The dualist policy, as the thought of Ter Haar demonstrates, posited a number of sovereign law systems, but at the same time political sovereignty rested in the institutions of only one of these systems. A codification of some sort would probably have been the answer to such a theoretical difficulty but this was never achieved,[34] and the contradiction persists to some degree even into the present.

Contemporary Legal Thought on Adat

Adat legal theory did not change drastically upon the establishment of independent Indonesia,[35] although many nationalists identified the *rechtskring* concept of law with the colonial opposition to the formation of a unitary state of Indonesia. Indeed, the attempt to set up the federal Republik Indonesia Serekat (United States of Indonesia) was seen by many as a continuation of the colonial policy of divide and rule.[36] Between 1945 and 1960 attempts were made to adapt and modify the Dutch colonial legacy by piecemeal legislative and administrative amendment, but the outcome of this was generally unsatisfactory. In 1960 the Provisional People's Consultative Assembly met to consider and establish the principles which should govern the recently inaugurated National Development Plan. Important amongst the goals of the plan was the establishment of a national law,[37] and the Consultative Assembly stated quite specifically that:[38]

ADAT IN LEGAL THOUGHT

... the principles (governing) the establishment of national law should accord with the political direction of the state and be based upon adat law *that does not retard the development of a just and prosperous society.* [Emphasis added.]

This raised, in an acute form, the colonial question of the relationship between adat and the state. The jurists associated with the Institute felt that the first task was to dispose of the Netherlands East Indies laws which were seen as 'an anvil for the exploitation... of the Indonesian people'.[39] This proved to be easier to accomplish in theory than in practice,[40] and the issue of national law remains as cloudy now as in 1960 or indeed at independence. Even before the national law issue was directly raised there had been an extensive debate on adat in the new Indonesia. Possibly the earliest commentator was Supomo who coined the term '*hukum adat*' as a replacement for, but with the same content as, the Dutch *adatrecht*.[41] But in 1950 the same author used the term[42] to mean the unformalized adat of the traditional system, possibly with the same sort of reference as van Vollenhoven. This has continued to be the view taken of adat by this writer.[43] His descriptions concentrate upon the principles of social structure and upon the ontology of law described in the second section of this chapter. Particular attention is given to the stress which adat lays upon the preservation of harmony within the group,[44] and an attempt at a philosophy of adat law based upon indigenous principles is made.[45] The institutions of adat are specifically compared with those of Western law.[46] These are interesting in themselves because they illustrate not just a method of analysis but also a distinction in principle between two clearly differentiated systems of law. Adat is said to lack institutions which provide for the possibility of an individual exercising a right against any other individual, a theme which appears in other authors of the period (see below). Rights, especially to land resources, are described as communally based. Adat is said to be characterized by mediation, the purpose of which is not to establish an individual right but to re-establish peace and harmony in the community.[47] With all this, however, Supomo holds the opinion that the scope of adat principles should be confined to matters of family law and inheritance; in other branches of the law the principles of foreign law, that is, Western law, should be adopted into the national law.[48]

This work is clearly an attempt to come to grips with the dichotomy which for long exercised the Dutch: the reconciliation between indigenous views of adat and the demands of a territorial law. In the new context of Indonesia, however, the question had an immediacy and urgency which it never attained in the colonial period. The new legal unit is the individual, not the adat law group, and the qualification for the law's attention is not race but citizenship. Supomo's solution was a fusion of law systems retaining adat only in family law with the expectation that even here future change would be possible. On the other hand, a slight variation on this view was presented by his contemporary, Kusumadi Pudjosewojo,[49] who distinguished between *adatrecht* and *hukum adat*. The former, broadly speaking, is the colonial complex of adat legislation and decision which is abolished because of the attainment of independence. *Hukum adat*, on the other hand, consists of the unwritten legal rules governing the conduct of the individual in free Indonesia. This view would amount to a definition of adat as 'usage' except for one thing: in Kusumadi's explanation of *hukum adat* his criterion for identification is that this adat is law proper when it has become the decision of a bearer of authority.[50] This position amounts to a restatement of Ter Haar though approached from a slightly different angle. However, it tends to lay more stress on the indigenous content of adat than was common in the immediate pre-war era. To a large extent it represents a reaction against the influence of Western law concepts.

Perhaps the most outstanding and certainly the clearest post-war example of this reaction is to be found in the work of M.M. Djojodigoeno. In the immediate pre-war era he had co-authored what is still the standard account of the adat private law of central Java.[51] But in the early 1950s he turned his attention to what he saw as the real needs of Indonesia in legal development, which were quite different to the laws which Europe had developed for its own social and economic systems. This appears clearly in the following passage:[52]

... individualistic and liberalistic views do not live in the minds of Indonesians. We are socio- and traditio-bound people: everyone of us has to act and to behave as all others do; one has to be common, *biasa* (Javanese *lumrah*). Being different from others is being strange, astonishing, wicked, condemnable. In this course of ideas an individualistic state of mind and an individualistic pattern of behaviour and action will arouse opposition, disapproval and condemnation. Freedom of contracting and competition is out of place, as are definite actions in law, containing definite claims.

The rejection of the individualism inherent in the laws of the West led Djojodigoeno to formulate a new basis for the laws of Indonesia in which adat was seen as having a primary role. He accepted

ADAT IN LEGAL THOUGHT 65

Ihering's notion that 'law is a work of an entire people in the sense of limiting human actions and behaviour in contractual relations'[53] which is intended to secure order and justice. It is clearly similar to the later views of van Vollenhoven, but Djojodigoeno has gone further in clarifying the implications of this idea for independent Indonesia. In a later and important paper on the re-orientation of adat[54] he lists the most important factors in the legal process as follows:[55]

(a) *The 'static' element*. This is the judicial reference to existing rules and statutes by the judge. It is identified as the dominant factor in Western law and is criticized as often producing absurd judgments. It is seen as a kind of legal automation involving intricate concepts of positive law, the result of which is often a travesty of justice. It should have no place in an Indonesian court.[56]

(b) *The 'dynamic' element*. This is a reference to existing social conditions amongst the various Indonesian peoples. These are seen to consist mainly of adat principles of the type formulated by van Vollenhoven. This is a call, in other words, for the acceptance of adat principles and, most important, to oppose a codification of the law on the principles of the Western law codes.[57]

(c) *The 'plastic' element*. This is a reference to the importance of considering each case as a unique combination of individual facts and personalities. The important underlying implication of this is that a series of abstract principles based upon formulations of positive law (either 'precedent' or statute) is not a desirable feature for the law of Indonesia.

The result of this threefold approach to the process of law is a formal distinction in the manifestations of adat. Adat has a 'material sense' which is a reflection of the indigenous sense of justice (in the adat universes) of the Indonesian people. It founds its authority in the practice of the villages although this may also be given effect to by the agencies of the state as in judicial decision.[58] Adat also has a 'formal' sense as a matter of legal classification and in Indonesia the basic distinction is between written and unwritten law. Adat has its source in the latter form, mainly in the facts of social structure.[59] This is more than just a distinction of sources of law; it represents a view of law as being founded in social process and to this extent it has obvious links with the thought of van Vollenhoven and Ter Haar.

The bulk of Djojodigoeno's work was written in the period immediately after the successful independence movement and it represents an attempt to found a philosophy of law in Indonesian tradition suitable for use in a state system whose ideology was a sort of modified socialism. The emphasis upon the dynamic and plastic elements in his discussion of the judicial process is only fully understandable when it is realised that in the Indonesia of the time social justice for and economic equality amongst the Indonesian people were to be attained through a mass consultation between people and government. The principle of Pantjasila was new and in its call for unity and social justice, jurists such as Djojodigoeno turned away from the positive law system of the West to indigenous adat cultures in the belief that this would provide a means for the practical implementation of the revolutionary ideals.[60] Unfortunately these have proved somewhat difficult to implement and there remained a wide and possibly increasing gap between such theories and the actual administration of adat, particularly in the courts.[61]

There has been little or no guidance from the legislature or political authorities in terms of legislation or judicial practice on these questions, and although later work continues in the tradition of Djojodigoeno,[62] its practical effect on legal policy must be accounted slight. It is only fair to say that contemporary work concerned with establishing the general character of adat within specific Indonesian communities does have its own value in a number of fields. For example it is essential data in the implementation of national modernization programmes, such as family planning and so on.[63] To this extent it contributes something both to the preservation of the legal *status quo* and to an understanding of particular adat institutions.

To a large extent current legal thought on adat continues in the tradition of van Vollenhoven and Ter Haar.[64] The questions with which they were concerned—the definition of adat and its relationship to the state continue to exercise contemporary jurists, but apart from attempted accommodations with political philosophy, such as that of Djojodigoeno, little that is original has been produced. The classifications established in Dutch colonial scholarship remain although the links between the state and adat have been drastically reduced. There is no longer an adat law policy as such and in matters of public law there is an equality of administration in contrast to the variety of jurisdictions current in the colonial period. The main connecting factor remains the presence of vast numbers of adat cases in all levels of the court system. This is a demonstration not just of the vitality of adat but also of the fact that the formal framework of Indonesian law with its Western derived principles has had little success in penetrating the countryside. However, it is precisely in this area that current legal thought is most inactive. Apart from collections of such cases[65] there has been little in the way of organized

ADAT IN LEGAL THOUGHT

discussion of the future role of adat in the national legal system.[66] Indeed the adat position may even go by default in that elements of state sovereignty may be stressed to the extent that adat will be confined to rules specifically admitted by organs of the state and to no other principles.[67] This is an argument which is put by the opponents of adat and it is based on the ground that to permit adat would contribute to uncertainty in the law.[68] It is a view of adat which is not unpopular at national level and which demands that law be written and rational on the Western pattern. It is between such persons and those who wish to see the continuance of adat, at least for some transition period, that the adat cases in the courts form a common ground for discussion and for the elaboration of a process-based theory of adat in modern Indonesia. It is in the development of such ideas, and not in repetitive discussions on the nature of adat, that the future of adat law theory lies.

1. This is its primary reference in the Arabic language from which the word originates.
2. For a convenient dictionary summary see van Hinloopen Labberton, 1933: 4–10.
3. See Chapter 2.
4. This class includes Indonesian scholars using the forms and techniques of European legal thought.
5. cf. Snouck Hurgronje, 1924: 411, Maharun Batuah & Bagindo Tanameh n.d: 57, Chairul Anwar, 1967: 57, Kusumadi Pudjosewojo, 1961: 43.
6. cf. Liaw (1967). See also Djojodigoeno, 1950: 6–8 on adat as oral tradition.
7. See Korn (1940) (1960).
8. cf. van Dijk, 1954: 7.
9. cf. Djojodigoeno, 1950: 10; van Dijk, 1954: 8.
10. Wirjono Prodjodikoro, 1957: 142. See also Supomo, 1966: 26–8.
11. cf. Supomo, 1952: 8 ff.
12. This was certainly the assumption of a group of Netherlands Indies jurists in the early years of this century who supported a programme of codification. See the next section in this chapter.
13. cf. Ter Haar, 1948: 81 ff for a brief description.
14. Koentjaraningrat (1961), Slamet (1963), Geertz, 1963: 244.
15. cf. Supomo, 1966: 22 and for a further elaboration see Djojodigoeno, 1958: 7–8.
16. cf. Nederburgh (1896) (1933).
17. cf. van Vollenhoven, 1933: 719–43 which contains his famous 'Juridisch Confectiewerk'. Also van Vollenhoven, 1931: 22–59 on 'Geen Juristenrecht voor den Inlander' originally published in 1905.
18. This was the main reason for the founding of the 'Adatrechtbundels' and the series 'Pandecten van het Adatrecht'.
19. When an 'enlightened dualism' became firmly established as official policy; see Ter Haar, 1948: 13.
20. cf. Snouck Hurgronje, 1893(i).

21. Comprehensive studies were presented at the 1939 Indies Juridical Conference. cf. Guyt (1939), M. Slamet (1939).
22. Snouck Hurgronje, 1893: (i) 357.
23. cf. J.P.B. de Josselin de Jong, 1948: 4.
24. van Vollenhoven, 1918: 14.
25. van Vollenhoven, 1931: 236, 400.
26. J.P.B. de Josselin de Jong, 1948: 4–5. Jaspan, 1964–5: 245.
27. cf. Chapters 1 and 2.
28. cf. Ter Haar, 1937: 4. For a contemporary critique see Holleman, 1938: 428–40, Logemann, 1938: 27–36.
29. See below Chapters 7 and 8.
30. See the following: Enthoven (1912) for adat law decisions of the period 1849–1912; van der Meulen (1924) for the period 1912–23; Boerenbeker (1935) for the period 1923–33. See further Chapter 7.
31. Ter Haar, 1948: 228–33.
32. ibid: 228.
33. John Chipman Gray (1927).
34. Some authors, for example Logemann, 1947: 44, see this failure as a broken pledge to the Indonesian people.
35. See Chapter 1.
36. cf. Kahin, 1952: 196.
37. cf. Depernas, 1960: 497.
38. *Ringkasan Ketetapan* MPRS, No. II, 1960: 82.
39. Suprapto, 1963: 42. This somewhat obscure writer does not seem to have published since 1963.
40. See Chapter 6 where the maintenance of colonial legislation is briefly discussed.
41. cf. Supomo (1947).
42. This reference appeared in a commentary by him on the Provisional Constitution of Indonesia, entitled 'Undang undang Dasar Sementara Republik Indonesia' and is cited in Kusumadi Pudjosewojo, 1961: 64. Also separately published, see Supomo, 1950: 53.
43. cf. Supomo, 1966: 5. See also Soepomo (1952).
44. See generally *ibid*. See also Supomo, 1952: 8 ff.
45. Supomo, 1965: 117.
46. Supomo, 1966: 22 ff.
47. ibid: 36 ff.
48. Supomo (1947).
49. cf. Kusumadi Pudjosewojo (1961).
50. ibid: 65.
51. Djojodigoeno & Tirtawinata (1940).
52. Djojodigoeno, 1952: 13.
53. For a more recent statement of Djojodigoeno's view of law see his *Wat is Recht?*—Djojodigoeno (1971). See also Djojodigoeno (1972).
54. Djojodigoeno (1961).
55. ibid: 13–14.
56. See below Chapter 7 on the judicial process where it is clear that this view was never accepted to any great extent by the judiciary and at present shows to an even lesser degree.
57. cf. Djojodigoeno, 1952: 17.
58. Djojodigoeno, 1958a: 7, 8.
59. cf. Djojodigoeno, 1950: 6.
60. cf. Djojodigoeno (n.d.).
61. See below Chapter 7.
62. cf. Koesnoe (1969).

63. cf. Koesnoe (1972).
64. See the following sources: Soetikno (1971), Wignjodipuro (1971), Hakim (1967).
65. See Chapter 7.
66. It is worth pointing out as these pages go to the printer, that an officially sponsored seminar on adat and national law has just been held. Its proceedings are reported briefly in *Sin. Har.* 29/1/75 and *Pelopor Yogya* 19/1/75.
67. See Gautama, 1970: 161.
68. cf. Alisjahbana (1968).

4

ADAT AND INDONESIAN LEGAL PLURALISM

Introduction

THIS chapter is really a continuation of the last in that colonial and contemporary adat thought is intertwined with the general legal theory on racially-based law groups.[1] From the earliest period of Dutch colonization, and more especially from the mid-nineteenth century, the different racial groups in the Netherlands East Indies (Dutch, autochthonous Indonesians, Foreign Orientals and various refinements on these) formed discrete legal groups. The attribution of obligation in all matters was determined by the law of the racial group to which an individual belonged. The motive for these divisions has been and remains a matter of dispute. Colonial apologists saw it as providing for the freedom for each ethnic group to follow its own special laws and religions. Later commentators, particularly in contemporary Indonesia, see it as a device to divide Indonesian society in order to ensure the domination of Dutch interests. In support of this argument they often cite the position of the Chinese who were made subject to European regulations, thus facilitating their economic function, although Chinese law was naturally quite different from the Dutch civil law. This argument ignores the fact that the Chinese were assimilated only in 1917, comparatively late in the history of the Netherlands East Indies. However, the rights and wrongs of the legal pluralism policy are not the subject of this chapter, but the issue does raise strong emotions on both sides and it is as well to be aware of this fact. The law-population divisions have survived into the Republik Indonesia and the major theme of law reform for the past twenty-five years has been legal unification in which racial criteria would be replaced by citizenship as the connecting factor between the individual and the legal system. Some progress has been made toward this goal, e.g. by the Agrarian Law of 1960 in respect of land matters, but in the absence of a uniform civil code a large part of Indonesian private law is still pluralistic in character.

The origin of the system lies in the early history of Dutch commercial enterprise in Indonesia in which the Dutch retained their own law and provided special regulations and caveats for those Indonesians who lived in regions controlled by the *Vereenigde Oost-Indische Compagnie* (East Indies Company).[2] This situation became a topic for discussion amongst the jurists of the sixteenth and seventeenth centuries and we find Grotius saying in his *Mare Liberum*:[3]

> Java, Sumatra, the Moluccas have their own kings, public institutions, laws and rights and they have had them always. One is not entitled to deprive these infidels of their will and princely power because they do not believe. Indeed it is even heresy to assume that the infidels should not be master of their goods, for it is no less theft and robbery to deprive them of their goods than it would be if a Christian were concerned.

The administrative system which made possible juristic work of this type continued but it was not until 1848 that legal pluralism in Indonesia became formalized in the constitution of the Netherlands East Indies. In that year the *Algemene Bapalingen van Wetgeving*[4] was enacted, classifying the inhabitants of Indonesia into two groups, European and Native. This classification was supposedly adopted on religious grounds since the classes were defined respectively as Christian or non-Christian. However, inconsistency almost immediately arose with Indonesian Christians being classified as Natives. In 1855 this system was replaced by Art. 109 of the *Regerings Reglement*[5] which confirmed the earlier arrangement but included the Chinese, Arab and Indian inhabitants within the Native group. In practice the latter tended to be treated separately from the natives so that there were three law groups in existence. This continued until January 1920 when Art. 109 was amended by Art. 163 which defined the racial groups and was later incorporated unchanged into the *Indische Staatsregeling* of 1925. Art. 131 of the same law defined the law in force for each group.[6] All persons were classified into one of three groups, Europeans, Natives and Foreign Orientals.

These classifications continue to be valid in modern Indonesia by virtue of the Transitional Articles of the Indonesian Constitution which provide that all regulations in force continue until replaced in a manner prescribed by the Constitution, that is, by statute.[7] It has been argued from time to time that pre-independence regulations are valid only to the extent that they are not contrary to the Constitution; indeedt his was an interpretation of the Constitution put out by an executive order in 1945,[8] but the provisions of Arts. 131 and 163 continue to be observed. In 1966 a Cabinet Instruction directed the Office of Civil Registration to cease recording distinctions based upon race,[9] but this does not affect the subjection of the different ethnic groups to separate laws. A more serious attempt was made in 1963 when the Supreme Court issued a circular letter[10] purporting to identify a number of provisions in the law as being contrary to the constitution. The validity of this has been disputed and may not be binding on the lower courts. On the other hand the Supreme Court has given judgments which specifically declare some articles of the earlier law to be invalid.[11]

Two questions arise in relation to adat: first, the content of adat in terms of this system and second, the relationship between the rules of the different systems particularly where transactions involving persons from more than one law group are in question: the problem of *intergentielrecht*.

Adat in the Plural Law System

One may look at this topic in two ways: first, in describing the formulation of adat rules specifically within terms of the regulations of the state. Second, by considering the options and possibilities open to an individual subject to adat to submit himself to the rules of some other system. Both these questions will be discussed in this section but with the caveat that the subjects discussed in the preceding chapters be kept firmly in mind.

First then, the question of adat rules in terms of the state regulations. This is a matter primarily governed by Art. 131 para. 1 of the *Indische Staatsregeling* of 1925 which came into effect in 1926 and laid down as a matter of general principle that the civil law of Indonesia was to be written law including the law for the Native group. However, para. 2(b) provided a set of guidelines for the legislator respecting the Native population. The natives were subject to written law only when their social need demanded it. In other words, adat continued in force subject to this provision. Thus European law might apply or a special law applicable to all groups might be promulgated depending upon circumstances. A current example of the practical working of this proviso is illustrated in the Basic Agrarian Law of 1960. Although it is stated in Art. 5 that this law is based on adat it does apply to all groups in Indonesia and, in fact, its connection with adat is a little tenuous.[12] The Agrarian Law is not, in terms, based upon the provisions of para. 2(b) but these may be said to have been in the minds of the legislature.[13]

Para. 2 says nothing about what law is in force for the Native group pending the promulgation of new regulations. This is regulated by Art. 131(6) which came into force on 1 January 1920 and which preserved all Native law already in force subject to later regulations under para. 2(b). In effect this refers to the adats and those European regulations promulgated prior to and after 1920 and declared applicable to the Native group by the Governor-General. There were relatively few European regulations so declared, the most important of which were Book II, Ch. 4 of the Commercial Code on shipping and some articles of the Civil Code concerning labour contracts and wagering.

In the period 1920-1938 a number of civil and commercial regulations were promulgated exclusively for the Native group but these were not based upon adat. Some of them however had the effect of drastically affecting the administration of adat and hence struck directly at the roots of adat. Such, for example, were the regulation on the law to be applied in the religious courts,[14] the regulation on marriage for Christian Natives in Java, Minahasa and Ambon,[15] and the regulations on Native corporations[16] and associations.[17] An extremely important regulation is that on Indonesian mortgages (*credietverband*) promulgated in 1908[18] and still in use. This permitted Natives holding Native land to give mortgages on the land to specified European banks although no banks were actually specified until 1937. The regulation, however, clearly contemplates a relationship between corporate bodies subject to European law and land held under adat tenures by members of the Native group. In the contemporary period a number of Indonesian banks which are incorporated on civil law principles may take adat land as security for credit.[19] All of these regulations illustrate the impossibility of preserving one law, here the Native law, as a self-contained entity.

The influence of Western law is apparent in this brief description, and this was an issue of which colonial jurists were well aware and on which they spent a good deal of energy. An early leading paper on this question and one which still has a good deal of contemporary relevance is that of Ter Haar, written in 1929.[20] He traces the means by which substantive principles of European law directly influence the Native group even though the greater number of the regulations are only enabling laws. First of all, there was the influence of European procedure, as in the courts, which formalized adat rules to an extent unknown in the traditional sphere. Second, specific concepts of European law were introduced via this procedure and in terms of the regulations themselves. This was a potent source of confusion particularly where the Native institution being regulated was misunderstood. The interpretation put upon the supposed Muslim office of 'priest' and the function given to such an official in Native court procedure is a well-known example. But it is in the specifically European context of regulation that adat was most affected. For example, in the matter of crime, Ter Haar demonstrates that although the same class of wrongdoing might be recognized in Native and government laws, the penalties under the latter were not those which accorded with the facts of Native society. The most striking example is the use of imprisonment which was largely unknown in pre-colonial days and which had consequences for which Native society had no answer. Connected with this was the introduction of the idea that fault, classified by Western jurists as penal, need not necessarily give rise to compensation; the latter is a feature of all adats which, in general, prescribe restitution either in the form of payment or in the form of services.

Ter Haar defined Western influence on the adats in the following way:[21]

... In all cases where—owing to the presence of the Dutch group of the population in the Indies and as a result of the administration of the government over the Indonesians by Dutchmen—ready-made Western law institutions or juridicial interdictions and injunctions appear to have been included in the law of the native population in such a manner that the *adat* law would not have arrived at that stage by independent development, in all those cases we can speak of Western influence on the *adat* law.

This is an extremely wide definition covering situations which would now commonly be classified as administrative or executive, substantive and procedural. It also takes account of the situation, common in Indonesia, of indigenous tribunals refusing to admit an adat rule on the basis, justifiable or not, that to do so would infringe some government regulation. Ter Haar admitted this possibility and proposed that any investigation into this topic should be conducted by ascertaining the methods through which Western law can (i.e., is able to) influence Native law. He isolated five such methods for Indonesia, of which the two most important were the influence of the administrator, particularly in reducing adat rules to writing, and the developed body of jurisprudence (judicial decision) which became established.

These last two factors continue to be important today as avenues through which the regulations of the Republik Indonesia come into contact with the adat. Jurisprudence is dealt with in a separate chapter,[22] but so far as administration is concerned we may instance a 1946 statute which requires that the contract of marriage must be witnessed by at least two persons.[23] This was originally a requirement at Islamic law and the witnesses are usually officials of the Department of Religious Affairs.[24] Absence of such witnesses does not invalidate the marriage as such, but the parties are under an obligation to prove their marriage in court. In other words, the demand expressed in a regulation which does not formally raise questions of validity, in actual fact does so, and an adjudication outside the adat world becomes necessary to determine validity.

This brings us now to the options and possibilities open to an individual subject to adat to enter into situations involving the rules of some other law system. This situation, generally known as 'transfer', arose in four main ways.

(i) *Equalization.*[25] Prior to independence it was possible for a Native to make application to the Governor-General[26] to become a member of the European group. To qualify the applicant had to show that by reason of his superior education he had become alienated from his own society and (until 1894) he had also to undergo conversion to Christianity. After the turn of the century equalization was applied for and granted on the basis of the type of legal transactions most commonly entered into by the applicant. In effect this meant the types of contract relationship known to European law. It was also possible for equalization to be attained through judicial action and the criteria was a combination of such factors as following a European way of life, marriage to a European, and so on.[27]

(ii) *Voluntary Submission.* This was provided for by Art. 131(4) of the *Indische Staatsregeling* and the procedure was regulated by a Royal Decree dated 15 September 1916.[28] Of the various sorts of submission possible (total, partial, *ad hoc* and presumptive), only two are of real significance to adat. These are the *ad hoc* and presumptive submissions.[29] An *ad hoc* submission was where the individual submitted himself to European private law for purposes of a specific legal transaction. Generally this was possible only in that area of the law known as *hukum hartabenda* (*vermogensrecht*) which, broadly, was the law relating to commercial transactions, contract, corporations and partnerships and, in some cases, civil wrongs. It does not extend to family law, including inheritance, or land law.

Presumptive submission is rather similar and occurs when a member of the Native group participates in a transaction unknown to adat law but found in European law. This submission is also confined to the area of *hukum hartabenda* and, further, the transaction must be one entirely unknown to adat; it is not sufficient that adat would regulate the matter in a different way.

In both these situations the assumption was that European law was superior to adat, and this opinion seems to have been based upon three factors. First, the European law provided greater scope and flexibility in taking account of transactions which were either unknown or imperfectly known to adat law. The area of commercial operation is the obvious example and indeed, the regulation specifically limits submission to this area. Second, since most of the activities involved in these submissions were matters of contract, the European law, being written, provided the certainty of terms and conditions necessary for commercial intercourse. Third, and following from the two points already made, there was a conscious policy to protect European financial interests in contracts between European and Native.

(iii) *Involuntary Submission*. This occurs when a person from one population group becomes subject to a law not normally applicable to him arising out of a transaction with a person from another group. This was dealt with both in legislation and through the courts, and the specific problem to which these institutions directed themselves was the choice of law issue. In such transactions the law applicable was, by the nature of the transaction, uncertain. Legislation was passed which provided, *inter alia*, that where persons subject to different laws married, the law of the husband governed the incidents of marriage such as property, the status of the wife and so on.[30] This regulation applied not only to marriage between persons of different population groups but also to marriages between Natives from different law areas. There are also regulations making similar provisions for illegitimate children as well as regulations on labour contracts. The regulations providing for choice of law in land matters were repealed in the Agrarian Law of 1960.[31]

In addition to regulations such as these the courts have, over the years, developed a body of jurisprudence dealing with conflict of laws problems (*hukum antargolongan*) arising out of contracts between persons of different population groups. This is considered in more detail in the next section of this chapter.

At this point it is as well to remember that, as with other aspects of adat in Indonesia, the courts and legislature did not function in a vacuum but had the benefit of a complex body of legal theory on pluralism. This will be described briefly here because it both puts what has been said already into some sort of perspective and introduces us to the complexities of the conflicts problem.[32]

The introduction of the term 'conflict' is of importance for at least two reasons. First, many obvious conflict situations did arise given the multiplicity of legal systems. This was most apparent in contract, either for the sale of goods or in contracts of marriage. The second reason was that the existence of a number of legal systems and the conflicts of principle which arose were often thought of either in terms of or as strictly analogous to principles of private international law. Toward the end of the nineteenth century there had been a marked growth in this subject within the wider international community, and the existing legal pluralism in the colonial empires of the day had not escaped the attention of leading jurists. The French jurist, Arminjon, for example, described the colonial situation as 'le droit international privé *interne*' and discussed it as an integral part of private international law.[33] Other jurists such as Neumeyer and Goadby held similar views.[34] The French jurists, especially those concerned with the French North African territories, also devoted a good deal of time to the subject, and a further reference is made below to the work of Henry Solus whose theories attracted the attention of the Dutch jurists.

If we turn now to the position in Indonesia, a convenient starting point is the proceedings of the Congress of the Netherlands East Indies Jurists' Association held at Batavia in 1887.[35] One of the main features of this Congress was the debate which arose as to whether a new statutory regulation regarding mixed marriage was desirable. In the event the Regulation Governing Mixed Marriages of 1896[36] was promulgated and provided that where the parties to a marriage were from different population groups the status and incidents of the marriage were to be regulated by the law of the husband. So far as the conflicts question was concerned, this was interpreted by some commentators, notably L.W.C. van den Berg, as demonstrating a general principle that the law from one group could not apply to an individual from another without special legislation to that effect. This view of course rested upon a belief that all law is an expression of the will of the sovereign, that is, statute. This opinion is incorrect not just because submission to European law was possible for a Native in the absence of legislation[37] but also because this was not the view of adat adopted in Dutch colonial legal policy.[38] Van den Berg's arguments were rejected by contemporary jurists but they gave rise to a considerable conflicts literature.

One of the most prominent contributors was Nederburgh who, while rejecting van den Berg's position,[39] pressed for a '*ius constituendum*', a general law for all the population groups in the Netherlands East Indies. In the absence of express legislation establishing this it had to be assumed that for the proper regulation of the relationships between the different legal systems there existed a 'higher' law. This was applicable not just to the formation of the laws of each of the population groups but was also the instrument by which the legal systems as a whole were defined. Since the adat laws were inferior to European law in utility and scientific value, the higher law could only be European law at least until the legislator acted.[40] This position led Nederburgh to press further for the codification of a law suitable for all population groups including the Indonesian, and brought him into conflict with van Vollenhoven.[41] However, as Kollewijn points out,[42] Nederburgh did not see the issue as one of existing conflict between higher and lower laws as such but as the relationship between dissimilar laws. His classification 'higher and lower' was a classification directed toward and in support of his codification thesis.

The actual use of the classification in the solution of conflict between the various laws in the Netherlands East Indies had to await the advent of André de la Porte.[43] He saw the situation of pluralism as basically being one of conflict. The object of his work was to discover whether the rules of private international law could be used in solving problems in interracial law but in so doing he developed the thesis that private international law was directly applicable as a matter of principle. He reached this conclusion by adopting the principle that private international law applies by virtue of a territorial connection, whereas interracial law is a matter of personal and not territorial attachment. His solution was to make use of the following fiction:[44]

> I act as though each of these laws [for the various population groups] possesses its own territorial jurisdiction in the same way as the legislations of various states have their own jurisdictions. Europeans are then presumed to have their actual place of residence in the jurisdiction of the European legislation and therefore to exercise their civil rights in that place.

This has been criticized by Kollewijn[45] on the ground that it rests upon an unproved axiom—that it is proper to follow or apply the rules of private international law so far as is possible. This is a valid objection because, as has been repeatedly demonstrated, a reference to the *lex fori,* the *lex loci contractus* or the *lex domicilii* of itself settles nothing.[46] These are territorial connecting factors and are not of themselves decisive in a territory characterized by personal laws.

Kollewijn, who has been described as the 'father of inter-personal law in Indonesia', maintained successfully that European and Indonesian laws were equal in status. Neither of them could be applied as a higher law and nor could the private international law analogy apply because the courts of the Netherlands East Indies had to treat both systems as equally part of the *lex fori*. On the other hand, if the needs of interracial law demanded it, there was no reason why some rules of private international law could not be utilized. It was also open for the courts to give priority to one law as against another if the circumstances of the case demanded it. Further, if one rule was more effective than another in the same field then that might also be preferred.[47] Kollewijn also specifically rejected[48] the French doctrine of '*conflit colonial*' which was most fully expressed in the work of Solus.[49] Kollewijn's position is not so much *sui generis* as an abstraction from judicial and legislative practice. The source of interracial rules is found, as described earlier in this section, in a number of special forms, judicial decision and statute, resulting in a group of clearly stated rules defined for a comparatively narrow class of circumstance. In this respect Kollewijn's views are a representation of legal reality and for this reason, if for no other, they have stood the test of time.

Adat Law in the Context of Pluralism

There are two major classes of plural relationships which are important for Indonesian adats. First, adat law is not uniform throughout the archipelago and, as pointed out in Chapters 1 and 2, the adats were organized into law circles on the basis of cultural differentiation. The Native law group was and is fragmented; individual adat systems often recognized the existence of 'foreign' systems but do not always provide rules dealing with such systems. The social construction of adat was such that the issue was not the adjustment of a foreign *principle* with one's own principles but the accommodation of an individual *person* within the system. This arose primarily in matters of marriage or residence, because the internal processes in adat were and are epistemologically naive in nature (see Chapter 2). Second, legal pluralism arose out of the system of racial laws which obtained in the Netherlands East Indies. This aspect only came into being with the imposition of European authority, the whole legal basis of which was posited on the exclusiveness of territorially based legal systems. Having introduced such an idea the issue of the conflict of principle became primary to the extent that one could speak about inter-local conflict of laws. This involved a contradiction to the extent that Schiller could say that 'interlocal law depends primarily on a legal system *territorial in origin* that *attaches to the person of a member of the group...*'.[50] This represents a considerable distortion of the traditional adat view in which a territorial exclusiveness was not primary. On the contrary, the law was personal in origin and process but under the twin demands of a territorial administration and a territorial system of law (including law-making) a contradiction arose. The colonial system therefore introduced conflict as a principle in the legal process and the courts were concerned to answer such questions as how one attaches a person to a system, what are the consequences of marriage or commercial contract between members of different systems and so on.[51]

This sort of adjudication could not be a matter for the legislature simply because they could not legislate for the number and variety of conflicts which arose. There was a further reason also and a more interesting one: this is that the administrative system encouraged the possibility of conflict within the Native group but the legal policy of non-interference within the adat universes made intervention impossible. The issue arises solely in judicial decision. This raises an interesting question: to what extent was the inter-local conflict problem a creation of the courts? It was not an issue in the traditional systems but it might be argued that the forum by its inability to follow indigenous principles of compromise made the conflicts question inevitable. It is also notable that the cases commonly cited in the literature[52] concern individuals who, by reason of their profession or business, are emigrants from their own group and had considerable means. The question was therefore confined to a small minority of the Indonesian people; to some extent, then, the 'inter-local law', while prescriptively valid, lacks a full descriptive validity. It may more properly be considered as part of the whole interracial question, not least because the conflict question in issue is a European legal issue. In addition, the extent to which interlocal law problems now exist is a function of the interracial question, given the current preoccupation with unification and legal modernization.

The second major class in Indonesian legal pluralism is the interracial question proper, with which the rest of this chapter is concerned. As a preliminary some attention should be paid to the term 'interracial' itself. This is a direct translation of the Dutch '*inter-*

gentiel', and was first used in English by Kollewijn in 1929; the term *intergentielrecht* (interracial law) came into use amongst Dutch jurists about the turn of the century and referred to the following relationship:[53]

> These interracial juridical conflicts [arise] when subjects of the same country, within the borders of that country, are subject to different private laws....

The term has been criticized[54] but its use is now firmly established and there seems little point in further objection. However, one must be careful in its use, particularly when one is writing in English, because its reference is to a particular type of legal system: the civil law system in its Dutch version. The two outstanding points which must be borne in mind by a common lawyer are both contained in the passage just cited. The references there are to the [political] 'subjects' of a state and to 'private' law. Neither of these classes is properly known to the common law; a political status is not essential to the common law jurisdictions where the issue is domicile. Private law is again not a category of importance except possibly in analytical works of jurisprudence. Further, the common law is always the law of general application; it does not admit of separate legal systems in the same territory. It does of course recognize principles of personal or religious laws but these form part of the common law in precedent although confined to (judicially) defined classes, either racial or religious. For this reason principles of private international law are not properly to be applied where cases of apparent conflict arise, because the conflict is internal and within the territorial common law system and is able to be solved only in terms of that system.[55] In common law colonial and post-colonial jurisdictions, therefore, the discussion is about 'personal law', its place in and relationship with the principles of the whole common law system. One may explain the distinction in terms of the language of normatives;[56] the Netherlands East Indies version posits two norm systems—adat and European, which exist separately and touch at various points. The point of contact is called *intergentielrecht*. Such systems, however, are self-contained and internally consistent. The common law in its colonial manifestations posits only one norm system which contains within itself sets of inconsistent prescriptions. According to many jurists, amongst them Kelsen and von Wright, an inconsistency could not or should not occur, but the common law is anything but consistent, especially in its personal law aspects. It is, however, an operable system in the sense that it works, although its judges are not known for their respect for either jurisprudential analysis or jurists!

It is with these points in mind that we return to interracial law,[57] that is, to the situation where the norms of the mutually exclusive adat and European laws intersect. The colonial legal system identified two processes in such a situation. First, it was necessary to establish the factors which could create the interracial law situation. Secondly, once this had been identified as an existing situation the problem was to decide what law was to apply. Both processes were a matter for the legislature and the courts, though the latter were more decisive in determining the issue.

(a) *The identification of an interracial issue.* Traditionally there were four primary points[58] of contact, any one of which identified an interracial law situation. The first and most obvious was where the parties to any transaction were from different population groups. Since independence this distinction has become less important. Many regulations are put out for the citizens of Indonesia as a whole though in some cases earlier divisions retain a functional significance.

The second point of contact was the status of land; the Agrarian Act of 1870 and later amendments[59] created a complex system of land classifications which had reference to the division of the population into racial groups but was not wholly consistent with it. For present purposes, land was classified into 'Indonesian' and 'Western' land, but these classes did not arise from the racial group of the owner but from the legal system (adat or Civil Code) which defined the characteristics of the land. The position was further complicated by a Royal Decree of 1870[60] implementing the Agrarian Act and providing in effect that all land held under adat rights was part of the state domain. This meant, *inter alia*, that the state could dispose of uncleared land over the adat rights of a village or kinship group. Indonesian land was subject to adat law except in the face of special legislation, and most of it was unregistered. European land was registered and was subject to the Civil Code as to ownership and possession. However, the complication was that land, whether Indonesian or European, could be possessed by individuals without reference to their population group. Europeans could acquire adat land by way of inheritance or mixed marriage and once acquired it could be later transferred to non-Natives without restriction. It was in this sort of situation that conflict problems arose. With the introduction of the Basic Agrarian Law in 1960 the status of land is no longer a decisive point of contact. This law abolishes the dual system of land rights and prescribes that the only rights which can be exercised in respect of land are those set out in the law itself.

The third method of identifying an interracial situation is where the parties to a transaction specify that a certain legal system shall govern the transaction. This was mentioned earlier in this chapter but it is worth emphasizing that it retains something of its importance in contemporary Indonesia. For example, it is open to Indonesian parties to a contract to specify that the agreement shall be subject to the (European) Civil Code. The court will apply European law even though in all other matters both parties are otherwise subject to adat.

The final point of contact in the colonial period was the forum of a suit. Briefly, there were separate courts for the different population groups prior to independence and the choice of forum depended upon the population group of the defendant. Thus, a suit brought by a Native Indonesian against a European was tried in a European court. This system was abolished under Japanese rule and there is now a unitary system of court process throughout Indonesia.[61]

Of the four methods of identification just sketched only the choice of law factor and, to some extent, the significance of different racial groups continue to be important. However, even with the absence of land and forum issues, the position remains complex enough, particularly in the question of choice of law. It might also be said that these so-called points of contact are juristic classes based exactly on the facts of legal pluralism in Indonesia.

(b) *Choice of law*. This is the more interesting and complex aspect of Indonesian legal pluralism, involving as it does the circumstances determining what law should be selected from among the systems present in the interracial situation. The area of law in which these questions arose was and remains in contract and, to a lesser extent, in the law relating to 'unlawful acts'. The latter is a category not properly known to common lawyers; an 'unlawful act' (*onrechtmatige daad*) is fairly closely analogous to tort although it can also refer to public law matters arising out of state activity. For example it is possible for the state or for a state organization to be sued by a person who does not submit to European law. The general rule in the unlawful act cases is that in an interracial suit the law of the wrongdoer applies and if, in this case, the state is the guilty party then liability and damages will be assessed according to European law.[62] The principle that unlawful acts be judged according to the law of the wrongdoer has not, however, received a consistent application in the period of independence. For example, in a Supreme Court decision of 1957[63] the law of the Chinese defendant, which would have been the Civil Code at that time, was rejected in favour of the adat, which was the law of the injured party. The reason given was that the adat was more flexible because it made possible the apportionment of responsibility for damage done while the relevant article of the Civil Code provided only that damage should be made good exclusively by the wrongdoer. This decision has been criticized[64] as not being in line with previous (colonial) authority and, more important, it represents a new criterion for choosing a law, which is insufficiently supported either by practical need or by juristic refinement of its implications. The decision is, however, in line with the prevailing legal climate of the time in which it was given, because at that time (1957) there was a conscious and critical assessment of the suitability of the colonial legal heritage, in this case the Civil Code for Indonesia.[65]

Turning now to the major field of interracial law—contract—it is clear that the categories established in the colonial era persist. The most important determining factor was the intention of the parties with regard to the choice of law governing their relationships.[66] In determining intention the courts took account of such circumstances as the nature and form of the contract, the place of contracting, its economic and social aspects, whether one of the parties was in a dominant bargaining position, and the acceptance by one party of the law of the other.[67] These factors are known collectively as the 'secondary points of contact' or the 'determinate points of contact'[68] in contrast to the primary points of contact discussed under (a) above.

It was well-established in the colonial period that labour contracts, although they did not form a special class, were usually to be governed by European law. This was particularly true where one of the parties was a limited liability company.[69] In a decision given by the Court of First Instance (Pengadilan Negri) of Semarang in 1951,[70] the law governing a contract between a company and an Indonesian managing director was settled at European law on the basis of the authorities just indicated. The managing director was taken to have accepted the applicability of European law because not only was this the law governing the affairs of the company but the individual involved had voluntarily submitted himself to this law. A similar result was reached involving a loan from a bank operated on European law principles.[71]

This principle has been held to apply to a commercial contract between two Native Indonesians where, *prima facie*, adat would govern. In a case decided by the Court of First Instance of Djakarta in 1956,[72] the question of what law was to apply arose between two Native Indonesians concerning the sale and purchase of some trucks. It was argued, on the basis of population groupings, that adat should apply. This was rejected by the court which applied the Civil Code on the following grounds. First, the objects involved in the contract were not such usually known to adat law[73] and were to be used for the benefit of all population groups. Second, and possibly an even stronger ground, the contract was a commercial contract concluded in Djakarta and both parties must, therefore, have intended the law ordinarily applicable in that place to apply. It is difficult to accept this decision as a proper example of interracial law. There was no conflict of interracial law in fact because the issue was between two persons subject to adat. The court in effect seems really to have been looking for reasons to avoid adat in favour of a more advanced and commercially suitable law; it was not properly considering interracial law at all. On the basis of the facts it is difficult to show that there was a voluntary submission to the Civil Code, the concept of sale and purchase is after all well-known to all adat systems.

A further illustration of the problems in ascertaining the intentions of the parties to a contract is provided in a Supreme Court decision of 1956[74] concerning the question of a disputed sale with right of re-purchase. This is a well-known adat institution[75] and it is not properly a sale but a contract of loan with a transfer of property as security, and this was recognized by the court who looked to intention and not to the form of the contract. The transferor was in fact a native Indonesian woman; intent was therefore said to be primary.[76] Difficulties sometimes arise where the existence of any contract is itself disputed. In such a case the Supreme Court has indicated[77] that it will determine the issue on circumstances surrounding the agreement including place, time, and the station of the parties.

If we turn now to marriage these points may be developed further. When persons who live under different laws marry, the law applicable to determine status and incidents of marriage was the Regulation on Mixed Marriages—the R.G.H.[78] The basic principle in the R.G.H. was the equality of the systems of private law in Indonesia. This principle was put to the test in a well-known case decided by the Supreme Court in 1955[79] on the validity of a marriage concluded in conformity with the R.G.H. between an Indonesian Muslim female and an Indonesian Christian male. Such a marriage was of course invalid according to Islamic law, under which a woman has capacity to marry only a Muslim. The court adopted the following reasoning:[80]

Considering that it is a fact, which we cannot in any way deny, that in our country, for a long time ... have been living together people of different religions and cultures, and consequently of different marriage laws; and that his difference of religion is in accordance with the constitution, which admits freedom of religion.

Considering, that with regard to what will be said later, it is appropriate for the security of the people, that as a principle of all law systems, there should be a regulation determining the law applicable to marriages between people of different religions without bias.

Considering that in the interests of society there should be no prohibition of marriage between people of different religions, for such a prohibition would render a great number of children illegitimate, and consequently—besides having no protection in his right to substance and inheritance—each child would perhaps suffer throughout his life by being despised as an 'outcast' (*anak gampang*).

Considering that in the R.G.H. there is no provision favouring any single religion, for in article 6 (1) it is clearly stated that a mixed marriage should be celebrated according to the law of the male spouse, and this means—if the act has been influenced by the law of a religion—that according to the particular circumstances one religious law is to be applied or another.

Considering that, whilst the Supreme Court is aware that Islamic law opposes the possibility, admitted by the R.G.H., of a legal marriage between an Islamic woman and a non-Islamic male, it should not be forgotten that every law in this world is intended to regulate the relationships of the human community—sociological phenomenon—and is not aimed at the well-being after death, which becomes the primary interest of every religion.

The position would of course have been different had the marriage been celebrated under the Marriage Ordinance for Christian Indonesians,[81] section 75 of which provided that when a marriage takes place between two Indonesians, one of whom was Christian, then the law of the non-Christian party is not to determine validity but on the contrary the civil (European) law was the determining law.[82] To this extent, the R.G.H. and the Marriage Ordinance for Christian Indonesians were themselves in conflict.

Another contemporary case relating to the R.G.H. is the decision of the Special Court of First Instance of Djakarta given in 1956[83] concerning the guardianship of a child who was born of a mixed marriage between a Minangkabau male and a Dutch female. It was held that under section 2 of the R.G.H. the mother had lost her Dutch status and thus European law no longer applied to her. The law applicable to this marriage was therefore the Minangkabau adat and this would determine the issue of guardianship.

Summary

The main issue in contemporary Indonesia is the unification of law and, as such, it is designated a question of legal policy (*politik hukum*). In other words, political rather than legal solutions are necessary simply because the law as it now stands cannot solve the problem on its own. Such solutions will of course be those which are practical politically rather than ideal in law. In the mid-1950s legal pluralism was seen as an undesirable part of the colonial legal heritage and was even described as 'monstrous'.[84] But in many areas a partial unification has already been achieved; in land matters the Basic Agrarian Law of 1961 (see Ch. 6) provides a unified scheme for land holding and transfer. In mercantile and commercial law there is an effective codification in practice (though not perhaps in strict law) based upon the old civil code.[85] The one area remaining is family law, particularly the vexed question of inter-religious marriage and the accommodation of Islamic precepts within an avowedly secular legal system. The new Indonesian Marriage Law (No. 1 of 1974) attempts to come to grips with these difficulties. It does not of course solve or determine these difficulties; like all Indonesian legislation it is concerned with principle rather than establishing strict provisions. In the case of this law, political considerations also figured largely. Earlier drafts providing for unified legal process and common grounds for divorce were progressively whittled away in favour of Muslim views, to the extent that Islamic principles were preserved and matters contrary to Islamic law in the proposed bills were dropped. Thus, the original Art. 2(1) providing that registration was necessary for a valid marriage was dropped, as were Arts. 3 and 40 requiring permission from a *civil* court for the taking of more than one wife and for divorce. Instead jurisdiction was limited to the Islamic courts (Art. 63), an interesting reinforcement of the status of Islamic courts *vis-à-vis* the civil courts (see also Chapter 5). On the question of mixed marriage the draft bill, in Art. 11(2) repeated the old Art. 7(2) of the R.G.H. (discussed above in this chapter) in providing that religious differences might not stand in the way of marriage. This also was dropped as were the sections dealing with the status of adopted children (Arts. 8(c) and 62) and the rights and obligations of engaged persons (Arts. 13 and 49).

What then, is its effect on the existing pluralism? The answer is not clear. Art. 66, on repeals, revokes three existing laws[86] 'insofar as they contradict the new law'. This proviso of course creates more uncertainty than already existed. It is not helped by the failure to issue the necessary implementing regulations (*peraturan pelaksanaan*) although some regulations were issued in April 1975, effective from 1 October 1975 (Reg. 9/1975).

However, given these uncertainties, some conclusions are relatively clear. First, Islamic law has been incorporated to some degree into state legislation. This is a considerable change from the earlier position, in particular its authority does not now depend upon whether it is a part of, or recognized by adat. In addition, as already noted, the Islamic court now has an increased function and, hence, importance. Second, a degree of unification has been achieved in that common rules for the whole population on minimum age, rights and duties of spouses, marriage agreements and so on,[87] are now in force for the first time. However, this is a limited unification, differences based upon religion still exist—'there is no marriage outside the respective religions and beliefs'.[88] It is at this point, specifically in the case of mixed marriages, that pluralism might well still persist.

To say more would be mere speculation; one thing however is clear. In all the major fields of law the principle of unification has now received legal formulation and, whatever the demerits of the particular laws, legal pluralism as a principle must now be on the defensive.

1. *Golongan rakjat, bevolkingsgroepen.*
2. See Widjojoatmodjo (1942–3) for a sample of Dutch orders.
3. Cited in Kollewijn, 1951: 309.
4. Staatsblad, 1847, No. 23.
5. Staatsblad, 1855, No. 2.
6. Staatsblad, 1925, No. 415.
7. Constitution of 1945. Trans. Arts. Art. No. 2.
8. P.P. 1945, No. 2.
9. Instruksi Presidium Kabinet No. 31/U./IN/12/1966.
10. Surat Edaran, 3/1966.
11. See Gautama & Hornick, 1972: 8–9.
12. See below Chapter 6.
13. See, for example, the views of Gautama & Harsono, 1972: 22–3 on the 'indirect' repeal of earlier colonial land legislation which was based upon racial classification.

14. Staatsblad, 1931, No. 53.
15. Staatsblad, 1933, No. 74.
16. Staatsblad, 1939, No. 569.
17. Staatsblad, 1939, No. 570, No. 571.
18. Staatsblad, 1908, No. 542, Staatsblad, 1909, No. 584.
19. cf. Gautama & Harsono, 1972: 87–8 for the regulations.
20. cf. Ter Haar (1929).
21. ibid: 165.
22. See below Chapter 7.
23. Undang2 No. 22/1946.
24. See below pp. 87–8 on the new marriage law.
25. *Persamaan-hak, gelijkstelling.*
26. Art. 163(5) Indische Staatsregeling.
27. cf. Gautama & Hornick, 1972: 16 for case references.
28. Staatsblad, 1917, No. 12.
29. The other two rarely had relevance to adat because they involve a more or less complete separation of the individual from adat. cf. Gautama & Hornick, 1972: 17–18. See also Gautama (1971).
30. Staatsblad, 1898, No. 158.
31. See Gautama & Harsono, 1972: 24.
32. The distinction between the European private law of the Indies and that of the Netherlands is not of moment here. See Schiller, 1942–3: 34–6 for a brief outline and for references. The leading texts on the nineteenth century and for the first decades of the twentieth century are those of Abendanon (1891), Wagener (1932) and Kollewijn (1938).
33. cf. Arminjon (1925 (i)).
34. Kollewijn, 1929: 207–8, 216–19 for references.
35. The proceedings are reported in *Handelingen der Nederlandsch-Indische Juristen-vereeniging* (1887).
36. Staatsblad, 1898, No. 158.
37. See Kollewijn, 1929: 210.
38. See Chapters 1 and 3.
39. cf. Nederburgh, 1896: (i) 293 and later papers in *Het Recht in Ned.-Indie* 1899–1903.
40. See also Cassutto, 1936: 66–9.
41. See Chapter 3.
42. Kollewijn, 1929: 213–14.
43. cf. de la Porte (1908).
44. ibid: 329.
45. Kollewijn, 1929: 215–16.
46. Bartholomew, 1952: 326, Hooker (1968).
47. cf. Kollewijn, 1929: 233–5.
48. ibid: 223–4.
49. cf. Solus (1927).
50. Schiller, 1942–3: 44. Italics supplied.
51. See ibid: 43–6 for references to judicial answers to these questions. See also Gautama (1973) for the more recent cases.
52. See Gautama (1973).
53. Kollewijn, 1929: 204. See also Kollewijn, 1939: 194.
54. cf. Schiller, 1942–3: 37.
55. cf. Hooker, 1976: 1–18.
56. cf. von Wright (1963) for a description by a leading contemporary jurist of norm systems.
57. '*Hukum antargolongan*' in Indonesian.
58. *primaire aanknopingspunt, titik taut primair, titik taut pembeda.*
59. See below Chapter 6 for details.

60. Staatsblad, 1870, No. 118.
61. See below Chapter 7.
62. cf. de la Porte, 1908: 348 ff., Gouwgioksiong, 1965: 564–5 and the decisions there cited.
63. In (1957) *Hukum* 7/8: 61.
64. Gouwgioksiong, 1965: 566.
65. cf. Wirjono Prodjodikoro (n.d.) who accepted the applicability of the Civil Code in such cases but stressed the sometimes artificial and rigid categories of fault in the code. See also Utrecht (1955) (1959).
66. cf. Gouwgioksiong, 1960: 50 ff.
67. Before 1960 the status of land was also fundamental.
68. This is the term preferred by the Official State Committee for the Drafting of Legal Terms.
69. cf. Kollewijn, 1934: 789.
70. In (1952) *Hukum* 4/5: 114.
71. cf. Gouwgioksiong, 1965: 550 and n.21 for references to judicial decisions.
72. In (1957) *Hukum* 1/2: 137.
73. In passing it might be said that there is no reason why principles of adat could not *in theory* be extended to new objects.
74. In (1957) *Hukum* 3/4: 73.
75. *Jual Janji* and other terms.
76. For other cases on this point see (1955) *Hukum* 4/5: 24.
77. In (1950) *Hukum* 1/2: 62.
78. *Regeling op de Gemengde Huwelijken*. Staatsblad, 1898, No. 158. Repealed in 1974, see below n.86.
79. In (1955) *Hukum* 3: 44.
80. Cited in Gouwgioksiong, 1965: 558–9. On Christianity and adat see Prins (1973).
81. Staatsblad, 1933, No. 74.
82. See further (1959) *Hukum* 3/4: 176.
83. In (1958) *Hukum* 9/10: 121.
84. The speech of the Minister of Justice reported in (1957) *Hukum dan Masjarakat*—special congress issue 2 (3/4): 12.
85. cf. Gouwgioksiong, 1965: 571–2.
86. The laws specified are: Kitab Undang-undang Hukum Perdata (Burgerlijk Wetboek); Ordonansi Perkawinan Indonesia Kristen (Huwelijks Ordonnantie Christen Indonesiërs, Staatsblad, 1933 No. 74); Peraturan Perkawinan Campuran (Regeling op de Gemengde Huwelijken, Staatsblad 1898 No. 158).
87. See Katz & Katz, 1975: 672 ff.
88. Elucidation, Art. 2.

5
ADAT AND ISLAM

Introduction

THE religion of Islam, from its inception, has never posited a distinction between things of the spirit and things of the world. One does not distinguish between God's and man's world. Islam is a religious and a civil and political system of thought. Islamic law, the *sharī'a*, governs man's relations with his fellows as well as his relationship with God.[1] Within the context of the Islamization of the East Indies this theory of social and religious organization had elements of continuity with the earlier Indian influenced political organization. It continued the idea of relating the individual to political authority through a belief in religious ideals. The specifically Islamic content of such a belief, however, varied from place to place in the Indonesian archipelago. The main centres of a full adherence to the tenets of Islam lay outside Java, especially in north Sumatra. In its purely religious aspect Islam demonstrated an ability to come to some accommodation with other systems of belief, especially animism in its various forms.[2] This was possible because in the version of Islam introduced there was a lack of the excessive legalism characteristic of Middle Eastern Islam, and the dominant missionary role was taken by Sufi mystics who were prepared to allow some accommodation between orthodoxy and indigenous religious beliefs. However, even with all this, Islam remained a system of thought and belief which claimed an exclusive jurisdiction in social and political matters as well as in religion. It is here, in this claim, that it represents a break with the past Indian-derived traditions of the archipelago, especially Java[3] (and Bali where it never penetrated). The organization of states such as Srivijaya and Majapahit did not claim to organize social structure in wholly religious terms.

In Indonesia the realities of social life were not reflected in the *sharī'a* to any extent except possibly in the trading stations of north Sumatra where the simplicity and austerity of Islamic rules were suitable enough given the absence of class distinctions. Further, in these stations, the forms of property were basically all movable property both in physical and in legal terms, and to this the rules of Islam on death or divorce could apply without too great a difficulty. Such, however, was an exceptional situation; in the rest of Indonesia pre-Islamic institutions provided a good deal of difficulty as indeed they did and still do, not just in Indonesia but in all Muslim countries. In Indonesia this is the problem of adat. In the *fikh*, adat may refer to or be used in reference to a customary usage which is not strictly a *source* (*usūl*) of law but an example of an ordinary standard or usage. Again, as a matter of practical jurisprudence, the administrative institutions of Islamic law may allow the application of adat in non-religious matters as in penal law or the law of obligation. These two instances keep separate the concepts in the *fikh* and the idea of adat as a reflection of an existing social structure, but in many cases it is difficult, if not impossible, to accomplish this. For example, courts dealing with religious matters generally may sanction a local adat because of some legal artifice (*hila*), such as where the act enforced is in a legally unchallengeable form, e.g. the conditional repudiation in favour of the wife in Java. Again, one finds principles of adat which are enforced in religious courts because they are considered as part of the law and religion of Islam; e.g. some forms of marriage arrangement in Java.

In other words the relationship between adat and Islam in Indonesia can, in some cases, be considered as an opposition of legal systems. This is true in some instances, as in Minangkabau adat and Islam. Here there are two systems: one claiming an exclusive jurisdiction and the other claiming to determine obligation as an element of social structure; one defining and attributing obligation in terms of the individual, the other in terms of a wider grouping.

In other parts of Indonesia such a clear-cut opposition of systems is much rarer. In Java one has a complex of classifications such as *santri*, *abangan* and *putihan* which relate the depths of one's convictions as a Muslim to issues such as social class and village organization. Such complexes have been discussed in terms of religion[4] and of politics.

In this chapter attention will be given to the issues in law which adat and Islam posit for Indonesia. To some extent this chapter is a specific field or example in which the issues raised in the preceding four chapters come together.

Adat and Islam in the State—Colonial Period

The nature of the relationship between the realities of social life or social structures in its widest sense and the dictates of Islam has been of the utmost importance not just to commentators on Islam but also to the institutions of state. This is particularly important in respect of sovereignty. So far as sovereignty is concerned the following passages are significant as to the attitude of the Dutch administration to Islam. The first is a Church Order of the Municipality of Batavia given on 7 December 1643:[5]

> The high officials should see to it, that the Moorish circumcision and schools will be forbidden and Chinese and other pagans will be prohibited from having their services of pagan superstition and devil's worship, which they have especially in their temples and also at night in the streets. Also their devilish knowledge of fortune-telling should be forbidden, for in no Christian republic such a violation of God's Honor should be permitted for whatever reason it might be, for it will only give joy to non-Christians and annoy the Christians.

In 1716 a prohibition was issued against the transport on ships of the Vereenigde Oost-Indische Compagnie of 'pilgrims, who have visited the tomb of Mohammeth in Mecca'. It was further stated 'that vagabonds like that are harmful because of their influence among the Mohammedans'.

The post-Napoleonic years gave the Indies more liberal regulations with regard to non-Christian religions. Clause 97 of the 'Regulation for Commissaries-General' (N.E.I. Gazette 1818 No. 87) stated that 'the prayer meetings of all religions in the Netherlands Indies have the protection of the High Government, provided that this prayer meeting is of no danger for public order'.

This regulation apparently acknowledged the principle of freedom of religion and became the forerunner of later state regulations and the following clauses of the New Indies Constitution:

> 173. Everyone professes his religious opinions in absolute freedom subject to the safeguarding of society and its members against infringing of the regulations on criminal law.
> 174. (1) All public religious services inside buildings and private places are allowed, as long as they do not disturb the public order.
> (2) The consent of the Authorities is required for public religious services outside buildings and private places.
> 175. The Governor-General sees that all religious sects will obey the general regulations.[6]

The variations in government regulation just set out are illustrative of the early uncertainties as to the treatment of Islam which persisted in Dutch minds until the close of the nineteenth century. The threat of an Islamic religious uprising was always real and in the colonial wars, which were a feature of the nineteenth century East Indies, the banner of revolt was more often than not raised in the name of Islam.[7] These factors mitigated against any extensive recognition of Islam in the legal sphere, and this is reflected in the paucity of Islamic legislation, especially when compared with that of adat. Apart from the regulations cited earlier, the only regulation in force for many years was a 'Regulation on Court Organization and the Administration of Justice', Art. 7 of which provided that a Muslim 'priest' should act as adviser in the native court where persons of this faith were litigants: this was an advisory role only. This regulation was made in 1808 by Governor-General Daendels. The Basic Law (*Regeringsreglement*)[8] had preserved this position by sanctioning a continued duality between adat and Islamic law although the boundaries between these two systems were never properly settled.

In Java and Madura where the problem occurred in its most acute form, provision was made for what was known as a 'Priest Court' (*priesterraad*) by regulations dated 1882.[9] These provided that Islamic law was to be administered by a collegiate tribunal, the *priesterraaden*, but was based, as was Daendel's original legislation, on misunderstandings of Islam and of Islamic law. First, there are no 'priests' in Islam in the Western sense. The attribution of such a function to the mosque director and Muslim judge (entitled *penghulu* in Java and *kadi* in other areas) was thus a fundamental error and led to the attribution of a priestly function not only to the *penghulu* but also to other mosque officials, who were then combined into the official *priesterraaden*. As constituted, this body, which purported to be merely a formalization of an existing Islamic institution, ran directly counter to Islamic practice which gave to the *penghulu* a sole jurisdiction in such matters as marriage, divorce and inheritance. A second and more fundamental error occurred in that the areas of competence of the Islamic official were never clearly defined *vis-à-vis* the other indigenous law courts. The Basic Law of 1855 had merely continued what was originally an administrative duality. The problem, however, was that although the *priesterraaden* were given jurisdiction in family law and inheritance, their pronouncements had to receive approval from the judges of the ordinary native courts. The practical result of this was that it was not uncommon for the native court to ignore the advice of the *penghulu* in its judgment,[10] so that the *penghulu's* judicial competence was reduced to that of Muslim adviser. This state of affairs was naturally resented by the Muslim leaders and agitation was more or less constant, ranging from requests for more effectiveness to threats of boycott of the *priesterraaden*.

It is against this background that new steps were taken in the formulation of an Islamic policy with the creation of the office of Adviser on Arabian and Native Affairs in 1889, the first incumbent of which was Snouck Hurgronje. He was the foremost Islamic scholar of his day and, moreover, was inspired by the best features of nineteenth-century liberalism. His recommendations to the authorities on an Islamic policy were followed and resulted in an initial accommodation between the Muslims and the colonial authorities. As Benda explains it,[11] this policy was basically one of tolerance in religious matters together with a vigilance and firmness in countering attempts at extending Islamic political control. However, and probably more important, Snouck Hurgronje foresaw that Indonesia would still have to make an accommodation with the new age and neither adat nor Islam could, on their own resources, provide the mechanics for such an operation. An accommodation by means of colonial institutions only could provide the key to modernization, and this demanded the association of Indonesians with Dutch culture focusing first upon the *priyayi*-élite of Java. This fitted in well with the new policy officially adopted by the Netherlands Government toward Indonesia—the 'Ethical' policy formally adopted in 1901. The essence of this policy was the assumption of a moral responsibility for native welfare and the exclusion of past colonial exploitation. At grass-roots level Snouck's policy of toleration for Islam worked well though legislative initiative was lacking at the higher levels of the judiciary. So far as the Ethical policy itself was concerned, it almost immediately gave rise to a political agitation which became known as the *Sarekat Islam* movement. This movement symbolized Indonesian protest, from a wide ideological spectrum, to colonial conditions, and though short-lived (1919–24/6) it fused Muslim disaffection with urban leadership. It gave rise also to later movements which concentrated attack on pre-Islamic institutions such as adat. It was followed by a retreat of the authorities into a more conservative policy to some extent based, as in the nineteenth century, on the adat official and buttressed by an ideology of the preservation of indigenous welfare.

It was in this light that a series of enactments on Islamic judicial administration became law in the period 1929–1938. Although this legislation resulted in a definition of Islamic legal competence, it also narrowed the field of jurisdiction especially in the light of the Islamic demands which had been initiated by *Sarekat Islam* and continued by a variety of Islamic parties,[12] of all shades of opinion from conservative to reformist. The legislation thus succeeded in alienating Muslim opinion in general, especially in that it tended to strengthen the authority of adat officialdom.

The first piece of legislation of note was the Marriage Enactment of 1929[13] which declared the *penghulu* to be a government official subject to the Regent's control. In addition a fixed procedure was set up for the registration of marriage and divorce and the fees to be paid for such. A second bill introduced in 1931[14] was far more serious in its effects on Islamic law. This had three major provisions. First, it proposed the abolition of the *priesterraaden* which were to be superseded by *penghulu* courts, i.e., courts of a religious official sitting alone as was the normal Islamic practice. Further, the *penghulu* was to be paid a salary and have the status of a government servant. However, this part of the bill never became law, adverse conditions being asserted in excuse. The second proposal was the establishment of a court of appeal to review the decisions of the *penghulu* court. This, the *Hof voor Islamietische Zaken* or *Mahkamah Islam Tinggi*, came into existence in 1938, too late to influence effectively the colonial development of Islamic law. The third provision,[15] and the one which aroused direct Muslim hostility, was the transfer of inheritance jurisdiction from the religious court to the native courts where claims were to be adjudicated not according to Islamic law but to adat. The *priesterraaden* were thus to be limited in jurisdiction to matters of marriage and divorce only. It had originally been recommended that inheritance matters be transferred to native courts but that these courts were to base themselves on the Islamic laws of inheritance. As Westra said,[16] 'Muslim law has been further pushed back by the school of customary law ... the question is whether the authorities have not gone too far along this road'. It is interesting to note that Snouck Hurgronje had advocated respect for both Islamic religious and inheritance law.

A final piece of 'reforming' legislation was a draft bill entitled 'Ordinance Concerning Registered Marriages' of 1937 which proposed the virtual abolition of polygamy. Despite the merits of such legislation it was withdrawn in the face of Muslim opposition, the first time that Islam in Indonesia had succeeded in halting government interference.[17] Provision was also made at this time for religious justice in areas outside Java with the creation of 'Kadi' courts in Bandjermasin and South Borneo but their competence was limited largely to matters of marriage and divorce.[18] Property questions only fell within their jurisdiction when they referred to the marriage gift or to the dowry.

In the colonial administration Islamic law was in an inferior position *vis-à-vis* the adats. The reasons for this were first, political fears on the part of the Dutch,[19] and second, the fact that Indonesians did not owe a sole adherence to this religion. This was first demonstrated by Snouck Hurgronje who showed the importance of adat and the limitations which it imposed upon the social and legal precepts of Islam, especially in matters relating to property. The difficulty was that although Islamic law, or something imagined to be such, did regulate marriage matters, the institution of marriage could not really be understood apart from or in separation from property questions—hence adat. The Dutch solution was to attempt the separation of the inseparable, and to a large extent this was dictated by colonial policy within the Netherlands East Indies. At the same time it was justified on the ground that the adats were working systems and must be supported particularly where the adat and Islamic officials in various areas came into open conflict.[20] The Muslim position was that the institutions of adat were in some instances—those involving family law—contrary to Islamic teaching, and must be reformed. The intensity of this sort of conflict varied from place to place, and it seems to have reached its greatest intensity in Minangkabau. In other areas, such as in most of Java, it hardly arose in this extreme form.

Given the administrative, legal and political framework constructed by the Dutch in the first decades of this century, the Islamic legal policy which they pursued could be said to have a certain inevitability about it. The legal system itself, by making provision for decisive adjudication, made a choice of law, and hence a conflict of laws, mandatory. The system, in other words, not just implied conflict but demanded it. In this respect it represented a violent change from traditional practice. In the *kampung* and *desa* of Indonesia the adat and Islamic systems though occasionally opposed— as in Minangkabau—were typically fluid as to their respective jurisdictions. Some parts of adat were regarded as part of the *sharī'a*, and in the processes of village administration of justice, compromise based upon elements of both systems was the common solution. Indonesian thought, particularly that of the Javanese, has often been described as 'syncretic' and the peoples of Java have sometimes been accused of holding two or more contradictory beliefs at the same time, but if this facilitates the peaceful solution of important matters such as inheritance, then why not? On the other hand, even in areas in which there was an obvious opposition of systems, as in Minangkabau, attempts at accommodation were both consistent and wide-ranging except when political advantage was to be got by stressing points of conflict. In the literature on the adat of Minangkabau there are commonly attempts to show two things. First, that in the real life of the individual the theoretically possible conflict between adat and Islam does not in fact occur. Second, adat and Islam are not just complementary but are part of the same system, both finding their origin in God and Islam is the perfection of adat.[21] These attempts at the reconciliation of adat and Islam both in the practical context and also in intellectual commentary are but one example of a general desire for accommodation in traditional Indonesian legal practice. More often than not this was able to be realized, but the necessity for choice demanded either on political grounds or in a Western-designed legal system has created major difficulties.[22]

Adat and Islam in Legal Pluralism—Contemporary Indonesia

The political position of Islam changed decisively in Indonesia during the Japanese occupation and Islam came to be of major importance in the nationalist and anti-colonial movement.[23] The enhanced power of the Islamic movement received political expression in 1946 with the formation of the Ministry of Religion as a department of state in the fledgling Indonesia. The Ministry took over the functions exercised by the former Religious Affairs Officers of the Residencies and its jurisdiction has been defined as follows:[24]

(1) Realizing the principles of the faith in the best manner possible.
(2) Watching over individual freedom of religion.
(3) Giving guidance and support so as to promote healthy religious movements.
(4) Maintaining relations with religious movements and currents not belonging to the Islamic and Christian (Protestant and Roman Catholic) religions.
(5) Advancing the general development in social life and in religious life.
(6) Administering, guiding and supervising religious education in government schools.

(7) Administering, guiding and supervising, as well as promoting education in the home, teaching in religious schools, and private teaching of religions.
(8) Training personnel necessary for religious education in government schools, for government officers and for jurisdiction, in the capacities of teachers and of religious judges.
(9) Administering and supporting everything pertaining to spiritual education in boarding establishments, prisons and other places where this may be deemed necessary.
(10) Regulating, administering and supervising everything pertaining to registration of marriages, repudiations and retractation of repudiations by Muslims.
(11) Providing material support for the improvement and maintenance of buildings destined for worship (mosques, churches, etc.).
(12) Administering, regulating and supervising all matters pertaining to religious jurisdiction and the Islamic High Court.
(13) Investigating, deciding, registering and supervising as well as administering legacies under Islamic law (*wakaf*).
(14) Administering and supervising matters pertaining to pilgrimages.
(15) Appointing and announcing holidays.
(16) Regulating official events relating to religion, with the proviso that freedom of religion is to be maintained.

In fact the Ministry has acted as a guardian and promoter of the Islamic ethic in the political field in modern Indonesia. Indeed, it was for some years and remains something of an arena for competing Muslim ideologies concerned with the place of Islam in Indonesia and with the nature of the Indonesian state. Its most important single achievement in the early period was its promotion of Law No. 22 of 1946 which aimed at unifying the administration of marriage and divorce throughout Indonesia under the control of the Ministry.[25] It was provided that all marriages, divorces and reconciliations of Muslims must be brought under the formal supervisions of Registrars appointed by the Ministry. Fines were to be levied against persons who undertook to change their status without registration and fees for registration were imposed. The statute clearly looked for a uniform administration throughout Indonesia, but it was admitted that until conditions permitted its implementation must be confined initially to Java and Madura. The motive behind the statute was to provide some measure of certainty and stability in marital relationships as well as to assert a political control in the name of Islam. In promoting certainty it is probable, as Prins suggests,[26] that the model for registration was found in the existing European civil registry, but registration alone did not determine the validity of one's personal status. Substantive rules of Islamic law were not mentioned in the law on the view that the substantive law was already stated and, for Muslims, was fixed and immutable in the Holy Koran. Neither the Ministry nor the statute changed the relationship between Islam and adat, the forum for this lying in the courts.

The importance of Islam in the political sphere was further demonstrated by the fact that while the adat courts were abolished, never to be reconstituted, during the Japanese occupation, the Islamic courts not only survived but were extended to territories never before under their jurisdiction. The Religious Court systems in Java and Madura[27] and in Bandjermasin[28] were transferred from the Ministry of Justice to the Ministry of Religion in 1946[29] under the control of the Bureau (later Directorate) of Religious Justice; courts in the remaining territories were transferred in 1957.[30] The jurisdiction of the courts in Java and Madura is limited to disputes between Muslim spouses and to matters concerning marriage, repudiation, reconciliation and divorce. The courts may deal with property or maintenance claims only if *mahr* or *nafakah* are in dispute. Other property matters must be referred to the secular courts. In the Outer Provinces similar restrictions exist although the jurisdiction is substantially wider and may extend to matters of inheritance (see below). This remains the position at the moment although the new law on the Basic Provisions of Judicial Authority[31] of 1970 provides that the Supreme Court may take proceedings in cassation from the Islamic courts.[32] It remains to be seen what effect this provision will have, but its mention here serves to introduce us to the relationship between the Islamic and secular judicial organizations.

The administration of [secular] 'public justice' is governed by Law No. 13 of 1965[33] which created a three-tier system of courts: the District Court (*Pengadilan Negri*), the High Court (*Pengadilan Tinggi*) and the Supreme Court (*Mahkamah Agung*). The District Court has a general jurisdiction in civil and criminal matters and the civil jurisdiction includes matters subject to adat laws now that the colonial adat courts no longer exist.[34] Further, the Supreme Court in its jurisdiction in cassation entertains appeals which claim that (a) a relevant rule of law (*written or unwritten*) has been applied wrongly or not at all, or (b) the court below has exceeded its jurisdiction, or (c) a mandatory rule of procedure has not been applied.

The structure of the courts is dealt with in more detail later[35] but with this background—of Islam's political position and the existence of separate judicial systems—which differs considerably from the pre-independence background, we can now go on to look at adat and Islam on their (at present) common meeting ground, that is, in the courts. The issue is one well-known in legal pluralism in South-East Asia and quite simply is the choice of which of two laws, religious or secular, administered in two jurisdictions, religious and secular, is to apply to an individual who is subject to both. Stated thus baldly, the answer in a secular nation state is obvious: the law of the religion is and can only be a limited exception to the general law; and so the highest judicial organ in the Republik Indonesia has held. In 1960 the Supreme Court handed down a decision, on appeal from the High Court of Makasar,[36] the relevant portions of which are as follows:[37]

In consideration ... that the original claim was brought before the Pengadilan Negeri in Makassar and registered on 31 June 1958 ...;
... that the basis of the claim is an inheritance dispute, in which the claimants argue that the land in dispute is the estate of the late woman Saida and that the claimants and the respondents are her heirs, and that, moreover, they are all Muslims;
... that for all areas outside of Java and Madura ... Government Regulation No. 45/1957 is in force, in which regulation it is provided, *inter alia*, that Islamic courts are competent to examine issues of inheritance which according to the living law should be decided according to Islamic law, but that these courts shall not have jurisdiction if the applicable law is not Islamic law;
In consideration that the Supreme Court regards it as clear that in all of Indonesia with respect to inheritance it is essentially the Adat law which applies, which in areas where the influence of Islam is strong contains more or fewer elements of Islamic law;
In consideration that therefore it can be said that, in accord with the law applicable to Java, Madura, and the area of Bandjermasin in Kalimantan, it is the Pengadilan Negeri which is competent to decide inheritance cases;
In consideration that the Pengadilan Tinggi of Makassar distinguished two matters in the original claim....
In consideration that the Pengadilan Tinggi ... then determined that it is the Pengadilan Negeri which is competent to determine the first matter and the Pengadilan Sjar'iyah [Islamic court] the second matter;
In consideration that the Supreme Court's view does not distinguish these two problems and is of the opinion that both matters are concerned with an inheritance issue and that both ... fall under the jurisdiction of the Pengadilan Negeri to decide....

The essential point is that the Supreme Court took to itself the right to decide the claims of two competing systems, a right which must always lie in the highest level of the secular judiciary in a non-religious state. This is a claim which the recent Ch. II, Art. 10(3) of the Basic Provisions of Judicial Authority, 1970 expresses clearly. In the 1960 case the Supreme Court made much of the fact that the action, though involving inheritance, was commenced in the secular courts. More fundamental, the Supreme Court was not prepared to *admit as a matter of fact* that Islamic law was the proper law applicable to inheritance issues in the area from which the case came. This is an important proposition because the Court is denying that 'inheritance' may be equated factually with 'Islam' in the Outer Territories although this is the assumption made in the regulations. It stems probably from the long held view dating back to the nineteenth century that Islam is somehow stronger or more pervasive in these areas than in Java and Madura. The Supreme Court's attitude may indeed be seen as a formal denial of such a proposition, a denial which was made in the early 1950s in South Sumatra to the extent that a Court of First Instance refused a request for an executary decree from an Islamic court on the basis that the latter properly had no existence in law![38] It is worth remembering also that the Ministry of Religion did not finally succeed in getting Law No. 22 of 1946 extended to all areas outside Java and Madura until 1954,[39] and in the intervening period secular courts often refused to recognize Islamic jurisdiction even in marriage and divorce, a situation which created a good deal of difficulty.[40] This tension has continued into the contemporary period; the colonial separation of competence between Islamic and adat authorities has become formalized into a division of judicial jurisdictions in which, however, the residual power lies in the secular system.

The jurisdiction of the Islamic courts is restricted to Muslims but there is little if anything on the definition of who is a Muslim. This is an important point because, as described in the last chapter, it is possible for Indonesians to become subject, or to subject themselves, to the civil code. In the matters with which Islamic courts properly exercise jurisdiction—marriage and divorce, reconciliation and maintenance—this may potentially give rise to some difficulty in modern Indonesia. It is perfectly feasible, for example, for an individual to claim civil code status and for this to be denied, *inter alia*, on the grounds of at least formal adherence to Islam in matters concerning family law. The Islamic courts themselves have no means, either theoretical or jurisdictional, for dealing with this sort of question. Indeed, they tend to assume a jurisdiction over Muslims on the sole ground that an individual is such by public repute and his own opinion.[41] This is perfectly justifiable given that the very great majority of individuals who come to the Islamic courts are the non-Westernized urban and rural lower classes for whom conflicts of laws do not really arise. However, if the Islamic courts are to face the future with any confident expectation they must be prepared to devote some attention to this question.

A further difficulty directly related to the adat question arises from the terms of Law No. 45 of 1957 providing for the jurisdiction of the *Mahkamah Sharī'a* in areas outside Java and Madura, and Southern Kalimantan. The legislation is ambiguous on the issue of jurisdiction in that the important Art. 4(1)(2) provides for jurisdiction in marriage, divorce, reconciliation and inheritance (excluded in Java and Madura) to the extent that 'according to the living law they are resolved according to the law of Islam'. This qualification formed an important part of the Supreme Court judgment cited a little earlier and the effect of the judgment and of this qualification is to remove the determination of these matters from exclusive Islamic jurisdiction. 'Living law' is a reference to adat and the extent to which some local adat does or does not admit elements of the *sharī'a* in the matters listed is for the secular courts to determine. The result is that the individual has a choice of forum and this choice is specifically given in legislation. It is in this context that colonial publications on adat exert an important influence. This work is consulted in the secular courts in determining what the context of the living law is, and since much of this work denies an Islamic content, especially in inheritance matters, the effectiveness of Islamic rules is further restricted.[42]

On the other hand the structure of the court system itself should not be allowed to disguise the fact that the individuals who come to the courts do not themselves often realise the limited jurisdiction which the Islamic courts possess. As one commentator instances,[43] plaintiffs, particularly women, approach the Islamic courts with requests for such things as the division of property subsequent to divorce.[44] This of course is a matter for adat, and although the court has no jurisdiction and would probably refuse to adjudicate, the jurisdictional lack of competence and the reasons for it are not clear to the applicant. This is the sort of situation often cited by proponents of adat to demonstrate the unrealistic nature of the Islamic rules on family law, although the lack of reality may more properly be ascribed to the political compromises facing the drafting of legislation and the establishment of courts with split jurisdictions. It is impossible to separate family and property matters.

This impossibility finds its most provocative form in the issue of inheritance on which the adats and Islam diverge sharply. All the major forms of kinship organization—unilineal and bilateral—are found in Indonesia, and there is a diversity of adat inheritance laws corresponding to greater or lesser degrees to these kinship patterns.[45] Islamic law, with its emphasis upon agnatic kin and certain classes of female, is uniform both in theory and in practice;[46] the latter because all heritable property is expressed in the Koranic shares which theoretically provide an exact distribution. Equally important is the fact that the adats generally distinguish between different kinds of property classing land in a category of its own. Ter Haar claimed[47] that the Javanese adats even regarded land as an indivisible whole. Whatever may be the truth of this last proposition, there is no uniform law of inheritance in Indonesia[48] and any discussion of the issue revolves around the respective proponents of adat and Islam.

The general arguments adduced by each side may be summarized as follows:

(i) *Adat*

(a) Only adat truly reflects the sense of justice of the Indonesian people.[49]

(b) Islamic law has not been received as part of the living law (*hukum hidup*) of the Indonesian people in respect of inheritance.

(c) Islamic law on inheritance is in fact rejected by the Indonesian peoples—usually instancing the Minangkabau inheritance system and citing also the rights which adopted children have under the adat.

(ii) *Islam*

(a) Indonesians are predominantly Muslim and have thus accepted Islamic law in its entirety.

(b) Islamic law is superior to adat which is primitive and old fashioned—this argument is usually based on the fact that Islam has a developed system of written jurisprudence governing vast numbers of people whilst adat was originally oral in form and is still localized.

These are the main battle lines in argument but there is one significant difference in the types of argument put forward which should be noticed here. This is that the adat arguments are arguments from experience: adat does do the things claimed for it. It is an argument from expediency in contrast to the Muslim argument which really amounts to little more than a confession of faith; be-

ADAT AND ISLAM

cause Indonesians are Muslim they accept or have adopted the whole of Islamic law, including the rules of inheritance. This is not in fact true but it is understandable as the assertion of an ideology which must, in its own terms, be accepted *in toto* or not at all. The position is further confused by the well-known Indonesian ability or propensity in this argument to be at the same time a devout Muslim and yet reject the inheritance rules in favour of some adat.[50]

These comments are valid enough as they have just been stated but they need to be put into some sort of context. The formulations just described are those which would occur to an outside observer with some legal training but the same observer would also notice that the opposition of views just described is not how many people in Indonesia actually operate the rules. As one commentator has recently shown,[51] Islamic courts do deal with inheritance matters which are formally outside their jurisdiction. Many such cases are not disputes at all but requests for a *fatwa* on the death of a proprietor. This is a process not regulated by statute and compromise settlements based more or less directly on the rules of Islam are commonly made. This is a case of voluntary acceptance of jurisdiction by the individuals concerned although it is not described by them in these terms. Islamic courts also deal with disputes proper although again these often result in settlements described as *fatwa*. Strictly speaking these are unenforceable and a dissatisfied party may apply to the secular courts. No full data exist on this sort of situation throughout Indonesia and the extent and varying practices of this are only known now in a somewhat impressionistic way. However, these processes of adjustment do leave large areas in which a mixing and adjustment rather than an opposition of rule systems is possible.

An explanation for this and a further comment upon it is that it is not common to find clear-cut applications of the rules (of adat and Islam) amongst the generality of the population. An inheritance is distributed in a way which tries to satisfy all parties and which makes economic and agricultural sense. There is room for adjustment and compromise, both of which are values in themselves in most adat systems. A too legalistic description of adat alone tends to obscure this point as it tends to obscure the sociological fact that most matters of inheritance are settled peaceably and do not result in judicial proceedings. Proponents of adat never tire of pointing out that the agriculturally inconvenient Islamic fractions are often avoided in this way but sometimes neglect to illustrate the converse: that an adat 'principle' is often avoided by another adat 'rule'. For example, the Toba Batak patrilineal principles which exclude females from inheritance are often circumvented by a 'gift' of property which 'must or ought to be' made.[52] There are many other examples which could be cited and they all tend to show that a textbook summary is or can be misleading. Some of the colonial work may be justly criticized on this ground although its emphasis upon the prescriptive statement of rules is understandable when one remembers that their prime use was as administrative handbooks. A statement written for the purpose of descriptive validity is bound to be much less satisfactory from the point of view of bureaucratic certainty, but it is a much more reliable guide to legal reality,[53] especially in an area where a conflict of systems is assumed but does not always take place.

This last is a particularly important point in contemporary Indonesia because, as Prins demonstrates with a wealth of data,[54] in a situation of rapid social change, adat and Islam are not seen as formally irreconcilable opposites but as alternatives between which one may choose for one's own advantage. Changing patterns of social organization, the loosening of traditional social bonds and values may tend to favour one system as against the other. This is especially important in that the nuclear family is increasingly becoming the primary unit in urban areas and Islamic law is more suitable in this context. This very point is illustrated in a recent account of dispute settlement among the Minangkabau.[55] Islamic courts do almost no inheritance work in the villages where inheritance is a matter for the matrilineal adat, but in the cities of Padang and Bukit Tinggi they do get cases involving Minangkabau. This is one field in which the effect of economic changes has had demonstrable legal effects.

Summary: Islam and Adat in Contemporary Legal Thought

Contemporary legal thought on Islam and adat, like the problem itself, is basically a legacy from the colonial period although new aspects have arisen since independence. The primary fact conditioning the colonial analysis and solution of the issue was an opposition to the universalist claims of Islam in both the social and (especially?) the political spheres. Among the Indonesian peoples, on the other hand, there remains a willingness to aggregate or compromise the rules of the systems, even extending to the highly developed sophistic arguments characteristic of the Minangkabau where the opposition of systems is probably at its most extreme in Indonesia.[56] However, the colonial legal policy was quite clear, that Islamic rules could be considered as law only insofar as permitted by adat in its various systems. This, the so-called reception theory, was stated by van Vollenhoven[57] and reiterated by Ter Haar[58] whose views, particularly on inheritance, were accepted by the colonial authorities. This view was maintained by Indonesian jurists during the Japanese occupation, particularly by Supomo.[59] However, with the political position achieved by Islamic organizations during the occupation and postwar period, Islamic views could be put forward from a new standpoint: the promotion of Islamic law as the proper basis for an Indonesian national law. The reception theory was described as a 'theory of the Devil' in affronting the faith of Muslims and the majesty of God.[60]

The argument proceeds by asserting that the primacy of Islamic law over Western law or adat law is established by the will of God expressed in the Koran.[61] From this point two things are necessary for a law reform proper to modern Indonesia. First, the abolition of adat law, which might be done gradually, in the interests of social progress. The leading proponent of these views, Hazairin, sees this as necessary because the laws of Islam, particularly in family matters, are more in line with the sort of social structure necessary for the economic and social development of the state. He instances the suitability of bilateral or cognatic social systems, the confinement of inheritance to the nuclear family, and he purports to find Koranic authority to show that various features of patrilineal or matrilineal social organization are forbidden.[62] These arguments are somewhat specious and rest upon rather strained interpretations of the Koran. For example, while it is true that parallel and cross-cousin marriage is neither enjoined nor prohibited in the Koran,[63] this is by no means evidence that such marriage practices should be abolished together with the principle of clan exogamy. In the event, Hazairin's arguments against adat on religious grounds amount to little more than a re-affirmation of acceptance of the rules of Islam because, and as a necessary consequence of religious adherence.

However, from this position Indonesian Islamic lawyers have developed a second plank for the reform of Indonesian law. This is no less than a reform of Islamic law itself along the 'modernist' lines adopted throughout a large part of the Middle East. Some have argued that instead of relying upon Shafi'i doctrine alone, Indonesian Islam should choose elements from among the four Sunni schools.[64] This has not met with any great success in Indonesia, at least up to now. The second proposal for reform is doctrinally much more radical. It asks for an extensive exercise of *ijtihad* (a reasoned application of the Koran) in respect of the principles of the *fikh*. This view is associated particularly with Hazairin and has met strong opposition from the more conservative elements in Indonesian Islam.[65] It has had no influence in national legal policy.

The problems and complexities involving adat and Islam continue to persist in modern Indonesia but in discussing them three contexts must be kept separate.

(i) First one may investigate the nature of the relationship in formal legal terms. Within this context and only within it, is there an obligatory conflict of systems with residual power located in the secular judiciary. From this point of view the structure of the formal legal system is primary and the basic data consists of legislation and judicial decision. Of these two the latter is the most important because, amongst other reasons, the dictates of the legislature are often not enforced or even communicated properly in Indonesia as a whole. There has been and there still remains a fundamental inefficiency in judicial administration, illustrating once more the gap between prescriptive and descriptive validity. On the other hand full data on the issue in case terms is lacking. Apart from a few collections of cases there is no system of law reporting although one can gain some idea of the relationship from current data. These, however, are confined to reports from the secular courts; for the Islamic courts we have to rely upon accounts in books written primarily for analytical purposes. Unfortunately, the data from the judicial process are still not sufficient to demonstrate fully the nature of the relationship.

(ii) The second context of the relationship consists of descriptions in the social sciences—particularly anthropology—of how the rules are seen and operated by the Indonesian peoples. In this respect it is impossible to generalize for all of Indonesia. There are cases, such as Minangkabau, where the opposition of systems is almost as formal as in the state institutions just discussed. In other cases, however, adjustment and a mixing of concepts is the norm. Again, the range of data necessary for a proper description is lacking. For this reason exaggerated claims by one side or the other in argument must be treated with the utmost caution.

(iii) Finally, there is the political context in which proponents of one view or the other attempt to promote their views as a national policy. At the moment it seems reasonably clear that adat has become identified as being a component of secularism and hence it is in a powerful political position. Islam, on the other hand, is somewhat on the defensive in contemporary Indonesia.

In any discussion of adat and Islam these three contexts, and variants of them, are commonly mixed; arguments drawn from one or the other field are used to mutually justify each other. The end result of course is confusion because the arguments are different in type and significance. Before rational decisions can be taken more data on (i) and (ii) above must be obtained.

1. This is well recognized both by commentators in general, cf. Levy (1957), and also by Indonesian Islamic writers, cf. Natsir (1951).
2. cf. Noer, 1973: 16–17 and the references there cited.
3. cf. Geertz (1960).
4. Noer (1973).
5. Cited in Widjojoatmodjo, 1942–3: 55.
6. ibid: 56.
7. Wertheim, 1964: 202 ff.
8. 1815: Art. 78.
9. Staatsblad, 1882, No. 152.
10. Legislation with a similar restrictive aspect was also common; e.g. Art. 4, para. 2B of Staatsblad No. 482 of 1932 forbade the Muslim marriage official to assist in a marriage which violates the adat of Minangkabau and Batak.
11. cf. Benda, 1958: 20–6.
12. See Boland (1971) for an outline of political and legal development.
13. Staatsblad, 1929, No. 348.
14. Staatsblad, 1931, No. 53.
15. Staatsblad, 1937, No. 116.
16. cf. Westra, 1939: 166. See also Lev, 1972: 19–30 for a full discussion of the political implications of these proposals.
17. See Prins, 1954: 94–8, Noer, 1973: 244–5 and the sources there cited.
18. Staatsblad, 1937, No. 638.
19. cf. Noer (1973) for a general description.
20. cf. Noer, 1973: 216–20 for an account from Minangkabau.
21. cf. Nasrun, 1957: 21–7. See also Taufik Abdullah (1966).
22. cf. chapters 7 and 8.
23. cf. Benda (1958) for a full account. See also Lev, 1972: 33–41.
24. See Lev, 1972: 43–61. See Ahmad Ibrahim, 1971: 125.
25. cf. Prins, 1954: 99 ff.
26. ibid: 100.
27. Pengadilan Agama; Staatsblad, 1882, No. 152, Staatsblad, 1937, Nos. 116, 610, Mahkamah Tinggi Islam.
28. Pengadilan Kadi: Staatsblad, 1937, No. 638.
29. Penetapan Pemerintah No. 5/S.D. March 25, 1946.
30. Mahkamah Sharia: Penetapan Pemerintah 1957, No. 45. See Lev, 1972: 75–92.
31. Undang2 tentang Ketentuan2 Pokok Kekuasaan Kehakiman No. 14 of 1970.
32. Ch. II Art. 10(3).
33. Lembaran Negara 70/1965. Tambahan Lembaran Negara 2767/1965.
34. cf. Schiller, 1956: 99–102, Damian & Hornick (1972). The adat courts were abolished or their abolition was anticipated everywhere in Indonesia by Emergen-

cy Law No. 1 of 1951 'except Religious justice where according to the living law [hukum yang hidup] such justice forms an independent part of Adat justice.' Art. 1(2) (a & b).
35. See below Chapter 7.
36. Decision Reg. n. 109 K/Sip/1960.
37. Cited in Lev, 1972: 68–9.
38. On somewhat legalistic grounds. cf. Lev, 1972: 84.
39. Law No. 32 of 1954, L.N. 98/54, November 1954.
40. cf. Lev, 1972: 86–9.
41. cf. Notosusanto, 1963: 27–30.
42. It is worth pointing out here that colonial adat studies circulate quite extensively in a variety of Indonesian language translations—often mimeographed and bound in a soft cover. The quality of the translations varies widely but they are cheap (averaging about 20–30p. English) and easily available in bookstalls.
43. Lev, 1972: 180–1.
44. That is property acquired during coverture: *gono-gini, guna-kaja, harta (barang) (sa) pencarian.*
45. cf. Ter Haar (1948). See above Chapter 2 on the social construction of adat.
46. cf. Nawawi (1914) for the Shafii rules.
47. Ter Haar, 1948: 199–200. See also Westra, 1939: 158–9.
48. Although the Eight Year Plan of 1960 looked to the creation of a uniform system. See Rantjangan Dasar Undang-undang Pembangunan Nasional Semesta-Berentjana delapan tahun 1961–69. Vol. IV: 2624. The Basic Agrarian Law of 1960 has not materially altered this situation. Indeed the Government Regulation No. 56 of 1960 Art. 10(1) setting 2 hectares as the minimum which may be owned for purposes of agriculture specifically excludes transfers of smaller amounts by way of succession.
49. cf. Koesnoe, 1971: 38.
50. See below the concluding section of this chapter.
51. Lev, 1972: 199–205.
52. cf. Vergouwen, 1964: 60–1.
53. Vergouwen, whose book on the Toba Batak is today recognized as one of the most valuable in the whole of Dutch adat literature, saw this clearly. See Vergouwen, 1964: 143–4 on the question of 'rules [of law in the positivist sense]'.
54. cf. Prins (1954).
55. cf. Tanner, 1969: 51.
56. cf. Taufik Abdullah (1966) for a general description.
57. cf. van Vollenhoven, 1918: 675 ff.
58. cf. Ter Haar, 1948: 27 ff. But see Carpentier Alting, 1926: 336–9 for objections.
59. cf. Lev, 1972: 20–1 citing a paper to this effect by Supomo which was written in 1944 for the Japanese authorities who accepted this view.
60. cf. Hazairin, 1962: 4.
61. Hazairin, 1950: 10.
62. Hazairin (1950) (1962).
63. Surah IV: 24.
'Forbidden to you are your mothers, and your daughters and your sisters, and your father's sisters and your mother's sisters, and the daughters of your brothers and the daughters of your sisters and your foster sisters, and the mothers of your wives and your step-daughters who are your wards by your wives with whom you have consorted....'
64. cf. Notosusanto (1963), Muhammad Hasbi (1961/1381).
65. cf. Lev, 1972: 239–42 for a description of the conflict, particularly its political aspects.

6

ADAT AND THE LEGISLATURE

Introduction

THIS chapter is concerned with the one major piece of legislation which has had a direct bearing upon the adat systems of Indonesia. This is the Basic Agrarian Law of 1960,[1] one of the few major pieces of reform legislation in the Republik Indonesia. Before going on to the subject proper of this chapter it is necessary to outline here the major forms of law-making and law enforcing documents in the Republik Indonesia. The present situation is complicated mainly because Indonesia has had three Constitutions in the past quarter century and each has provided for varying types of legislation, executive decrees and instructions. However, each Constitution has affirmed the continuing applicability of Dutch colonial law.[2] The forms in which this law appeared were the Royal Decree (*koninklijk besluit*) and General Administrative Regulation (*Algemeen Maatregel van Bestuur*), both for the period 1814–55. From 1855–1926 the Royal Decree continued to be used but was constrained by the Statute (*Wet*) enacted by the Dutch Parliament. In addition, the Governor-General promulgated the Crown Ordinance (*Kroon Ordonnantie*) given with the approval of the King and the Ordinance (*Ordonnantie*) given with the approval of the colonial parliament (*Raad van Nederlands Indie*). These forms continued to be used in the period 1927–42 and in addition the Governor-General promulgated regulations (*Regeringsverordeningen*) for the purpose of implementing one of the other forms.

The forms used in independent Indonesia have varied as the constitutions have varied and as presidential government became fully established as the normal form of government. The latter has led to an extensive array of executive law-making instruments, particularly in the period of President Soekarno.[3] In 1966 the People's Assembly adopted the following forms of law.[4]

(i) *The Constitution of 1945—Undang-undang Dasar 1945.*

(ii) *Decree of the People's Assembly—Ketetapan MPR.* A decree fixes the outlines of a national policy for the legislative and executive spheres of government. In respect of the former it must be implemented by Statute and if it concerns the executive it must be put into effect by a Presidential Decision.

(iii) *Statute—Undang-undang*. These are enacted by the House of Representatives and ratified by the President. They implement either an article of the Constitution or a Decree of the People's Assembly.

(iv) *Government Regulation—Peraturan Pemerintah*. These are promulgated by the President for the purpose of implementing a statute and they are one of the most common and important forms of law for day-to-day administrative purposes.

(v) *Presidential Decision—Keputusan Presiden*. These are also promulgated by the President to give effect to an article in the Constitution, to implement a decision of the People's Assembly in the executive sphere or to implement a Government Regulation.

(vi) Regulations and Instructions of a Minister—*Peraturan/ Instruksi Menteri*. These are orders promulgated by a Minister for the purpose of implementing a higher order, particularly statutes. In addition Ministers also put out 'Decision of the Minister'—*Surat Keputusan Menteri*—with the same function.

(vii) *Circular Letter—Surat Edaran*. This is an internal memorandum issued by the Head of a Department in a Ministry to interpret or clarify a regulation or decision of the Minister. It is not published in any State Gazette and is technically for internal use only but on occasion it can be extremely important in that it interprets key provisions in the regulations.

The forms of law listed here are in a descending order of competence; indeed, one may say that as one goes down the list one is proceeding from the general policy statement to the specific implementation of a legal policy. The system is basically a system of executive orders with strong centralist tendencies, and important powers of law-making are delegated to functionaries.

Adat, Law Reform, and the Basic Agrarian Law

The Agrarian Law of 1960 is a statute (*Undang-undang*) drafted to accomplish a set of specific reforms in respect of land. This is particularly apparent from Articles 7, 10 and 17, which anticipate detailed legislation on land reform. These Articles declare as a matter of general principle that there will be maximum and minimum limitations on land ownership, and they provide that agricultural land must be cultivated by the owner himself. The question of maximum and minimum limits has been regulated for in a detailed regulation,[5] as has the issue of absentee ownership.[6] The policy motive behind this legislation was to deal with the social and economic problems caused by land hoarding and land fragmentation within the framework of rights of land ownership and use as defined in principle in the Basic Agrarian Law.[7]

The major legacy bequeathed to Indonesia by the colonial authority was a dual system of land tenures and the interracial law questions which they often occasioned. With the replacing of race by citizenship as the determinate point of legal reference it was both logical and necessary that the land tenures be unified.[8] The Basic Agrarian Law specifically revokes the principles of colonial agrarian law as set out in the Agrarian Act of 1870[9] and later regulations. The existence of a dual system of tenures, one based on adat law and the other on European law was specifically described in the preamble to the Basic Agrarian Law as 'a consequence of the law policy of the colonial government'. In addition, the Law invalidates all of Book II of the Civil Code which set out the principles of land tenure in the European law sense. The only exception has been the rules on mortgage (*hypotec*) which are retained,[10] although the rights in land on which a mortgage can be affected are now confined to those specified in the Basic Agrarian Law. The general principle of revocation of earlier law is contained in Art. 58 of the Basic Agrarian Law, and as well as providing for the specific revocations just outlined it contains also a general qualifying principle that previous laws should remain in force 'so long as they are not contrary to the spirit (*bertentangan dengan djiwa*) and stipulations of this law and are interpreted accordingly'. This provision has given rise to a good deal of uncertainty because any judgment as to the validity of a law cannot be other than subjective. One may even speak, as do the leading commentators on the Law, of a special class of 'regulations indirectly invoked'.[11]

The effect of the Law has therefore been to inject a good deal of uncertainty into Indonesian land law. The former European rights of Book II have gone and the basis of the new unified tenure is specifically stated to be 'adat law'.[12] This term is used in a very wide and general sense and its reference is not clear. Is it to the concept of adat in general and, if so, what does this mean in relation to land tenure? Does it include, for example, Ter Haar's proposition that all land rights are 'communal' in nature?[13] On the other hand, does it refer to the specific local rules of some named adat? This uncertainty is not helped by the lack of data on a good many adats, and even where data do exist they are often in a form not readily assimilable in judicial proceedings. These comments contrast strongly with one of the stated aims of the Law which is to provide or improve security of tenure,[14] particularly for the Indonesian peasantry. The Law itself recognizes that its provisions provide only broad or general principles and it stipulates that implementing legislation should follow[15] and some has indeed been made (see below). At the same time, however, there are still broad areas of uncertainty though transitional articles[16] attempt some regulation; for example, Article 56 provides that pending the provision of new regulations, rights of ownership in land are governed by the 'local adat law' and by old regulations concerning similar rights in land. The same Article goes on to qualify this, however, by requiring that these laws must not be applied contrary to the spirit of the Law. Uncertainty seems to have been compounded in no uncertain manner! We now go on to look a little more closely at the proposition that 'adat is the basis of the new Law'.

Adat is specifically mentioned in Article 5 of the Basic Agrarian Law where it is said 'to be the basis of' the subsequent system of rights in land. However, the generality of this proposition is extensively qualified in the same Article. The Explanatory Memorandum to the Law takes this proposition a little further, although it does say that the basic adat must be reshaped by and adjusted to the needs and interests of the people in the new state.[17] Principles of existing adat laws which do not conform to such interests and needs should not be enforced. On this point the Explanatory Memorandum specifically says that the relationship of Indonesia with the international community must not be hindered by an adat law unsuited to the needs of a modern state. The overwhelming implications of the Memorandum and of the statement of principle itself are as follows. First, the legislation recognizes that, for the moment, the existing law which governs a large portion of Indonesian agricultural land is one or another variety of adat. This fact is acknowledged and, second, the Law looks forward to the formation of a concept of adat which must be refined out of the present adats and adapted to meet the economic needs of an independent state. This is a call, in other words, for a modernization in principle and in practice. The Basic Law itself sets out what are to be the guidelines in this attempt in its qualifications to the general principle that adat is basic. These are as follows:[18]

(i) *Adat must not be contrary to the National Interests of the State.* The interest of the state is defined as being the protection of 'national unity'. The thrust of this qualification is twofold; first, it is a reaffirmation of the principle of state sovereignty as being superior to adat. Adat is but a part of the state system and exists by its fiat; it can be limited or abolished by the institutions of state.[19] Second, and more immediate, it means that national (economic) development will not be thwarted by the specific or local rules of some adat which interfere with regional development. The example quoted in the Explanatory Memorandum[20] is the adat right of disposal (*hak ulajat*)[21] which is considered to have been an obstacle in regional development. The Law recognizes the right but stipulates that its implementation must be adjusted to state interests.[22] It is clear for example that this right cannot be exercised by any adat community so as to pre-empt the government right to dispose of land for any purpose which it thinks fit. This issue raises two interesting questions which are not dealt with in the Law itself. First, the adat right of disposal is not a right which is regulated in detail in the Law and indeed, is only mentioned very generally in Article 3 and in the Explanatory Memorandum. It is not properly one of the basic rights in property defined fully in the body of the Law. Its formal status is thus uncertain. Second, and of particular economic relevance, where the state does dispose of land for some development purpose, for example, to erect a factory, the local adat community insists upon payment to itself from the new proprietor. This is not compensation from the state to a dispossessed occupier because the state is not involved in payment. The payment comes from the new proprietor and is not compensation for loss of ownership, for none exists legally, but is a payment for loss of the (future) right to dispose. This payment is in no way sanctioned by any law but it is a matter of practical necessity and is always made.[23]

(ii) *Adat must not be contrary to 'Indonesian Socialism'*. The term 'Indonesian socialism' remains relatively undefined. It appears in Articles 6 and 15 of the Law but is merely restated in forms such as 'all rights over land have a social function'. Its basic reference in the Law seems to be toward limiting the unrestricted use of natural resources, including land and water, by providing that such resources be utilized for a general benefit. It is not possible to go much beyond this at the moment. It is not a prescription for socialist forms of control over the means of production, either in a Marxist sense or even in a Socialist sense. As a statement of policy it appears to refer to the mixed type of economy, and the Explanatory Memorandum stresses that individual and general interests must be kept in harmony so as to achieve the goals of justice and equality for the people.[24]

Possibly the clearest practical expression of the principle is the land reform programme which Articles 7, 10 and 17 of the Law describe. It prohibits unlimited land ownership (Art. 7) which would violate the interests of the people as a whole, and Article 10(i) provides that each occupier must cultivate his land himself. Absentee landlordism is, in principle, avoided, although Article 5(3) does allow the government to authorize exceptions to this principle.[25] Article 17 provides for the maximum and minimum areas of land that may be owned by any individual.[26] The criteria in fixing the limits are population density and soil fertility and type. The conversion rights in the self-governing areas of Jogjakarta and Surakarta were of course abolished well before the 1960 legislation.[27]

(iii) *Adat must not be contrary to the Principles of the Basic Agrarian Law or to other Government Laws.* This is dealt with in rather more detail in the next section but there are two comments which should be made here. First, the Basic Agrarian Law is primarily concerned to lay down general principles which anticipate detailed implementing regulations. Therefore the place of adat in the Law is a matter of principle (as described above), the working out of which is planned as a gradual process contingent upon detailed regulation and the provision of supporting institutional machinery, e.g. land registration offices. Many of the articles in the law are formulated in apparently vague and idealistic terms which are quite different in nature and function from laws with which a European jurist is familiar. For example, it is unlikely that there is any land law in the West which commences by saying that (Indonesian) land, water and air are a 'blessing of God'.[28] To a certain extent this can be explained by the fact that Indonesia is consciously stating an indigenous point of view in reaction to the views of the former colonial régime. It can also be said that the vagueness of statement in the Law is an attempt to provide a general framework within which the variety of indigenous adat tenures may be included and through which a common set of fundamental principles of land tenure might be developed.

Second, and following from this, although the Law looks toward a unified set of tenures, it does not deny the continued existence of different 'interests of law'. Article 11(2) provides that 'differences in the social conditions and legal interests of population groups should be observed if they are significant and not in contradiction with the national interest'. The Explanatory Memorandum goes on to state clearly that the aim of this Article is to recognize systems of interests which are of importance to population groups.[29] For example, Article

11(2) distinguishes between the economically weak and strong and guarantees a special protection for the former. More important, however, later articles of the Law perpetuate distinctions between adat and European land which the Law itself supposedly abolishes. Article 58 provides that former regulations requiring a licence (or now the approval of the Minister of Agrarian Affairs) for the transfer of rights derived from European law concerning land are still valid. Although this distinction ceased to be of importance after 1961,[30] it does illustrate that the Law clearly contemplates the retention of such distinctions, at least for a transitional period and pending the drafting of new regulations. This point should be kept in mind because although the distinction between land types is now no longer valid, the rights which arose out of or were derived from different land types continue to be governed by regulations taken from colonial practice.[31] For example, in the very important area of mortgage (*hypothec*) the provisions of Book II of the Civil Code remain in force.

Bearing these general comments in mind, perhaps the clearest example of what is meant by the proposition that adat should not be in conflict with the provisions of the Basic Agrarian Law or other government regulation can be got from the procedure providing for the conversion of adat rights into new rights under the Law.

The procedure for conversion is regulated by the following rules:

(a) The Conversion Provisions of the Basic Agrarian Law[32]
(b) Regulation of the Minister for Agrarian Affairs No. 2 of 1960[33]
(c) Regulation of the Minister for Agriculture and Agrarian Affairs No. 2 of 1962[34]
(d) Government Regulation No. 10 of 1961 on land registration[35]
(e) Decree of the Internal Affairs Minister 1970 on conversion and registration of titles on land.[36]

The applicant for conversion must show that he is an Indonesian national and apart from this the main burden of the regulations just cited is to require that the area and use of the land in question and the identity of its proprietor be specified and registered in the Land Registry Office where such has been established. This Office can register only rights specified in the Law itself, i.e. rights of ownership, exploitation, building and use. No other right is permitted and rights under adat laws must be subsumed under one of these heads.[37]

What then can be concluded from this brief description of adat and the new Law, particularly the provisions of Article 5? The answer seems to be clear—at least on the matters considered so far in this section—that the principle that adat should form the basis of the land laws of Indonesia is so heavily qualified in the three ways described that we must doubt seriously whether it can in fact continue to do so. There is certainly little room for the view that the legislature has supported or underwritten adat as a source of land law, except to the extent that it does not conflict with the limits imposed upon it. This appears clearly from the matter considered in the following section.

Adat Rights and Statutory Rights in Land

The changes brought about by the Basic Agrarian Law on rights in land have been extensive and far reaching. This is clear even if one does no more than glance at and compare the tables of contents of standard texts, such as those by Ter Haar[38] on adat land rights, and Harsono[39] on the new system provided in the Law. Perhaps the easiest and most logical way of describing the changes which have occurred is to take the classifications of rights in the Law and try to describe their effect upon the traditional adat system.

(i) *Ownership (hak milik).* This is the fullest and most complete right known to the Basic Agrarian Law and provides for the exclusive use of land, and the water and air attached to it if these are necessary to its utilization.[40] The interest is unlimited in time and the owner is entitled to transfer all or part of his interest to any other person including the right to transfer a limited interest if he so wishes. The right of ownership can be inherited,[41] conveyed as security for debt,[42] or made the subject of gift.[43]

This view of the concept of ownership is one with which the European lawyer, whether a civil or common lawyer, is quite familiar. However, it does represent a radical departure from traditional Indonesian views or indeed the traditional views found in South-East Asia. The adat systems of Indonesia treat the concept of land ownership in a distinct way. It is based on the idea, only imperfectly described in the term 'ownership', that the adat group (whether of a territorial or kinship nature) controls the allocation and use of land. At the same time all adat systems recognize that the effort and capital put into a piece of land by an individual create something of a personal tie between that person and the land. In some sense, as we would say, he had 'rights in and over' the land in question. The basic issue at the root of all Indonesian land systems is the relationship between the community and individual interest. It was van Vollenhoven who pointed out that the range of interests throughout Indonesia could not simply be described as 'communal', and it was he who coined the term *beschikkingsrecht* (right of disposal).[44] This term directed attention toward the means of organizing the utilization of land and away from jurisprudential classification which, being of European (civil law) origin, had a somewhat limited significance in the Netherlands East Indies. The elaboration of the right of disposal idea concentrated upon a variety of relationships between individual and community interests and resulted in descriptions of the man-land relationship focused around occupation, possession and usufruct.[45] Van Vollenhoven and later writers, particularly Ter Haar,[46] denied that the rights of an individual could amount to 'ownership' in the European sense by which they meant the availability of the right of a free and unrestricted alienation. Ter Haar indeed went further and refused to distinguish between an individual right of possession and the right of usufruct. Such is clearly based upon a definition of adat in terms of social structure,[47] and the indigenous view, common to all adat systems, that the individual is not the point of normative reference for legal purposes.[48] The essential element is instead the idea that obligation is attributed in fixed status terms. So it is with land, thus giving rise to specific adat terminologies which express the interests of groups and not of individuals: for example, the Minangkabau '*harta pusaka*'. The term '*milik*', commonly translated as ownership, in reality referred to little more than a usufruct when used in relation to an individual. It was not open to an individual to transfer such land except within a community, and even here we must distinguish between a transfer of the land itself and a transfer of the right to occupy and use. The former was uncommon because it was unnecessary and arose largely in relation to princely land.

The primary right was the right of disposal, i.e. the right to allocate as between individuals in the group and in relation to outsiders. This right, the *hak ulajat*, is recognized in the Basic Agrarian Law to the extent that it cannot be exercised contrary to the 'national interest of the State';[49] that is to say the community control of disposal is no longer *sui generis*. Instead the primary right has now become that of the individual, the new *hak milik* as described earlier. This right is defined in terms which are in no way cognizable to traditional adat principles; the restrictions on individual freedom of action similarly have no relation to adat principles. Under the new law the restrictions relate to maximum and minimum areas, issues of citizenship and the like. The right of *hak milik* can be created on the basis of the conversion regulations[50] or by government grant.[51] In neither case is any adat qualification required. The only duties on the individual in the case of government grant land are to erect a boundary mark, to pay a small sum, and to register the right of ownership at the local Land Registry.[52]

In addition, the implementing regulations have gone even further in that they bear directly upon the adat in relation to *hak milik*. Traditionally, the cultivation of land within the adat community gave rise only to a right of usufruct, but the same action since 1960 can give rise to a right to have the occupation and use of such land registered as *hak milik*. In other words, a new right of quite a different nature as defined by the Basic Agrarian Law can arise out of a traditional practice.[53]

In the light of these comments it is impossible to suppose that the proposition in Article 5 of the Basic Agrarian Law, that the Law is 'based upon adat', can be entertained as a serious working principle. For example, there are yet further restrictions on the transfer of *hak milik* which owe nothing to adat, in that they require a process of registration, the underlying premise of which is that only the individual proprietor is involved. On the other hand, in the case of sale and purchase of *hak milik*, a recourse to adat is not only possible but is necessary because of gaps in the Basic Agrarian Law itself. The Law does not define a contract so that there are two possible legal definitions which can be imputed in the formation of an agreement. The first is the definition in Art. 1457 of the Civil Code to the effect that a contract is in existence, given agreement as to object and price. The second is the adat view that a contract is completed only when payment (actual or imputed)[54] is actually made. It seems that the latter view of contract is the preferred one in relation to *hak milik*; the Supreme Court impliedly recognized the validity of the adat notion of contract in so far as land sales are concerned in a decision given in 1958.[55] Admittedly this is prior to the Basic Agrarian Law but it is a circumstance in which the provisions of Art. 5 of the Law may actually be a reflection of legal reality. This question is, however, by no means settled. Further, the actual process of sale and purchase is subject to registration, although there is no evidence that lack of registration would invalidate the contract; naturally, though, it would cause difficulty in later transactions.

It is open for an individual to transfer *hak milik* by testamentary disposition.[56] This is known in all adat systems and such arrangements may be either oral or written. In Java this disposition is called *wekas* (or *weling* in high Javanese) and by other names throughout the archipelago (*umanat* in Minangkabau). In all adat systems any such disposition is subject to the rule that such a bequest cannot be met unless and until all debts have been cleared. In addition the Basic Agrarian Law imposes a further condition which effectively disbars any such bequest from constituting an automatic transfer. Articles 21(3) and 26 provide that bequests must be to persons properly qualified in the Law and the actual putting into effect of the bequest is a legal action. This means that the conveyance of the land must be effected before the proper official specified in the Law. So far as intestate succession is concerned, this occurs automatically on the owner's death, although the regulations on land reform must be observed.

(ii) *Exploitation.* This right[57] (*hak guna usaha*) is a specific title in State land given to an individual to cultivate for a certain period of time and for a purpose stated in the grant. The right can be sold, inherited or used as a security for debt. The qualifications to acquire such a right are the same as those demanded for ownership. The title is granted by the Minister of Internal Affairs[58] who fixes an annual money payment. There is a connection here with adat in that much of the land classified as State land may also be part of an adat community's right of disposal. In this case it is necessary for the grantee to give the *recognitie* (recognition money) to the representatives of the community as an acknowledgement of the adat right. This is subject to agreement with the community concerned.[59]

(iii) *Use.* This right[60] (*hak pakai*) is a general right to use and obtain the products of a piece of land. The land in question can be either state land or land belonging to an individual, although the latter is unusual because more specific rights, such as lease, cultivation, or land pledging (see below), are the norm so far as land individually owned is concerned. The right, therefore, occurs mainly on state land. There is no definite time limit although it is possible to specify a fixed period of time in the grant.[61] In its present statutory form the *hak pakai* includes the adat right of village members in some adat systems to utilize village land under certain conditions: 'the *gogolan* right'.[62] This is an example of an adat title receiving a direct formulation in the Agrarian Law although the grant is now made by government agency.[63] The right is transferable.[64]

(iv) *Lease.* This interest in land does not apply to State lands, titles to which are given under *hak pakai*, but is confined to lands owned by an individual. The right of lease[65] entitles the holder to utilize land in compliance with an agreement which specifies a certain amount of rent. Lease is not properly regulated in the Basic Agrarian Law except insofar as Articles 44, 45, and 53 provide for further detailed regulations. Indeed, Article 53 of the Law states that leasing will, in the future, be prohibited in line with the provisions of Article 10 which provide that agricultural land should be cultivated by the owner himself. This provision has not yet been put into effect. The only detailed regulations which concern leases are the Government Regulation (in lieu of law) No. 38 of 1960,[66] as amended by Law No. 20 of 1964[67] on the utilization and designation of land areas for certain crops. The details of lease agreements are thus a matter for local adats to determine.

(v) *Sharecropping*. This interest is not directly regulated in the Basic Agrarian Law. It arises when an individual, who requires land for cultivation, agrees to submit part of the crop to the landowner in terms of some agreed share. The shares vary from area to area and they may also depend upon the type of crop grown and the yield of the harvest. The institution is widespread in areas of dense population, especially in Java. It is regulated by Law No. 2 of 1960[68] which substantially modifies local adat rules.[69] It does this in three ways: first, it specifies the minimum shares which can be agreed upon as either equal shares or a two-thirds share in favour of the sharecropper depending upon the type of crop. This replaces local practices which in some areas provided for as little as one-fifth of the crop to go to the sharecropper. Second, it was common in adat systems for the duration of the agreement to be limited to one year. Law No. 2 of 1960 specifies a minimum of three or five years, depending upon the type of land. Third, the law specifies that the village head should supervise sharecropping agreements—a new function for this officer—and to see that Law No. 2 is implemented.

The sad fact is, however, that these regulations have had little practical effect mainly because of the shortage of land available for cultivation.

(vi) *Landpledge*.[70] This practice (*hak gadai*), like the practice of sharecropping, is not directly regulated by the Basic Agrarian Law and it exists, as it has always done, subject to adat laws. Landpledge takes two forms: first, there is the practice of transferring land to another in return for an agreed sum of money. After an agreed period of time,[71] the land is restored without any obligation to repay the money received. This form of landpledge is known as *jual tahunan* or *jual odojan*. It may be described as a lease with pre-paid rent.

The second form of landpledge is the transfer of land for a sum of money with the condition that the land will not be returned except that the money be repaid. This is called *jual gadai* and it is also found under different names throughout much of South-East Asia.[72] The transfer of land in this way is not properly a security for debt although this is usually the motive; it is a complete transfer of title subject to a conditional retransfer. For example, the person who provided the money cannot demand repayment; it is up to the original transferor to determine the time of retransfer. In the event of death of one or both parties, the relationship is continued by their heirs, although the right to retransfer may be nullified by effluxion of time.[73] Both rights in the transaction are saleable so that the original parties are often replaced by different people who are, however, bound in the same terms.

The difficulty which arises in this latter form of land pledge, especially when a long period has elapsed, is to distinguish the transaction from sale and purchase. Landpledging is typically an oral transaction and disputes are common in the courts as to whether sale or pledge was intended by the original parties. A further difficulty was (and remains) the tendency of landpledge to contribute to rural indebtedness. For these reasons, and in pursuance of Article 53 of the Basic Agrarian Law, an attempt has been made to regulate it. In Government Regulation No. 56 of 1960[74] it is provided that where land has been pledged for seven years, then it must be returned to the original transferor without his having to repay the money originally received. The theory behind this rule is that the person who has provided the money will have got it back with interest in seven years simply because he will have had the produce of the land for this period. In addition, the regulation goes on to provide that the transferor may request retransfer within the seven-year period, and in this event he is obliged to repay only a portion of the money originally advanced, not, as in the traditional system, the whole amount. This regulation does not of course allow for the fluctuation in the value of money, and the Supreme Court has ruled that in assessing the amount to be repaid both parties must share equally in the risks of inflation.[75] Since 1961 it has been the law[76] that land pledges should be conducted in the Land Registry Offices and registered on the certificates of ownership. However, it is doubtful if this rule is enforced in more than a very small minority of transactions.

Summary

What effect has the legislation had on adat? First, it continues in modern statutory form some of the major principles of adat land holding. This is a modernized adat and as such may truly be a basis for a national law. However, in (a) asserting the rights of the State and (b) in the new concept of ownership, quite revolutionary changes have been made. These two changes are now well settled; much of the adat retained—as in pledge and so on—is retained for limited periods and is thus reduced to the status of transitional rules. Second, the administrative machinery necessary for the full implementation of the law has still not been provided. The adats may therefore continue to be valid for a longer period than the legislation anticipates. As is shown in the next chapter, the land cases which come to the courts not only involve principles of adat in conjunction with the provisions of the Law, but also require decisions in terms of adat alone. The legislation has not made adat any less important, indeed in some of its provisions it may well have strengthened the necessity for a grasp of adat principle. Indirect reinforcement of this type is not uncommon in modernizing legal systems although, needless to say, it is not often the intention of the legislature.

1. Undang-undang Pokok Agraria, No. 5/1960, Lembaran Negara 104/1960.

2. *Constitution of 1945*. This constitution, effective from 1945 to 1949, provided in Art. 2 of the transitional provisions that the colonial law in force as at 17 August 1945 remained in force and the later government regulation (*peraturan pemerintah*) No. 2 of 10 October 1945 retroactive to 17 August, interpreted Art. 2 to mean that colonial law was valid only to the extent that it was not contrary to the Constitution of 1945.

Federal Constitution of 1945–50. This was the Federal Constitution and in Arts. 192, 195 stated that the law in force at the moment of transfer was valid provided it was contrary to neither state sovereignty nor to the new constitution.

Provisional Constitution of 1950. This replaced the Constitution of 1949–50 and was valid for the period 1950–9. It provided that all pre- and post-independence legislation of the Dutch as well as legislation of the Federal Republic (1949–50) was valid for the new state. All legislation enacted by the first Republic (1945–9) was also declared valid.

The Revived Constitution of 1945. This, the original Constitution, was revived in 1959 and Art. 2 of the transitional provisions is now once again in force. Presumably the legislation made under the Federal and Provisional Constitutions is also still in force.

3. cf. Damian & Hornick, 1972: 525–6 for the forms of executive decree introduced by President Soekarno.

4. MPRS Decree No. XX/MPRS/1966 of 5 July 1966.

5. Government Regulation (in lieu of Act) No. 56 of 1960, Lembaran Negara 174/1960.

6. Government Regulation No. 224 of 1961, Lembaran Negara 280/1961 as amended by Government Regulation No. 41 of 1964, Lembaran Negara 112/1964.

7. For an assessment of the success of the land reform programme see Utrecht (1969) and for general source material see the *Bulletin of Indonesian Economic Studies*.

ADAT AND THE LEGISLATURE

8. Other reforms, such as the abolition of conversion rights in the former principalities of Jogjakarta and Surakarta in Central Java, the liquidation of private estates, the reform of the lease system and the problem of illegal occupation were also dealt with in the Basic Agrarian Law. cf. Gautama and Harsono, 1972: 3–18. On social change in Jogjakarta as this affects land, see Selosoemardjan, 1962: 215 ff.

9. *Agrarische Wet*. Staatsbladt, 1870, No. 55 including the principle of *domeinverklaring* contained in the same act and in later decrees and acts. This principle stated that all land within the territorial boundaries of the state was state land if no person could show sufficient title. Its validity was strenuously contested by the adat law scholars. cf. Wirjono Prodjodikoro, 1959: 65–6.

10. Art. 57.
11. cf. Gautama and Harsono, 1972: 22–3.
12. Art. 5.
13. cf. Ter Haar, 1948: 81 ff.
14. In the Preamble to the Law, and in the Explanatory Memorandum, Part A (1) (c), Tambahan Lembaran Negara 2043/1960.
15. cf. Arts. 22 and 50 for examples.
16. Arts. 53–58.
17. See Explanatory Memorandum Part A (III) (1), Tambahan Lembaran Negara 2043/1960.
18. Specified in Art. 5.
19. See the discussion in Chapter 1 on this question.
20. Explanatory Memorandum, Part A (II) (3), Tambahan Lembaran Negara 2043/1960.
21. cf. Ter Haar, 1948: 81 ff. for a description.
22. Art. 3.
23. See below footnote 59 on the *recognitie*.
24. Explanatory Memorandum Part A (II) (4), Tambahan Lembaran Negara 2043/1960.
25. See Peraturan Pemerintah No. 224 of 1961, Lembaran Negara 1961, No. 280.
26. This principle had been introduced prior to the Basic Agrarian Law by the Law on the Abolition of Private Estates, No. 1 of 1958.
27. Law on the Conversion of Land Lease Regulations in the Principalities No. 13 of 1948.
28. Art. 1.
29. Explanatory Memorandum Part A (III) (2), Tambahan Lembaran Negara 2043/1960.
30. Consequent upon the Regulation of the Minister of Agrarian Affairs No. 14 of 1961, Tambahan Lembaran Negara 2346/1961.
31. See Teluki (1966).
32. Arts II & VI, Conversion Provisions, 1960.
33. Peraturan Menteri, Tambahan Lembaran Negara 2086/1960.
34. Peraturan Menteri, Tambahan Lembaran Negara 2508/1962.
35. Peraturan Pemerintah, Lembaran Negara 28/1961.
36. Keputusan Menteri No. SK26/DDA/1970, 14 May 1970.
37. For a description of the process of conversion see Gautama and Harsono, 1972: 97–100.
38. cf. Ter Haar (1948).
39. Harsono (1970).
40. Art. 4(2).
41. Arts. 20, 24, 27, 49(3).
42. Art. 25.
43. See the Peraturan Menteri No. 11 of 1961, Tambahan Lembaran Negara 2384/1961.

44. In Indonesian *hak ulajat*. Van Vollenhoven, 1909: 19 ff.
45. The right to use and take possession of the produce of land.
46. cf. Ter Haar, 1948: 95 ff.
47. Chapter 2.
48. Chapter 4.
49. Art. 3.
50. See above pp. 118.
51. Peraturan Menteri No. 1 of 1967.
52. Basic Agrarian Law, Art. 23.
53. This is governed by the regulation on land registration, Peraturan Pemerintah No. 10 of 1961, Lembaran Negara 28/1961, by the Peraturan Menteri No. 2 of 1960 and Keputusan Menteri No. SK26/DDA/1970 of 14 May 1970.
54. For example, it is common for only part of the purchase price to have been paid. The payment of the balance is treated as a credit transaction having no relationship with the original contract.
55. cf. Subekti & Tamara, 1965: 166.
56. Art. 26.
57. Arts. 28–35.
58. Peraturan Menteri No. 1 of 1967.
59. Authority for the continuation of *recognitie* is unclear. It is stated to be in force by textbook writers—Gautama & Harsono (1972).
60. Arts. 41–43.
61. Art. 41(2).
62. Art. VII (2) of the Conversion Provisions of the Basic Agrarian Law.
63. Regulation of the Minister of Internal Affairs No. 1 of 1967.
64. Regulation of the Minister of Agrarian Affairs No. 14 of 1961, Tambahan Lembaran Negara 2346/1961.
65. *Sewa* and other terms such as *sewa-bumi* in South Sumatra, *chukai* in Borneo. See Ter Haar 1948: 118 ff. on the variety of obligations involving land.
66. Peraturan Pemerintah No. 38 of 1960, Lembaran Negara 120/1960.
67. Lembaran Negara 108/1964.
68. Lembaran Negara 2/1960.
69. This law was, however, made in pursuance of Art. 53 of the Basic Agrarian Law which looks toward the abolition of sharecropping and landpledging. The article directs that detailed regulations be made for the time being to regulate these institutions and protect the economically weaker party to such contracts.
70. ibid.
71. A period of years or, more commonly, a stated number of harvests.
72. *Jual janji* in Malaysia; see Hooker, 1972: 249n. In Vietnam it is called '*dien*'; cf. McAleavy (1958).
73. cf. the decision of the Supreme Court reported in Subekti and Tamara, 1965: 158.
74. Peraturan Pemerintah No. 56/1960, on the fixing of agricultural land area. Lembaran Negara 174/1960.
75. cf. Subekti & Tamara, 1965: 160.
76. Government Regulation No. 10 of 1961.

7

ADAT AND THE COURTS

Introduction

THE courts in both the colonial Netherlands East Indies and in independent Indonesia have been and remain an important source of adat; indeed, according to one influential school of jurisprudence, adat in the form of judicial decision was the only true or proper description of adat laws. The aim of this chapter is to describe the sometimes complex position of adat within the state judicial process.

The court system of the Netherlands East Indies was complicated by the existence of two distinct hierarchies of courts.

(a) *Government justice* (*gouvernementsrechtspraak*). The courts of government justice were created by legislation and were regulated by a statutory procedure. They existed only in directly governed territory and comprised European Courts, Native Courts and General Courts. The primary court so far as adat was concerned was the (Superior) Native Court (*landraad*) which had competence in all civil and criminal cases for Indonesians which were not assigned to other courts. From 1938 onwards, and largely as a result of the efforts of Ter Haar, a third chamber of the (European) Superior Court of Law (*Raad van Justitie*) in Batavia took appeals from the Native Courts. The jurisdiction of this court included Java, Madura and the Residencies of Palembang, Jambi, the Lampongs, Bangka and Billiton, all of Borneo, Bali and Lombok. The Native Court in these directly governed areas was regulated by its own code of procedure.[1] In the directly governed lands of the Outer Territories, Native Courts also existed under different names though with similar competence, but their organization and procedure were governed by different regulations.[2] Government justice also existed in self-governing lands.[3]

(b) *Native administration of justice* (*inheemscherechtspraak*). In various regions of indirectly governed territory designated by statute, native tribunals of various sorts were validated. They were to apply adat law to the indigenous people within their jurisdiction except insofar as adat had been replaced by legislation.[4] In the self-governing lands native administration of indigenous adat continued although from 1938 it was subject to colonial regulation[5] providing for court organization and judicial procedure.

With the advent of independent Indonesia, first in federal[6] and subsequently in unitary form, this position changed drastically. Gone were the distinctions between the separate administrations of justice, whether native or European; the Constitution of 1945 (Arts. 24 and 25) provides that judicial power shall be exercised by a Supreme Court and by other courts in accordance with statute. These Articles also provide for the appointment and dismissal of judges although, as is usual in Indonesian constitutional matters, leaving the detailed conditions and regulations to be established by later statutes.

The courts with which we are concerned are the courts of general jurisdiction,[7] that is, the District Court (*Pengadilan Negeri*), the High Court (*Pengadilan Tinggi*), and the Supreme Court (*Mahkamah Agung*).[8] The District Court is the ordinary court of first instance with jurisdiction in criminal and civil matters. A valid court session normally requires three judges although the general practice seems to be that one judge is sufficient except in especially difficult cases. The High Court is the appeal court with jurisdiction in civil and criminal matters from District Courts within its territorial jurisdiction (the province: *propinsi*). In addition, it supervises the administration of the District Courts in its region and resolves all jurisdictional disputes between such courts. The Supreme Court is at the apex of the judicial system and has both original and exclusive jurisdiction in the following matters:

(a) All jurisdictional disputes between courts of different spheres, between High Courts and between District Courts belonging to different regions.

(b) The Supreme Court has an overriding appellate jurisdiction in the form of cassation (*kasasi*) to annul or quash decisions of the High Courts. It may grant cassation where there has been procedural error, where a lower court has exceeded its jurisdiction or has wrongly applied the law. In addition, the Supreme Court has an important function in providing a sort of judicial leadership to subordinate courts; it issues circular letters (*surat edaran*) and personal letters (*surat tersendiri*) which, though not binding, set out a formulated judicial policy. The purpose is for the lower courts to take account of this policy in their decisions so far as is possible, given the variations in local conditions which exist in Indonesia.

ADAT AND THE COURTS 129

The procedure of the Courts is regulated by legislation originating in the colonial Period. The 1941 Code of Procedure—the *Herziene Indonesisch Reglement*[9]—was declared in force for all civil and criminal cases in the District and High Courts by Emergency Law No. 1 of 1951.[10] A separate law on Supreme Court procedure was enacted in 1950.[11] These two laws were the basic procedural statutes, though subject to minor amendment, until 1965. In that year Law No. 13 repealed the 1950 Supreme Court Law,[12] but no new rules of Supreme Court procedure have been enacted. In its decisions the Supreme Court has consistently held that the law of 1965 does not affect its jurisdictional competence as established in the 1950 law.[13] Article 17 of Law No. 13 of 1965 also repealed 'all other regulations' of the courts of general jurisdiction but to date these, contained in the Law of 1951, have not been replaced and all the courts have continued to use the amended *Herziene Indonesisch Reglement* on the assumption that it is still valid. This is particularly true of the District Courts with which the writer is familiar and extends to a most minute conformance with the details of civil procedure. The implications of this for adat are of the first importance because the role of the judge(s) is much more active than in the common law or even in comparison with other civil law systems, including the Dutch, from which the *Herziene Indonesisch Reglement* derives. It is not uncommon, for example, for District Court judges to go into the countryside, ostensibly to take evidence in civil suits involving adat matters, but actually to decide a suit on the spot by a process of conciliation. This is justified within the terms of the *Herziene Indonesisch Reglement*, which obliges the judge to use his best endeavours to achieve a settlement and which leaves him a fair amount of leeway in doing so.[14]

Stability and Change in Adat

It is commonly assumed, often on the basis of incomplete evidence, that adat rules are somehow changed drastically within the Indonesian judicial process. They become, as it were, subject to modernization because of the forum, particularly in the Supreme Court. There is some truth in this just as there is truth in the corollary that adat is not basically altered at the lower levels of the District Court. As with most things connected with adat in Indonesia, the true position is rather more complex—the District Courts are not bastions of the *status quo* nor is the Supreme Court always some sort of radical reform institution. All levels of the judicial hierarchy are after all concerned with doing justice to individual claims, and judicial reality is always rather more complicated than the attenuated versions of it which appear in textbooks or in the statements of judicial propagandists. A full demonstration of this would unfortunately require a complete analysis of Indonesian jurisprudence from the early 1950s to the present, much outside the scope of this book. However, if one looks at the reported jurisprudence[15] it becomes clear that at least as many decisions on adat are given in confirmation of adat principle as those which alter adat rules. For example, in a collection of cases for the year 1969 decided in the Mahkamah Agung,[16] well over half represent little more than an affirmation of adat. A more recent example is to be found in Civil Suit No. 358 K/Sip./1971[17] where the issue was solely decided on the detailed inheritance rules of Balinese adat. There is, therefore, a good deal of stability in adat in the sense that the judicial system does apply adat rules in the determination of suits. The perhaps undue weight which has been given to legal and social change in Indonesia has tended to obscure the important stabilizing function of the judicial system in adat matters. The importance of this function cannot be over-emphasized and it must be kept in mind in any discussion of adat and the courts.

Having said this, it is equally true to say that important changes have occurred in adat through the activities of the courts. In this context 'change' means the subjection of adat rules to legislative or administrative requirements, the precise scope and extent of which can be illustrated by looking at a series of annotated cases decided by the Mahkamah Agung in 1969.[18]

(i) *The Rights of the Individual and the Rights of the Adat Community.* In Civil Suit No. 75 K/Sip./1969[19] the issue was the right of an individual to hold and take the yield from *upa parik* land when he was no longer a resident of the area. The adat is quite clear, that such land is not in the ownership of the holder but is at the disposal of village members although the right to utilization may be inherited. This rule was affirmed by the Mahkamah Agung but with the proviso that the right of exploitation is now governed in its incidents by the Basic Agrarian Law. Although the judgment is not specific on this point, this may be taken as a reference to the provisions of Law No. 28/1956[20] providing that the transfer of this right is subject to the regulations of the Djawatan Agraria (Department of Agriculture).

A similar result was reached in Civil Suit No. 76 K/Sip./1969,[21] but what is not clear is whether the judgments are referring to the right of use or the right of exploitation under the Basic Agrarian

ADAT AND THE COURTS   131

Law.[22] It may well be that the basic reference is to the right of use (*hak pakai*), the definition of which is wide enough to encompass the lesser right of exploitation. There can be no doubt, however, that the courts require that the claimants to such rights conform to the principles of Articles 41–43 of the Basic Agrarian Law and accompanying regulations, particularly the Regulation of the Minister of Agrarian Affairs No. 14/1961[23] on the transfer of such rights.

(ii) *Landpledging*. The whole field of land law is now largely regulated by the Basic Agrarian Law of 1960 and its enabling regulations which, as we saw in Chapter 6, do provide for a limited implementation of adat laws. But in addition to this the courts have been faced with a series of problems which have required decisions about the effect of this legislation. Perhaps the most interesting is landpledging (*hak gadai*) of which there are two forms. In the first, the landowner conveys land to be cultivated by another and in return he receives a sum of money. After an agreed period the land is restored with no obligation on the owner to repay the money received. This form of pledging is known as *djual tahunan* or *djual ojodan* and, in its effects, is properly a lease with an obligation to pay rent in advance. The second form of pledge (*djual gadai*) is to convey land in return for money, with a re-conveyance conditional upon repayment of the money advanced. The initiative to request re-conveyance rests with the landowner, and the pledgor is not entitled to demand the return of his money.[24] Such contracts tend to continue for many years, and the obligations arising out of them are often inherited by the heirs of the original parties. Such obligations may also be sold to third parties. In Civil Suit No. 23 K/Sip./1969[25] a portion of *sawah* was pledged in 1946 and the pledgee later transferred his rights to a third party. In 1955 and later in 1961 the pledgor offered to repay the debt but this was refused by the then pledgee. The pledgor brought an action for the return of the land but the Pengadilan Negeri Palewali refused relief on the ground that the land had been in the possession of the pledgee for a considerable period. This was overruled by the Mahkamah Agung, who relied upon Government Regulation No. 56/1960, Art. 7,[26] providing that land which has been pledged for seven years must be restored to its owner without his having to repay the money received.

This decision, in giving effect to the legislation, alters the adat in that it does away with the need for repayment in the case of *djual gadai*. On the other hand, the adat principle that a long period of time does not convert pledge into sale was specifically approved in Civil Suit No. 261 K/Sip./1970,[27] despite the fact that the original pledge was entered into in 1903. The right to redeem is not abolished by effluxion of time (*kadaluwarsa, verjaring*).[28] The provisions of Art. 7(1) of Government Regulation No. 56/1960 providing for return after seven years may be taken as a statement of this principle because the motive behind the legislation is to protect the interests of the small landowner who is the person normally putting his land out to pledge.

The difficulties raised by pledge transactions often extend to matters of inheritance, and Civil Suit No. 8 K/Sip./1969[29] provides an excellent illustration. The owner of a plot of *sawah* which had been pledged died and one of his heirs redeemed it but, when he in his turn died, his heir sold the land. The purchaser and the seller were then sued by another heir of the person who redeemed it on the ground that he was entitled to a share in the inherited property. In the Pengadilan Negeri Wattansoppeng the court decided two questions in this claim: (a) an heir, to be recognized as such, had to show that he had full control over property one month after the death of the owner and that this control was not disputed by any person. In addition his name must be on the *surat landrente* (land tax certificate). (b) So far as the sale of the land was concerned, the only requirement was that the circumstances of the sale be clear and honest. Since both of these conditions were met by the seller of the land, the plaintiff's claim was refused. In the subsequent proceedings, the Pengadilan Tinggi took a different view. So far as control over inherited property was concerned, an undisputed occupation and dealing did not of itself evidence a right of disposal. On the contrary, undisturbed possession was merely evidence of the 'spirit of tolerance among relatives'. This view was also taken by the Mahkamah Agung, and this reasoning is a clear illustration of the primacy of adat concepts. The plaintiff's claim was allowed.

Transfer of land is subject to the provisions of the Basic Agrarian Law although the term 'transfer' in Art. 20(2) covers a wide range of transactions. It includes, for example, gifts *inter vivos*, the validity of which may very well depend upon principles of adat.[30]

(iii) *Marriage*. Marriage is probably the single most important topic in Indonesian legal pluralism,[31] particularly where interracial and inter-religious marriage is involved. A recent case in point is Civil Suit No. 371 K/Sip./1969[32] where a Christian Batak had married a Dutch woman in a civil ceremony at the *Burgelijke Stand* (Civil Registry) and had subsequently married his younger brother's widow in accordance with the adat Batak. The second marriage, however, was incomplete in form in that it was without *pagodangkon*, i.e., the presence and payment of witnesses who have participated in the conclusion of a contract. The issue was the legitimacy of the children of the second marriage for purposes of inheritance. The Pengadilan Negeri decided the question solely on the fact that the defect in the adat ceremony establishing the second marriage was not decisive. However, the Pengadilan Tinggi considered the wider question of whether or not a Christian Batak was bound to monogamy. It decided he was not in that the adat of the area (Simalungun) provided for the taking of a second wife under certain conditions. The court also considered the applicability of the colonial *Huwelijksordentie Christen Indonesiers*[33]—Marriage Ordinance for Christian Indonesians—to such a case. It was held not applicable in that the husband had remained subject to the adat Batak. The Mahkamah Agung concurred.

(iv) *Contracts*. In some areas of land transactions it has become necessary for the courts to supplement adat rules. For example, where there has been a *gadai* transaction and the pledgee has subsequently sold the land to a purchaser in good faith, the court has held that the purchaser should be protected.[34] The most striking example of the readiness of the courts to act is in those circumstances where rapid changes have occurred in the value of currency. In one case concerning the sale and purchase of land, a seller refused to complete, despite the fact that there was a written contract, on the ground of changes in the currency. He was upheld by the Mahkamah Agung[35] who stated that the two parties should each share half the change in the value of the currency as determined by its value in gold at the time the contract was made and at the time the action was brought.[36]

The courts are by no means unanimous in the extent to which they will allow alteration. In Civil Suit No. 477 K/Sip./1969 the court considered the status of a written agreement to buy and sell land where the vendor cancelled the agreement orally. Both the Pengadilan Negeri Sengkang and the Pengadilan Tinggi Makasar refused to allow the cancellation despite the fact that in the adat of the area such (known as *kegau-gau*) was allowed. The reason given by the court included, *inter alia*, that to enforce this provision of the adat would adversely affect the validity of transactions whether made under adat or not. The Mahkamah Agung refused to accept this ruling on the ground that the agreement was only a preliminary to sale, and therefore there was no contract in existence. This is a rather strict interpretation by the Mahkamah Agung of the well-known adat principle that a cash advance binding the individual in the future (*pandjar*) is necessary for the validity of any agreement. It amounts really to the equation of *pandjar* with *djual-beli*. If this equation becomes finally established as a general principle then it will represent a change of some magnitude in the field of contract.[37]

Judicial Innovation

Judicial innovation occurs where the court—in this case the Mahkamah Agung—introduces a new principle of law.[38] For example, the judicial establishment of the rule giving a widow a right to inherit is a creation of the Mahkamah Agung,[39] although the Provisional People's Deliberative Council in its Decree No. II/1960 also established that a widow and children are the 'heirs' of a deceased. The basic issue is to determine what the function of the judge should be in modern Indonesia. It must be remembered that Indonesia has inherited what is basically a civil law system from the Dutch, but the legal realities in Indonesia tend to complicate this inheritance. The courts are faced, for example, with such questions as legal pluralism, the creation of a national legal system, demands for economic and legal modernization as well as the fact that the bulk of the population is governed by one or other of the adat systems.[40] The relationship between the courts and codified law has, in the past quarter of a century, been difficult to determine. On one view the codes should be brief and leave areas of creative law-making at the discretion of the judge. This was the view adopted, to some extent at least, in the early years of the Republic. However, as Indonesia moves toward the second quarter century of its existence as an independent nation state, it seems that the contrary view providing for complete written laws is becoming established. The Basic Agrarian Law is only one example and the recent Marriage Law is another. Judicial innovation is likely, therefore, to be confined to the interpretation of legislation although large areas of discretion will remain in relating adat provisions to written law. The cases cited earlier in this chapter and the issues raised in chapters 3, 4, 6 and 8 bear out this view. One would like to be more precise so far as substantive principles of law are concerned, but this is not possible in the light of the present development of Indonesian jurisprudence.

The major factor in the existence and influence of judicial innovation is most likely to be found in the extent to which the courts, that is, the judiciary, in Indonesia develop a common policy on the nature of the judicial function. In the absence of clear directives specifying such a function, as is at present the case, this question turns upon the relationship between the Mahkamah Agung and the lower courts. There are regulations prescribing limits of competence in these institutions but the matter is far more complex so far as substantive principles of law are concerned. This is especially true in the case of adat which, as already mentioned, is known to the judiciary either through colonial publication or through the testimony of litigants whose interests are, of course, not free from bias. In a very real sense the question is one of the definition of law, not as an abstract but as a search for a relationship between concepts which exist in the daily lives of the Indonesian people, and hence are fundamental to the court, and written laws which find their ultimate validity in the existence of the state.

In some cases it is perfectly possible for the courts to perform their tasks within their own terms and administer adat law unperturbed by doubts and speculations about the theory of law, either its definition in general or the identification of its basic elements. For example, in Civil Suit No. 103 K/Sip./1969 where the claim was for the return of a piece of land loaned for use as a dwelling place, the court had no difficulty in deciding the suit on adat principle alone. The main contention was that effluxion of time (*kadaluwarsa*) made a return of possession unnecessary; this was rejected as not being in accord either with the adat of the area or the jurisprudence of the Mahkamah Agung. On the other hand in Civil Suit No. 13 K/Sip./1969,[41] given two months after the decision just mentioned, the issue also related to the status of land which had been transferred and had been in the transferee's possession for thirty years. The transferee did not, however, claim ownership but only a right of *hak usaha*—a right of exploitation—and so far as this right was concerned the court was prepared to allow the effluxion of time in substantiating such a claim. But in Civil Suit No. 499 K/Sip./1969[42] which involved a claim to unpaid rent for a piece of land, the Mahkamah Agung refused to allow that effluxion of time could determine the rights of an individual. The reason given was that the adat of the area did not recognize the concept of *kadaluwarsa* although, of course, other adat systems might do so. But the court also said, and here it seemed to be speaking in general terms, that *kadaluwarsa* was difficult to prove as a fact. This may indeed be the main reason why the Mahkamah Agung is reluctant to give effect to it.

These cases are all examples of the courts performing their function untroubled by definitional questions but, as commentators have often pointed out, the axioms and rationalizations of the court do not always operate so easily in practice. This has led to a situation in which there has been a widespread failure of confidence amongst jurists themselves in the court system. In the past this has been quite critical and it has compelled particular attention to what the definition of law is to be for the purposes of the courts. Within the judicial system itself there has been difficulty with this question, and this difficulty is directly related to the jurisdiction of the different courts. The Mahkamah Agung not only exercises broad powers of cassation (*kasasi*) but it is empowered to give (theoretically) non-binding opinions and advice to all lower courts. This is done by means of circular letters (*surat edaran*) distributed generally. Such letters provide guidance in difficult matters and are usually prompted by either government policy or by the hearing of a case of exceptional difficulty in the Mahkamah Agung. To the recipients of the letters, especially the judges of the Pengadilan Negeri, the instructions, which they commonly regard as binding, not unusually cause acute embarrassment. This is matched only by the embarrassment caused by some of the Mahkamah Agung's findings in cassation. The reason is that in some cases the instructions from the Mahkamah Agung in Jakarta are out of touch with what is realistically possible in the regions. By far the greatest number of cases in this category are naturally adat cases and commonly they concern inheritance, especially the widow's right to inherit land.[42] In addition the Mahkamah Agung has given decisions supporting the actions of local government functionaries which run counter to established adat practice. For example, in Civil Suit No. 19 K/Sip./1969,[44] the Mahkamah Agung overruled both the Pengadilan Negeri Gorontal and the Pengadilan Tinggi Makasar and supported a decision by the village headman (*kepala kampung*) that an individual had a right to undisputed possession of land despite evidence that the land was subject to an agreement concluded under local adat as to sharing the yield. The Mahkamah Agung said:

> The question of the decision of the government [here the local official] to give land to any person represented a policy of the government which could not be questioned by the court.... The authority of the government to alter its policy [cannot be] affected....

The relationship between the Mahkamah Agung and the lower courts is beset with difficulties such as these, which are rooted in disparate views of the nature and sources of law, and hence, of legal function. The decisions of the Pengadilan Negeri to be enforceable must have some relationship to the adat of the area and be accepted as valid in a world founded upon adat values. At the same time there is both a pressing need for reform and a duty upon the Mahkamah Agung to accomplish reform in the light of national policy. This problem is well recognized in Indonesia, but the legal writing of the last few years has not come to grips with the issue. Despite the publication of judicial decisions in a number of forums,[45] a complete analytical survey of judicial decisions in all courts has not yet been done. This is probably an essential prerequisite to establishing a workable relationship between all levels of the judiciary. Such data would do much to avoid the present somewhat sterile debates about the nature of the judicial function.

There has been one important development in this field which is potentially of major significance. In 1969 the Mahkamah Agung commenced publication of the *Jurisprudensi Indonesia*. This contains detailed reports of cases which have come to the Mahkamah Agung by way of cassation and which are regarded as important to the development of national law. In the introduction to the first issue the then Chief Justice, Soebekti, emphasized that its prime purpose was to provide information on modern developments to judges at all levels of the judicial system. Implicit in his statement is a recommendation that the decisions published be 'followed' in the lower courts. This does not amount to the creation of a system of precedent on the common law model; rather the judgments reprinted exemplify a set of standards felt to be suitable for the development of an Indonesian national law. The judgments themselves demonstrate an approach to the development of a national law which can best be described as gradual or even hesitant when compared with statute and political policy. However there have been remarkable and even revolutionary innovations in adat decisions (see footnote 39), although each of these has been followed by a period of consolidation.

The outstanding single characteristic of contemporary Indonesian jurisprudence is its fragmentation. This is true generally but it is especially striking in respect of adat. The jurisprudence on important points of principle varies from one District Court to another, as a consequence of course of localized adat rules being in existence. These variations also persist at (provincial) High Court level where adat appeals make up a substantial proportion of the work load. It is obvious that this fragmentation cannot be mended without direction from the centre of judicial administration, the Supreme Court. As we saw above a lead has been given, though perhaps it has been rather too tentative, but of recent years even this has faltered somewhat. The *Jurisprudensi Indonesia* appears to have ceased publication.

The need is for strong central direction which can (a) determine a consistent set of adat principles and (b) relate them to the institutions of state, and to legislation which impinges on adat and general principles of law. The jurisprudence now in existence would allow a start to be made on such a programme.

1. Het Herziene Indonesisch Reglement. Staatsblad, 1941, No. 44. See also Zorab (1954).
2. Rechtsreglement Buitengewesten. Staatsblad, 1927, No. 227.
3. See Ter Haar, 1948: 18–19 for a summary.
4. Inheemsche Rechtspraak in Rechtstreeks Bestuur Gebied. Staatsblad, 1932, No. 80 later amended, see Staatsblad, 1938, No. 371 and Staatsblad, 1941, No. 7.
5. Zelfbestuursregelen. Staatsblad, 1938, No. 529.
6. cf. Schiller (1955) on this.
7. Courts of special jurisdiction include the Military Courts (Pengadilan Tentara, Pengadilan Tentara Tinggi/and Agung), Religious Courts (Pengadilan Agama); see Chapter 5, and Administrative Courts including the Land Reform Court (Pengadilan Land-Reform) which was established in 1964 but abolished in 1970 and its powers and functions transferred to the general courts—Law No. 7 of 31 July 1970, Lembaran Negara 41/1970, Tambahan Lembaran Negara 2939/1970.
8. Law No. 13 of 6 July 1965, Lembaran Negara 70/1965, Tambahan Lembaran Negara 2767/1965; see also Law No. 6 of 5 July 1969, Lembaran Negara 37/1969.
9. Staatsblad, 1941, No. 44.
10. Lembaran Negara 9/1951 amended Lembaran Negara 36/1955. The law of 1951 is often cited as authority for the proposition that the colonial adat courts were abolished. On this point see the argument of Logemann, 1954: 129–30.
11. Law No. 1 of 1950, Lembaran Negara 30/1950 amended in Lembaran Negara 106/1958.
12. Art. 70 Law No. 13 of 1965, Lembaran Negara 70/1965, Tambahan Lembaran Negara 2767/1965.
13. See, for example, the decision of the Mahkamah Agung of 29 May 1971 in *Jurisprudensi Indonesia* IV/1971 at 108 and 114.
14. See also Civil Suit No. 358 K/Sip./1971 reported in *Jurisprudensi Indonesia* IV/1971 at pp. 1–20 citing later legislation, *viz.*, Undang2 No. 20/1947 Art. 15(1), Undang2 Darurat No. 1/1951 Art. II(1), Undang2 Darurat No. 11/1955, Art. 192 (3).
15. There are a number of collections of cases published in Indonesia of which the best known are: Adiwinata (1970), Badaruzzaman (1962), Suryadarmawan (1962), Poedjosoebroto (1964), Subekti & Tamara (1965), Gouwgioksiong (1959).
16. cf. Koesnoe (1970a).
17. Reported in *Jurisprudensi Indonesia* IV/1971 at pp. 1–20.
18. Taken from Koesnoe (1970a). The advantage of looking at a series is that one does not fall into the temptation of picking out 'illustrative' cases.
19. An appeal from the Pengadilan Tinggi Medan decision No. 13 of 4 April 1968.
20. Lembaran Negara 73/1956.

ADAT AND THE COURTS

21. Also an appeal from the Pengadilan Tinggi Medan decision No. 15 of 11 April 1968.
22. See above Chapter 6.
23. Peraturan Menteri, Tambahan Lembaran Negara 2346/1961.
24. See further Chapter 6.
25. An appeal from the Pengadilan Tinggi Makasar No. 499 of 10 January 1968.
26. Peraturan Pemerintah No. 56/1960, Lembaran Negara 174/1960.
27. An appeal from the Pengadilan Tinggi Makasar No. 208 of 16 July 1968.
28. See also the cases in Subekti & Tamara, 1965: 158–60.
29. Appeal from Pengadilan Tinggi Makasar No. 34 of 8 March 1968, from the first instance decision of the Pengadilan Negeri Wattansoppeng No. 113 of 27 October 1964.
30. See, for example, Civil Suit No. 271 K/Sip./1970 where a gift of *sawah* to an adopted child was declared valid by adat and not contrary to the Basic Agrarian Law.
31. See above Chapter 4.
32. Appeal from Pengadilan Tinggi Medan No. 247 of 31 August 1967.
33. Staatsblad, 1933, No. 74.
34. Civil Suit No. 262 K/Sip./1969.
35. Civil Suit No. 340 K/Sip./1969.
36. See also Civil Suits No. 74 K/Sip./1969, No. 340 K/Sip./1969.
37. cf. Ter Haar, 1948: 140–1 on the question of 'panjer'.
38. Apart, that is, from giving effect to new legislation.
39. cf. Lev, 1962: 213–22, and the civil suit recently reported in *Jurisprudensi Indonesia* III/1971 at pp. 55–73.
40. It should also be remembered that until comparatively recently there has been little original research on adat since 1942. Much of the work which has appeared is little more than a recapitulation of colonial studies. This has obvious implications for the judicial application of adat. See also Chapters 3 and 4.
41. Appeal from Pengadilan Tinggi Medan No. 33 of 6 February 1966.
42. Appeal from Pengadilan Tinggi Medan No. 363 of 18 September 1967.
43. cf. Lev (1962).
44. Appeal from Pengadilan Tinggi Makasar No. 264 of 11 January 1968.
45. cf. n.15 above.

8

ADAT AND VILLAGE JUSTICE: AN ISSUE IN THE ETHNOGRAPHY OF LAW

Introduction

IN addition to the formal administration of justice described in the last chapter there is an equally important but far more informal forum for adat in Indonesia. Such is the system of voluntary mediation under which villagers submit disputes to some indigenous form of settlement process, the aptly named 'village justice' (*dorprechtspraak*). This form of legal administration was largely ignored in the Netherlands East Indies where attention was concentrated upon the organization and administration of formal court systems. It was not until 1935, and largely at the prompting of van Vollenhoven and Ter Haar, that some sort of formal recognition was given to this facet of adat process. In that year a regulation became law and provided that formal tribunals (*landraad*—Native Courts) were required to respect the decisions given by the 'judges of the small autonomous communities'.[1] The same policy was implemented also in the native states by separate regulation.[2]

The literature on village justice from the Netherlands East Indies is reasonably extensive,[3] and reference is almost invariably made to it in general accounts of adat systems.[4] Similarly in contemporary Indonesia the literature on the subject is not so much specifically written on the relationship of village justice to the formal court system, but as a description of an adat process in a specific locality.[5] However, the relationship is probably one of the most important for adat in contemporary Indonesia for two reasons. First, at the level of the District Court, it is open to the judge to refer any dispute for attempted settlement to a local process of mediation; only if this fails will the court give a binding decision in favour of one party or another. Village justice is or can be intimately linked with the lowest level of the formal process, and the grassroots nature of this link is of primary importance. Indeed at this level it is not uncommon to find an informal mixed process with the judges of the District Court adopting a mediation function in conjunction with village or kinship elders (see below, p. 142). The second reason is that, from published work, all those interested in the subject stress the importance of this process as a feature of Indonesian legal culture. The courts and the legislature are not the only sources of law in Indonesia. A student of Indonesian law ignores this fact at his peril; it even has its amusing side when one sees the unexpected effect that some 'unwritten' and therefore 'non-existent' adat rule has on foreign entrepreneurs who have been advised by lawyers in the cities solely on the basis of the written law! It is equally important that the judiciary be aware of the nature of village justice because it forms a part of the adats which, as judges, they are bound to know and administer in their own courts.

The Ontology of Village Justice

In both colonial and modern Indonesia village justice has a dual existence both in the ethnographer's notebook and in actual fact. The forms in which it is found are:

(i) As a formal part of the national legal system.

(ii) As a 'legal' phenomenon existing within the confines of a territorial or kinship group.

Each form merits separate attention although, as we shall see, they share many features in common. It may also be said here that, in the contemporary period at least, the studies of village justice have been largely the preserve of social scientists rather than of jurists.[6]

If we turn first to the formal relationship between the national judicial system and village justice we find the link to be established in the rules regulating the procedure of the District Courts. In this legislation, which is basically an Indonesian version of the colonial legislation, a duty is laid upon the judge(s) to attempt to effect a settlement of any dispute before a formal judicial determination is made.[7] This attempt may take place in court with the judge acting as mediator or, as not uncommonly happens, a case may be referred to some village tribunal or institution for an attempted settlement. The frequency of this practice varies in some sort of ratio, it seems, with the views of adat held in particular courts or by individual judges. Data on the scale of this process for all of Indonesia are lacking but it cannot be doubted that it occurs and is important. A fairly typical example of the reasoning adopted in such cases is demonstrated in the following passage:[8]

In Karo society there exists an institution of adat deliberation ('*lembaga musjawarah adat*'), called *runggun adat*, which has as its function to search for the termination of a dispute that has arisen between the two parties, and which in its complete composition consists of the three adat-groupings, i.e. of the *anakberu*, of the *senina* and of the *kalimbubu*.

That, beside doing justice in accordance with written and adat law (*'hukum/hukum adat'*), it is also the judge's task—in accordance with the Regulation on the Administration of Justice in the Outer Territories to further a settlement between parties (*'hakim ... berwadjib pula berusaha ... untuk memperdamaikan (merukunkan) kedua belah pihak jang berperkara'*), so that the request to attempt a settlement via *runggun adat*—as described by both parties—can be granted.

This passage comes from a dispute before the District Court at Kabandjahe[9] in Karo-land, North Sumatra, which occurred in 1969. The issue here was a claim by the members of a lineage that the defendant was attempting to acquire lineage land as though it was his own individual property. The sorts of evidence advanced by both sides related to issues of fact: whether the defendant was a member of the proper lineage and whether, as a matter of historical fact, the land was or was not *pusaka* (heirloom land). Essentially this appears to have been not merely a dispute over land allocation but a more fundamental quarrel over the definition of membership of a lineage and of the obligations occurring to lineage membership. This is an issue touching the essentials of Karo adat[10] and it was for this reason that the District Court referred the matter to adat deliberation (*lembaga musjawarah adat*). The underlying motive was a recognition that an official adjudication in coming down on one side or the other would inevitably split the lineage and disrupt the adat obligation system without replacing it with an adequate substitute. The solution was therefore to order a recourse to the Karo institution of *runggun adat*,[11] the formal process of discussing and settling an issue in dispute. Amongst the Karo-Batak the process is highly formalized, as it is also among the Sasak of Lombok and among the Balinese. It is not so formalized amongst the Javanese generally but the process does exist amongst all Indonesian peoples.

If we turn now to the second form of village justice, the indigenous tribunal which has no formal links with the national legal system, we find generally a similar situation. The tribunals operate by way of *musjawarah* and are composed of lineage or village notables. Very often disputes are put to some internal adjudication instead of to the formal courts with the clear motive of avoiding the formal process with its delays and difficulties.[12]

So far as the ontology of village justice is concerned, therefore, we may say that the term refers both to an internal process and to an aspect of the national legal system, that is, where it is related to District Court proceedings. In both instances the reference is to the 'case', which is both a means of description and a means of analysis. Village justice, in other words, finds its mode of existence in the case; this is the single most important issue in the study of Indonesian village justice.

The notion of case is a complex which may or may not include such elements as procedure, fact, argument, 'judicial reasoning', rule and status (i.e. how far and to what people the decision is regarded as 'binding' or applicable). The sorts of cases collected outside the administrative records of judicial decisions vary in quality and depth of reportage, and the variation may be described in terms of the elements set out above. But there are two things they do have in common, and these are that each decision is given in the context of a concrete situation, and the decision does not consist of the mechanical application of any formulae. This makes it probable that in any individual case there will be a wide range of judgment which is variable in application and in subsequent reference. Two further points should be made. First, it is said that any particular decision is the result of a relationship between material fact and the acceptance of materiality for a certain purpose. Second, it is said that a decision is the propounding of a principle (of law) which is the 'basis of' a finding in a particular case: this of course is also eventually fact-dependent. Both these propositions share two assumptions. First, that there is only one legal principle expressed in a case and which explains the material facts. Second, that a legal principle can be delineated from an examination of the particular case itself. Neither of these assumptions is justified because apart from any explicit or implicit assertion of materiality there will always be competing versions of the material facts.[13] Thus there may be many principles of law, each of which can explain the holding on the facts, but not one of which is (logically) necessary to explain it. Apart from the multiplicity of fact elements, each individual fact element is usually capable of being stated at various levels of generality, all of which may embrace 'the fact' in a particular case but each of which may give a different result in a different fact situation in a later case. In other words there is a unique concreteness, at least in the ethnographer's notebook, which later moves through a series of widening generalizations to form what is later thought to be a coherent statement of related legal principles.

Even here problems arise because the native usage of indigenous 'legal' terminology is not claimed by any investigator to be fixed and certain. Indeed, both van Vollenhoven and Ter Haar warned against any such assumptions. There are areas of shadow and conflict in all usage and the inbuilt range of interdeterminacy is increased by the choice of what is material, and by the generality of statement of material facts. Choice in any particular instance, then, involves choices arising from the nature of the terms used, from competing versions of a supposed principle on material fact, and from 'the fact' out of a group of (particular-general) material facts. Further, the method used in the case process, i.e. one judge or several, mediation or decision, will obviously also affect the situation.

In addition, and specifically in relation to ethnographies undertaken in ex-colonies, one must be careful to distinguish the situation where low-level judicial process is carried on in the expectation of judicial review. One of the results of this expectation will be the propounding of rules in full knowledge of later possible review and so there will arise a consciousness, if not of law-making then of law declaration, the statement of which, whether accepted or not, is going to remain relatively permanent.[14] Whilst this is not claimed to be a complete description of the case, in particular it does not include any reference to the technical function of the case in Western jurisprudence, it does seem to cover its major features as these are thought important in jurisprudence and ethnography.[15]

Within this complex of cases there is room for a variety of analyses, the nature of which can be said to depend primarily upon an initial choice of attitude to case material which must be made by the outside observer. The choice is this: does the material in the case and does the case phenomenon itself represent a logical structure of law or, on the contrary, does it merely state social fact, the assessment of which can only be accomplished in its own terms? It seems not impossible that, in the continuing debate on the ethnography of law, this is the most important issue. The question of language, in particular the language to be used in comparative study, has an immediate bearing upon this issue. The language of the law is typically composed of abstractions, and if this is to have a referent then it must be found in some usage which designates the 'thing meant'. Some would deny the possibility that concepts of Western jurisprudence can be used out of their own context on the grounds that any usage or referent is culturally confined.[16] However, this does not go to the heart of the problem, which is the propriety of an investigation into a foreign law which has to be (linguistically) described as such on the basis of proper or useful referents for the term 'law' itself. Even if some agreement as to this point has been reached, problems will remain, especially in the analysis of case, about whether any result reached embraces a meaning for the instant purpose of the case or whether this meaning is part of an extensive range of referents. A case is a 'complex purposive unit of discourse'[17] comprehending facts, normative propositions, elements of value and emotion and, occasionally, prior judicial discourse ('precedent'). It is difficult to believe that any one meaning of such a complex should present itself as the only correct meaning; some delimitation of meaning is of course possible, but this depends upon one's aim and upon the significance which one attaches to the referents of 'fact', 'law', and to how one conceives of the relationship between them. There are some scholars, for example, who conceive of law as a set of interrelated symbols and distinguish its behavioural referents;[18] the implications of this view for case analysis will obviously be vastly different from those who see law simply as a matrix of social relationships.

These comments illustrate two characteristics of the ethnography of law; first the ethnography of law is a branch of general jurisprudence in the sense that the issues which it raises are also issues in jurisprudence upon which debate continues. Second, the primary activity which is going on in legal ethnography is the search for criteria which are designed to identify legal systems. At present these criteria are being searched for within the context of the case, a proceeding which, in many respects, has parallels in current analytical jurisprudence.[19]

The Structure of Village Justice

Without exception, accounts of village justice are predicated upon the assumption that categories of law are dependent upon structures of society.[20] This means that the usual terminology of jurisprudence is used in a specific way. This is possibly the single most important issue in using data on village justice. The following topic heads do not purport to be exclusive but at least illustrate this issue.

(i) *Rights, obligations and sanctions: the definition of law*. These terms are of such general application and are possessed of so many nuances that their usage is constantly found in early ethnographies and in contemporary work. A common form of discussion proceeds on the question of the 'binding force' of rights and obligations and the interpretation of this binding force in terms of sanction.[21] Fairly typical examples are provided in descriptions containing legal elements which are based upon ethnographic data from a variety of sources; one thinks for example of the conclusions reached by Radcliffe-Brown,[22] that 'law' consists of social control through the systematic application of the force in a politically organized society; the force which constitutes this sanction is legal when imposed by some constituted authority.[23] Later authors have drawn from this the proposition that social control may be analysed into a set of binding rights and obligations and, under the influence of Malinowski, have stressed the positive aspects and variety of forms of sanctions. This involves a study of those institutions which fulfil the function of maintaining order and stability, that is, which are the binding force.

A not untypical analysis based upon data from one particular society, the Toba Batak,[24] illustrates the working out of these principles. In this study, a description of kinship, ritual and economic obligations is given and the point made that one of the main criteria of law is that it constitutes a system of binding rights and obligations. The latter are called 'law' and not 'custom' because a breach of any such obligation would result in social repercussions such as moral condemnation, withdrawal of co-operation, exclusion from activities, demand for compensation, or the infliction of punishment. However, there are equally important positive sanctions which contribute to the maintenance of the binding obligations; the point is made that an undue emphasis upon penal sanctions tends to distort the reality as presented in ethnographic data. On the point that non-penal definition of sanction tends to confuse moral, ritual and legal rules,[25] the author proposes that when the data are looked at in terms of rights and obligations, the use of categories such as legal, moral and so on, is not only unnecessary but a distortion of reality. The better approach is to regard as cultural sanctions all those factors which contribute to the maintenance of rights and obligations; all sanctions are legal in so far as they contribute to this maintenance,[26] and hence a 'moral' sanction fulfilling this function would be a legal sanction. This view of sanction, then, involves considerations of morality, religion, tradition, the conditioning of temperament and inculcation of sentiments, and the operation of rules in daily life, including those which control the settlement of disputes and the payment of compensation. A large part of Vergouwen's account is concerned with working out these views under a variety of topic headings which draw attention to the legal sanctions of kinship obligations, sentiment as a legal sanction, the 'moral' sanction of law, and the functions of institutions as legal sanctions. Sections are also devoted to penal rules and to the legal obligations in economic matters.

There are two features in this summary which perhaps we can pursue a little further. The first is the question of the distinction between law and custom, which is well-known as a hardy annual in the ethnography of law. A recent example speaks of the 'rule of law versus the order of custom'.[27] The following passage illustrates what one author feels to be the correct usage of the terms.[28]

> Law ... is symptomatic of the emergence of the state; the legal sanction is not simply the cutting edge of institutions at all times and in all places.... Custom—spontaneous, traditional, personal, commonly known, corporate, relatively unchanging—is the modality of primitive society; law is the instrument of civilization, of political society sanctioned by organized force, presumably above society at large, and buttressing a new set of social interests. Law and custom both involve the regulation of behaviour but their characters are entirely distinct; no evolutionary balance has been struck between developing law and custom, whether traditional or emergent.

This statement clearly depends upon an evolutionary progression: the increasing amount of data which is now becoming available on the relationship between written codes and living practice in ancient society make such evolutionary relationships difficult to support.[29] It is also difficult to see how a dichotomy between 'civilized' and 'primitive' based upon the particular form which sanction is said to take can be supported.[30] A discussion in these terms can lead to nothing but confusion in adat study. It does not fit the facts of contemporary adat cultures and it is a wild oversimplification of the historical relationship between the adats and state organization at all periods of Indonesia's history.

The second feature to which attention should be drawn here is the continuing question of the use of legal terminology. As was intimated earlier in this chapter, and as just illustrated, the use of legal terminology is often loose and incidental. That is to say, description and analysis does not proceed upon fixed referents for selected terminology, but in the description of foreign society legal terms are used in a general sense. The point is that such usages rest upon various assumptions, often unstated, as to certain characteristic features of society. For example, a common assumption is that strict liability, 'private law' and collective responsibility are characteristic features of primitive society. In contrast, the parallel assumption is often made that moral fault and individual legal responsibility is a characteristic of modern society. As a recent commentator[31] has convincingly shown, such assumptions on the facts of life in both sorts of culture are unwarranted:[32]

> ... Surely collectivity and individuality in legal matters are aspects of all systems, not alternative systems. To speak of the temporal precedence in legal development, of civil or criminal law, of public or private law, or of collectivity or individuality, does not make sociological sense.

The examples cited here are descriptions of the ways in which concepts possessing a certain (Western) cultural value are given a content on the basis of data abstracted from a foreign culture in the course of a sociological investigation. There are, however, also examples of attempts to construct specific systems based wholly in sociology as concepts which adequately describe the facts of some particular (legal) culture. This may be illustrated by looking at one examination of the concept of 'conflict'. In a study of dispute settlement amongst the Minangkabau[33] this concept is used as an independent criterion, thus:[34]

> Conflict is a patterned expression of the inherent polarities and incongruities of a culture and is based on opposing interests which arise from the very structure of the society itself. It is an expression of functional and historical processes which may be cyclical or repetitive.... As I see it, conflict is a social activity which should be regarded with considerable ambivalence—theoretically as well as by the people involved. The more usual way of making this point would be to say that there is some question as to whether conflict is dysfunctional or eufunctional, that is, whether it is good or bad for the society concerned. There can be little social or cultural change without at least minimal conflict. Therefore if we are to assume, as I would, that it is desirable for societies to adapt continuously, that is to change in response to the ecological-economic situations and international social and political contexts in which they find themselves, it must be assumed that some conflict will be necessary. Yet conflict is seldom pleasant even at low intensities, as in teasing and response, or competition, and often results in extreme emotional and physical pain. Thus conflict poses a problem for every society; it must be presumed necessary to the society's continued existence and prosperity; yet it is often disruptive, painful and ineffective. The real question for the people of a society—for their life or death, whether they will spend the years of their lives in peace or war, and with regard to the relative degree of human pain —is how ingenious they can be in devising workable compromises for dealing with conflicts *while* they are changing, for finding ways to keep conflict at an acceptable level, whatever that might be, or simply for devising modes of enacting conflict which maintain or enhance the society's potential for change but place some bounds on the inherent destructiveness of conflict.

The sociological standpoint could not be more clearly expressed in the passage just cited, and whatever its merits might be in the field of sociology, its formulation in the terms of that discipline effectively takes its assessment out of the hands of the jurist. At the same time the data provided are important in the study of the Minangkabau adat, and the issue for the jurist therefore becomes to what extent is he prepared to accept this view of conflict in its relation to the totality of the particular adat culture? The writer's view, *as a jurist interested in adat*, is that this sort of formulation must be accepted on its own terms as at least descriptively valid, but this is a view by no means shared by many lawyers interested (and practising!) in the Indonesian legal system.

(ii) *The 'jural' community.* The adjective 'jural' is one which is commonly used to indicate the social control functions in a group described in terms of legal ethnography. The characteristics of such communities are given in terms of sociological theory on social structures.[35] In more specific studies of social control the universe is defined in accord with the facts of a particular culture as expressed in sociological terms.[36] This was always the practice in the classic studies of adat produced in the era of Dutch scholarship,[37] but in that case sociological categories were subsumed into a legal terminology which ordered and classified such categories in its own terms. In the present instance, the sociological category is given a 'jural' meaning in terms of a social science construction of law. Law, in other words, is sociologically dependent; an early example of such dependence is shown clearly in the following passage:[38]

We see that descent is fundamentally a jural concept as Radcliffe-Brown argued...;[39] we see its significance, as the connecting link between the external, that is political and legal aspect of what we have called unilineal descent groups, and the internal or domestic aspect. It is in the latter context that kinship carries maximum weight, first, as the source of title to membership of the groups or to specific jural status, with all that this means in rights over and toward persons and property, and second as the basis of the social relations among the persons who are identified with one another in the corporate group. In theory membership of a corporate legal or political group need not stem from kinship, as Weber has made clear. In primitive society, however, if it is not based on kinship it seems generally to presume some formal procedure of incorporation.... It will be remembered that Radcliffe-Brown[40] related succession rules to the need for unequivocal discrimination of rights *in rem* and *in personam*. Perhaps it is most closely connected with the fact that rights over the reproductive powers or women are easily regulated by a descent group system. But I believe that something deeper than this is involved, for in a homogeneous society there is nothing which could so precisely and incontrovertibly fix one's place in society as one's parentage.

It is the sociological concepts, upon which the 'jural' is dependent, which are at issue here, not the nature of law as such. This has continued to be a not unusual viewpoint,[41] and may possibly stem from a conception of law as a set of rules obeyed or disobeyed with statistically measurable frequency; patrilineal descent, for example, may be called, as such, a 'jural rule'.[42]

The implication of such a view of law is that what the investigator should be trying to specify is the source or sources of some 'right'. This is clearly an influence derived from the particular nature of Western municipal systems in which this is the fundamental question in legal practice. The problem, however, is that in respect of non-industrial societies it is not always possible to do this in the precise terms one is accustomed to expect. Anthropologists commonly put forward a variety of mechanisms which the facts of a particular ethnography show as being relevant to the question of source, and in contemporary studies it is now becoming realised, on the basis of these data, that the specification of a single source is subject to serious qualification. Thus, as one commentator puts it, descent,[43]

... although relevant to many rights and duties, is in the instances examined neither exclusively nor absolutely determinative of them. Descent is seen, not as a principle that has clearly definable, invariable legal consequences, but rather as one of the more significant of a number of considerations pertinent to rights and obligations. Descent sometimes figures more prominently in the conceptualization of rights and obligations than in their operation. These facts—that rights and duties arise from the concatenation of a number of circumstances; that descent is not in and of itself an absolute definer of obligation, but rather a contributory definer of it—bear on the whole question of rules of law and what they are made of.

The important point which this statement and its supporting data illustrate is that rules are multiple and highly conditional in operation. They provide means for manipulating the social universe and also provide descriptions of that universe. This is not the view of rules adopted in, say, the Anglo-American court process where the whole emphasis is upon limiting the conditions which might affect the application of rules. The limitation is an essential part of the definition of a rule; it is easy to see how an assumption as to the nature of rule taken from such a system can distort the description of village justice in Indonesian cultures.

The two topics just discussed in this section illustrate various aspects of the law's dependence upon social structures as this is conceived in the social sciences. The importance of the sociological viewpoint lies in the particular view of law to which it gives rise. A social system is seen as a structure of persisting relationships between persons and groups which are objectively described in terms of obligations concerning things and individuals. The anthropological data adduced in a description of a social system is organized around and in terms of various usages of the idea(s) of obligation or of related terms such as 'rights', 'duties' and so on. The elements of these ideas are partially determined by whatever knowledge of his own legal system the social scientist has and partially by formulations made by himself and others in ethnographic studies and in the theoretical analyses which these studies have occasioned. This characteristic, if no other, is a persisting feature of legal ethnography and possibly explains the constant difficulties in the application of concepts from Western jurisprudence to ethnography. The reasoning behind this explanation is quite simple: it is that such concepts do not necessarily require a behavioural component in their definition. An aspect of this was mentioned earlier when it was said that the limitation of the conditions affecting the application of rules was part of the defining process itself. Indeed, some jurists have seen the sociological dependence upon observation and behaviour as a disqualification for jurisprudential analysis because this reliance predicates that externally observed behaviour constitutes a legal regularity. The objection is that regularity cannot be so ascertained but can only be sought in the internal structure of legal concepts themselves.[44] The behavioural practices by which the people in non-industrial societies live do not form a legal system in any sense but simply to constitute a set of standards; their only common feature being that they are accepted by most of the people for most of the time.[45]

Summary

The ontological and descriptive elements just described are concepts which 'categorize'[46] that which is law properly so called and which may be demonstrated by means of processes of dispute settlement. Such processes are accepted, at least as evidence of adat rules, at all levels of the formal judicial hierarchy.[47] It is difficult to decide, however, whether they are taken as demonstrating rules already known to exist, or as themselves constituting such rules. From the viewpoint of the individual judge it is probably the former, because in cases of doubt the judiciary tends to rely upon earlier works on *adatrecht*. The process of village justice is read in the light of such work and its validity judged accordingly. This need not necessarily be the approach of the student of adat; on the contrary one may regard the case as constituting the basic principles of legal structure. It demonstrates the relationship between an individual and a culture for which no scheme of norms or ideal rules can substitute. The cases offer a cumulative demonstration that the law *is* process; in other words, its ontology is, by the nature of that fact, also its structure. The case may be taken as a source of law from which one may extract principles which can only be understood insofar as they related to principles of social structure.[48]

These different approaches are not really alternatives. Adat is both local and a part of the national legal system. At the village level adat is particular and concrete and can only be understood in the principles of social structure, combined with an understanding of the processes of dispute settlement within the village. Adat is socially dependent, but at the national level the concepts of adat are beginning to be nationally defined by the judiciary and the legislature. The tensions to which this gives rise are a continuing feature of Indonesian legal life and at the same time the inspiration for the future development of adat.

    1. Ordonnantie op de Dorprechtspraak. Staatsblad, 1935, No. 102.
    2. Zelfbestuursregelen. Staatsblad, 1938, No. 529 Arts. 12 & 13.
    3. cf. Mieremet (1919), van Vollenhoven, 1931: 498 ff. See also the Adatrechtbundels.
    4. cf. Vergouwen, 1964: 386–423 especially at 410–12 on the amicable settlement of dispute (*pardamean*) and 417–18 on the administration of justice by the chiefs.
    5. cf. Cooley (1962), Koesnoe, 1971: 31–4, Koesnoe (1972a), Adhi (1972), Soepomo (1967), Soeripto (1973a).
    6. See, for example, Hofsteede (1971).
    7. See, for example, Art. 154 of the Regulation on the Administration of Justice in the Outer Territories amended by Emergency Law No. 1 of 13 January 1951, amended Lembaran Negara 36/1955 and converted into statute by Law No. 1 of 1961, Lembaran Negara 3/1961.
    8. From van den Steenhoven, 1970: 13.
    9. ibid. Case 43/S/1969.
    10. cf. Singarimbun, 1965: VI.
    11. Known also among the Toba-Batak as *harungguan*. Vergouwen, 1964: 413 translates this as 'court', which is slightly misleading but which does emphasize that the proceedings are formal and not an informal chat or 'get together'. This procedure has parallels in other parts of Indonesia, e.g. the Sasak *'begundem'*. cf.

van den Steenhoven, 1973: 711-13. See also Mieremet (1919) and van Vollenhoven, 1931: 498 ff.
12. cf. Jaspan (1971) on the Redjang village tribunal. Also Koesnoe (1969a).
13. See, for example, the formal analyses of native categories in the following sources: Metzger & Williams (1966); Black & Metzger (1965).
14. See, for example, R.E.S. Tanner (1966).
15. See the following sources: Epstein (1967), Groves (1937), Burridge (1957) and the contributions and sources in Nader (1965) (1969).
16. cf. J. C. Smith (1968). See also Nader, 1969: 337 ff.
17. Stone, 1964: 36.
18. cf. Barkun (1968).
19. See, for example, Hart (1961), Raz (1971).
20. This was largely though not entirely true in the Netherlands East Indies. It is true in contemporary Indonesia to the extent that much of the national law is either not known to or is ineffective in respect of the bulk of the rural population.
21. This remains a not uncommon approach in jurisprudence; for arguments as to the invalidity of any such analysis the works of the Scandinavian Realist school may be consulted.
22. cf. Radcliffe-Brown, 1952: 205-11, originally published in 1933.
23. For a comparative description including these elements see also Redfield (1964), originally published in 1941. See also the discussions in Chapter 3.
24. cf. Vergouwen (1964).
25. A criticism made of Malinowski as well as of Vergouwen.
26. Vergouwen, 1964: 349 ff. on offences. See also Cooley (1962) on Ambonese adat.
27. cf. S. Diamond (1971).
28. ibid. 47.
29. Moertono (1963).
30. See MacCormack (1973) on the particular topics of revenge and compensation.
31. cf. Moore (1972).
32. ibid. 100-1.
33. Nancy Tanner (1969).
34. ibid. 22, 23.
35. cf. Accounts of the Minangkabau—de Josselin de Jong (1951), Nancy Tanner (1969), Taufik Abdullah (1966). On other Indonesian peoples see Peacock (1973) for references.
36. cf. van den Steenhoven (1970), Jaspan (1971).
37. cf. Ter Haar (1948) for references.
38. Fortes, 1953: 30.
39. Radcliffe-Brown (1935).
40. ibid.
41. See the examples cited by Moore, 1969: 378-82 on the category 'descent'.
42. Moore, 1969: 378. For Indonesian examples see the sources cited in note 5 above.
43. Moore, 1969: 375.
44. cf. Ross, 1968: 88-9.
45. cf. Hart, 1961: 90.
46. cf. Levi, 1948: 4-5.
47. See Chapter 7.
48. See Chapter 2.

BIBLIOGRAPHY

ABENDANON, J. H. (1891) *Publiek-en Privaatrechtlijke verhoudingen tusschen Nederland en de Nederlandsche Kolonien.* Leiden.
—— (1908–1930) *De Nederlandsch-Indische Rechtspraak en Rechtsliteratuur* (4 vols.) Leiden, Den Haag.
ADHI, IDA BAGUS NGURAH (1972) 'Pengangkatan Anak Menurut Hukum Adat Bali.' *Hukum Nasional* 16: 63–76.
ADIWINATA, S. (1970) *Perkembangan Hukum Perdata/Adat Sedjak Tahun 1960.* Bandung.
—— (1972) 'Some Thoughts concerning the Renewal of the Indonesian Patrimonial Law Legislation.' *Hukum Nasional* 16: 49–62.
AHMAD IBRAHIM (1971) 'Administration of Muslim Law in Southeast Asia.' *Malaya Law Review* 13: 124–177.
ALISJAHBANA, S. TAKDIR (1968) 'Customary Law and Modernization in Indonesia' in Buxbaum (ed.) *Family Law and Customary Law in Asia*: 3–16. The Hague.
ALLEN, C. K. (1931) *Legal Duties and Other Essays.* Oxford.
ALLEN, D. E. (ed.) (1969) *Asian Contract Law.* Melbourne.
ANDERSON, A. R. (1956) *The Formal Analysis of Normative Systems.* Technical Report No. 2. Office of Naval Research, Group Psychology Branch, United States Navy.
—— and MOORE, O. K. (1957) 'The Formal Analysis of Normative Concepts'. *American Sociological Review* 22: 9–17.
ANDERSON, BENEDICT R. O'G. (1972) 'The Idea of Power in Javanese Culture' in Holt *et al.* (eds.) *Culture and Politics in Indonesia*: 1–70. Ithaca.
ARMINJON, PIERRE (1925) *Précis de Droit International Privé.* Paris.
BADARUZZAMAN, NJ MARIAM DARUS (1962) *Keputusan-Keputusan tentang Perkara-Perdata.* Medan.
BARKUN, MICHAEL (1968) *Law without Sanctions.* New Haven.
BARTHOLOMEW, G. W. (1952) 'Private Inter-Personal Law.' *International and Comparative Law Quarterly* 1: 325–344.
BASTIN, J. (1960) 'The Working of the early land rent system.' *Bijdragen tot de Taal-, Land- en Volkenkunde* 116: 301–312.

BENDA, HARRY J. (1958) *The Crescent and the Rising Sun.* The Hague.
―――― (1964) 'Political Elites in Colonial South East Asia: an historical analysis.' *Comparative Studies in Society and History* 7: 233–251.
―――― (1965–1966) 'The Pattern of Administrative Reforms in the Closing Years of Dutch Rule in Indonesia.' *Journal of Asian Studies* 25: 589–606.
BISSCHOP, W. R. (1934) 'Adat Law in Indonesia.' *Journal of Comparative Legislation and International Law* (3rd ser.) 16: 304–307.
BLACK, MARY & METZGER, DUANE (1965) 'Ethnographic Description and the Study of Law in Nader (ed.) *The Ethnography of Law*: 141–165. *American Anthropologist* 67 (Special Publication).
BOERENBEKER, E. A. (1935) *Het adatrecht der Inlanders in de Jurisprudentie, 1923–1933.* Bandung.
BOLAND, B. J. (1971) *The Struggle of Islam in Modern Indonesia.* The Hague.
BURRIDGE, K. O. L. (1957) 'Disputing in Tangu.' *American Anthropologist* 59: 763–780.
CARPENTIER ALTING, J. H. (1926) *Grondslagen der Rechtsbedeeling in Nederlandsche-Indië* (2nd ed.) 's Gravenhage.
CASSUTTO, I. (1936) *Handleiding tot de Studie van het Adatrecht van Nederlandsch-Indië.* Haarlem.
CHAIRUL ANWAR (1967) *Hukum Adat di Indonesia-menindjau alam Minangkabau.* Djakarta.
COOLEY, FRANK L. (1962) *Ambonese Adat: A General Description.* New Haven, Conn: Yale University, Southeast Asian Studies, Cultural Report Series No. 10.
DAMIAN, EDDY & HORNICK, ROBERT N. (1972) 'Indonesia's Formal Legal System: An Introduction.' *American Journal of Comparative Law* 20: (2) 492–530.
DANUREDJO, L. S. (1968) 'Declining Trends of Legal and Administrative Performance in Indonesia.' *International Review of Administrative Sciences* 34: 164–172.
DARMAWI, H. (1972) 'Land Transactions under Indonesian *Adat* Law.' *Lawasia* 3: 283–316.
DE LA PORTE, ANDRÉ (1908) 'Beschouwingen over Quasi-Internationaal Privaatrecht.' *Indisch Tijdschrift van het Recht* 91: 1–33.
―――― (1933) *Recht en Rechtsbedeeling in Nederlandsch-Indië* (2nd ed.) 's Gravenhage.
'DEPERNAS' *Rantjangan Dasar U.U. Pembangunan Nasional-Berentjana,* Vol. III, Bk. I 1960. Bandung.

DIAMOND, S. (1971) 'The Rule of Law versus the Order of Custom.' *Social Research* 38: 42–72.
DIMAAMPAO, P. D. (1966) 'Agama Courts of the Muslim Philippines.' *Lyceum Law Review*: 22–30.
DJOJODIGOENO, M. M. (n.d.) *Harapan Hukum Adat Indonesia*. Jogjakarta.
—— (1950) *Menjandra Hukum Adat*. Jogjakarta.
—— (1952) *Adat Law in Indonesia*. Djakarta.
—— (1953) 'Adat Law in Indonesia.' *Asian Review* 49: 38–44.
—— (1958) *Asas-Asas Hukum Adat*. Jogjakarta.
—— (1961) *Reorientasi Hukum dan Hukum Adat*. Jogjakarta.
—— (1971) *Wat is Recht?* Djakarta.
—— (1972) 'Naar aanleiding van Ter Haar's dies-rede van 1937.' *Bijdragen tot de Taal-, Land- en volkenkunde* 128: 235–256.
—— & TIRTAWINATA, Raden (1940) *Het Adatprivaatrecht van Middel-Java*. Batavia.
ENTHOVEN, K. L. J. (1912) *Het Adatrecht der Inlanders in de Jurisprudentie, 1849–1912*. Leiden.
EPSTEIN, A. L. (1967) 'The Case Method in the Field of Law' in Epstein (ed.) *The Craft of Social Anthropology*: 205–230. London.
FARID, ANDI ZAINAL ABIDIN (1969) 'Sekapur Sirih Asas-Asas Hukum Adat Pidana Sul-Sel Sebagai Bahan Pembentukan K.U.H.P. Nasional.' *Hukum Nasional* 6: 2–65.
FEDERSPIEL, HOWARD M. (1973) 'The Military and Islam in Sukarno's Indonesia.' *Pacific Affairs* 46: (3) 407–420.
FEITH, H. (1962) *The Decline of Constitutional Democracy in Indonesia*. Ithaca.
FORTES, M. (1953) 'The Structure of Unilineal Descent Groups.' *American Anthropologist* 55: 17–41.
FURNIVALL, J. S. (1944) *Netherlands India: a study of Plural Economy*. Cambridge.
GAUTAMA, SUDARGO (GOUWGIOKSIONG) (1970) 'Legal Developments in Independent Indonesia (1940–1970).' *Lawasia* 1: (3) 157–170.
—— (1971) *Hukum Antargolongan*. Djakarta.
—— (1972) 'The Role of Law in the Development Process and the Role of the Lawyer in Indonesia.' *Malaya Law Review* 14: (2) 259–275.
—— (1973) *Himpunan Keputusan-Keputusan Hukum Antar Golongan*. Bandung.
—— and HARSONO, BUDI (1972) *Agrarian Law: Survey of Indonesian Economic Law*. Bandung.

────── and HORNICK, ROBERT N. (1972) *An Introduction to Indonesian Law: Unity in Diversity.* Jakarta.
────── et al. (1973) *Credit and Security in Indonesia.* St. Lucia, Queensland, Australia.
GEERTZ, CLIFFORD (1960) *The Religion of Java.* Glencoe, Ill.
────── (1963) 'The Rotating Credit Association.' *Economic Development and Cultural Change* 10: 241–263.
────── (1968) *Islam Observed: Religious Development in Morocco & Indonesia.* New Haven.
GOODENOUGH, WARD H. (1965) 'Rethinking Status and Role' in *The Relevance of Models for Social Anthropology*: 1–24. A.S.A. Monographs 1, London.
GOUWGIOKSIONG (1959) *Himpunan Keputusan Keputusan Hukum Antargolongan.* Djakarta.
────── (1960) *Hukum Antargolongan* (2nd ed.) Djakarta.
────── (1962) 'Law Reform in Indonesia.' *Rabels Zeitschrift* 26: 535–553.
────── (1964) 'Marriage Law of Indonesia with special reference to mixed marriages.' *Rabels Zeitschrift* 28: 711–731.
────── (1965) 'Interpersonal law in Indonesia.' *Rabels Zeitschrift* 29: 545–573.
GRAY, JOHN CHIPMAN (1927) *The Nature and Sources of Law* (2nd ed.) New York.
GROVES, WILLIAM C. (1937) 'Settlement of Disputes in Tabar.' *Oceania* 7: 501–519.
GUYT, H. (1939) 'Enkele Opmerkingen Omtrent de Beteekenis van den Term Adatrecht in de Wetgeving.' *Indisch Tijdschrift van het Recht* (supplemental volume) 151: 5–62.
HAKIM, S. A. (1967) *Hukum Adat.* Djakarta.
HAN BING SIONG (1961) *An Outline of the Recent History of Indonesian Criminal Law.* The Hague.
HARSONO, BUDI (1970) *Undang-Undang Pokok Agraria* (3rd ed.) Djakarta.
HART, H. L. A. (1961) *The Concept of Law.* Oxford.
HAZAIRIN (1950) *Hukum Baru di Indonesia.* Djakarta.
────── (1961) *Hukum Kewarisan Bilateral Menurut Al-Qur'an.* Djakarta.
────── (1962) *Hukum Kekeluargaan Nasional.* Djakarta.
HEINE-GELDERN, R. (1942–43) 'Conceptions of State and Kingship in Southeast Asia.' *Far Eastern Quarterly* 2: 15–30.
HINLOOPEN LABBERTON, D. VAN (1933) *Dictionnaire de Termes de Droit Coutumier Indonésien.* Amsterdam.

HOADLEY, MASON C. (1971) 'Continuity and Change in Javanese Legal Tradition: The Evidence of the Jayapattra.' *Indonesia* 11: 95-109.
HOEBEL, E. A. (1954) *The Law of Primitive Man*. Cambridge, Mass.
HOFSTEEDE, W. M. F. (1971) *Decision Making Processes in Four West Javanese Villages*. Nijmegen.
HOLLEMAN, F. D. (1938) 'Het Adatprivaat Recht van Nederlandsch-Indië' in Wetenschap Praktijk en Onderwijs. *Indisch Tijdschrift van het Recht* 147: 428-440.
HOOKER, M. B. (1968) 'Private International Law and Personal Laws.' *Malaya Law Review* 10: 55-67.
―――― (1972) *Adat Laws in Modern Malaya*. Kuala Lumpur.
―――― (1976) *The Personal Laws of Malaysia: An Introduction*. Kuala Lumpur.
HUSSEIN ALATAS, SYED (1970) 'Religion and Modernization in Southeast Asia.' *Arch. Europ. Sociol.* 11: 265-296.
JAARSMA, S. (1936) *Grond voor den Nederlander*. Soerabaja.
JASPAN, M. A. (1964-65) 'In Quest of New Law: The Perplexity of Legal Syncretism in Indonesia.' *Comparative Studies in Society and History* 7: 252-266.
―――― (1971) *The Redjang Village Tribunal*. Nijmegen.
JAY, R. R. (1956) 'Local Government in Rural Central Java.' *Far Eastern Quarterly* 15: 215-227.
―――― (1963) *Religion and Politics in Rural Central Java*. New Haven.
JOSSELIN DE JONG, J. P. B. DE (1948) 'Customary Law: A Confusing Fiction.' *Koninklijke Vereeniging Indisch Instituut Mededeling* No. LXXX *Afd. Volkenkunde* No. 29, Amsterdam.
JOSSELIN DE JONG, P. E. DE (1951) *Minangkabau & Negri Sembilan*. The Hague.
KAHIN, G. M. (1952) *Nationalism and Revolution in Indonesia*. Ithaca.
KARTOHADIPRODJO, SOEDIMAN (1969) Hukum Nasional. *Hukum Nasional* 3: 45-54.
―――― (1971) *Hukum Nasional*. Djakarta.
KATHIRITHAMBY-WELLS, J. (1973) 'A Survey of the Effects of British Influence on Indigenous Authority in Southwest Sumatra (1685-1824).' *Bijdragen tot de Taal-, Land- en Volkenkunde* 129: 239-268.
KATZ, JUNE S. & KATZ, RONALD S. (1975) 'The New Indonesian Marriage Law.' *American Journal of Comparative Law* 23: 653-81.

KOENTJARANINGRAT (1961) *Some Social-anthropological Observation on Gotong-Rojong Practices in Two Villages of Central Java.* Ithaca.
—— (ed.) (1967) *Villages in Indonesia.* Ithaca.
KOESNOE, MOH. (n.d.) *Perkembangan dari Pemikiran dan Tjara2 Penjelesaian Masalah2 Hukum Antargolongan.* Surabaja.
—— (1969) *Hukum Adat dan Pembangunan.* Denpasar, Bali.
—— (1969a) 'Menetapkan Hukum dari Adat.' *Hukum Nasional* 3: 3–11.
—— (1969b) *Musjawarah.* Nijmegen.
—— (1970) 'Hukum Adat dan Pembangunan Hukum Nasional.' *Hukum dan Keadilan* 3: (1) 32–44.
—— (1970a) *Mahkamah Agung dan Hukum Adat dalam Tahun 1969.* Surabaja.
—— (1971) *Introduction into Indonesian Adat Law.* Nijmegen.
—— (1971a) 'Hukum Adat didalam pasal 5 U.U. Pokok Agraria dari tahun 1960.' *Madjalah Perguruan Tinggi* 3: (iv) 35–43.
—— (1972) 'Persoalan Keluarga Berencana dan Adat di Djawa Timur.' Surabaja.
—— (1972a) 'Saat Jadinya Suatu Perkawinan Menurut Adat "Ngerorod" di Bali.' *Hukum Nasional* 17: 51–68.
KOLLEWIJN, R. D. (1929) 'Interracial Private Law' in B. Schreike (ed.) *The Effect of Western Influence on Native Civilizations in the Malay Archipelago.* Batavia.
—— (1934) 'Het op Arbeidsovereenkomsten toe te Passenrecht.' *Indisch Tijdschrift van het Recht* 139: 789–806.
—— (1938) *Interregional en Internationaal Privaatrecht.* Bandung.
—— (1939) *Intergentiel Recht in Nederlands Indie.* Bandung.
—— (1951) 'Conflicts of Western & non-Western Law.' *International Law Quarterly* 4: 307–326.
KORN, V. E. (1940) *De Wetgeving der Indonesische Volksgemeenschappen.* The Hague.
—— (1960) 'The Village Republic of Tenganan Pegeringsingan' in W. F. Wertheim *et al.* (eds.) *Bali: Studies in Life, Thought and Ritual*: 301–368. The Hague.
KRISHNAMURTHY, S. (1960–61) 'Constitution making in Indonesia.' *Indian Yearbook of International Affairs* 9–10: 118–126.
KUSUMADI, PUDJOSEWOJO (1961) *Pedoman Peladjaran Tata Hukum Indonesia.* Djakarta.
LABBERTON, D. VAN H. (1933) *Dictionnaire de Termes de Droit Coutumier Indonésien.* Amsterdam.
LEGGE, J. D. (1957) 'Central Supervision & Local Government in Indonesia.' *Australian Journal of Politics & History* 3: 79–95.

——— (1964) *Indonesia*. New York.
LEV, DANIEL S. (1962) 'Adat Inheritance Law In Indonesia.' *American Journal of Comparative Law* 11: 205–224.
——— (1964–65) 'The Politics of Judicial Development in Indonesia.' *Comparative Studies in Society & History* 7: 173–199, 202.
——— (1965) 'The Lady and the Banyan Tree: Civil-Law Change in Indonesia.' *American Journal of Comparative Law* 14: 282–307.
——— (1972) *Islamic Courts in Indonesia*. California.
——— (1972a) 'Judicial Institutions and Legal Culture in Indonesia' in Holt et al. (eds.) *Culture and Politics in Indonesia*: 246–318. Ithaca.
LEVI, EDWARD H. (1948) *An Introduction to Legal Reasoning*. Chicago.
LEVY, R. (1957) *The Social Structure of Islam*. Cambridge.
LEYSER, J. (1954) 'Legal Developments in Indonesia.' *American Journal of Comparative Law* 3: 399–411.
LIAW, YOCK FANG (1967) 'Undang2 Luhak Tiga Laras.' *Nanyang University Journal* 1: 107–118.
LOCHER, G. W. (1956) 'Myth in a Changing World.' *Bijdragen tot de Taal-, Land en Volkenkunde* 112: 169–192.
LOGEMANN, J. H. A. (1938) 'Om de taak van de Rechter.' *Indisch Tijdschrift van het Recht* 148: 27–36.
——— (1947) *Staatsrecht van Nederlandsch-Indië*. The Hague.
——— (1954) *Het Staatsrecht van Indonesië*. The Hague.
MACCORMACK, GEOFFREY (1973) 'Revenge and Compensation in Early Law.' *American Journal of Comparative Law* 21: 69–85.
MAHARUN BATUAH, A. M. Datuk & D. H. BAGINDO TANAMEH (n.d.) *Hukum Adat dan Adat Minangkabau*. Padang.
MAINE, Sir HENRY (1861) *Ancient Law*. London.
MARETIN, IU V. (1966) 'Adat, Islam and the political struggle among the Minangkabau of Western Sumatra in the first half of the twentieth century.' *Soviet Anthropology & Archaeology* 4: 29–45.
McALEAVY, H. (1958) 'Dien in China and Vietnam.' *Journal of Asian Studies* 17: 403–415.
MEHREN, A. T. VON (1964) 'Comment on "The Politics of Judicial Development in Indonesia"'. *Comparative Studies in Society and History* 7: 200–201.
METZGER, D. G. & WILLIAMS, G. E. (1966) 'Some Procedures & Results in the Study of Native Categories.' *American Anthropologist* 68: 389–407.
MIEREMET, A. (1919) *De Hedendaagsche inheemsche rechtspraak in Nederlandsche — Indie en haar regeling*. Leiden.

MOCHTAR NAIM (ed.) (1968) *Menggali Hukum Tanah dan Hukum Waris Minangkabau.* Padang.
MOERTONO, SOEMARSAID (1963) *State and Statecraft in Old Java: a study of the later Mataram Period.* Cornell University Modern Indonesia Project.
MOORE, SALLY F. (1969) 'Descent and Legal Position' in Nader (ed.) *Law in Culture and Society*: 374–400. Chicago.
―――― (1972) 'Legal Liability and Evolutionary Interpretation: Some aspects of Strict Liability, Self-help and Collective Responsibility' in Gluckman (ed.) *The Allocation of Responsibility*: 51–107. Manchester.
MUHAMMAD HASBI ASH-SHIDDIEQY 1961/1381 *Sjari'at Islam Mendjawah Tantangan Zaman.* Jogjakarta.
NADEL, S. F. (1951) *The Foundations of Social Anthropology.* London.
NADER, LAURA (ed.) (1965) *The Ethnography of Law. American Anthropologist* 67. Special Publication.
―――― (ed.) (1969) *Law in Culture and Society.* Chicago.
NAGARI BASA, B. *Datuk* (1966) *Tambo dan Silsilah Adat Minangkabau.* Pajakumbuh.
NASRUN (NASROEN), M. (1957) *Dasar Falsafah Adat Minangkabau.* Djakarta.
NATSIR, M. (1951) *Islam sebagai Ideologie* (2nd ed.) Djakarta.
NAWAWI (1914) *Minhaj-et-Talibin* (trans. E. C. Howard). London.
NEDERBURGH, I. A. (1882) *Het Staatsdomein op Java.* Leiden.
―――― (1896-1898) *Wet en Adat.* Batavia.
―――― (1933) *Hoofdstukken over Adatrecht* (vol. 1). The Hague.
NOER, DELIAR (1973) *The Modernist Muslim Movement in Indonesia 1900-42.* Kuala Lumpur.
NOTOPURO, MH. HARDJITO (1969) 'Tentang Hukum Adat: Pengertian dan Pembatasan dalam Hukum Nasional.' *Hukum Nasional* 4: 36–59.
NOTOSUSANTO (1963) *Organisasi dan Jurisprudensi Peradilan Agama di Indonesia.* Jogjakarta.
PALMIER, L. H. (1960) *Social Status and Power in Java* (Reprint 1969). London.
PAÑGATO, H. S. (1960) 'Muslim Divorce Customs & Practices as recognized by Law.' *Far Eastern Law Review* 8: 481–505.
PEACOCK, JAMES L. (1973) *Indonesia: An Anthropological Perspective.* California.
PIGEAUD, THEODORE G. Th. (1962) *Java in the 14th Century: A Study in Cultural History* (5 vols.) 3rd ed. The Hague.

POEDJOSOEBROTO, R. SANTOSO (1964) *Jurisprudensi Indonesia.* Djakarta.
PRINS, J. (1951) 'Adat Law and Muslim Religious Law in Modern Indonesia.' *Die Welt des Islams* 1: 283–300.
——— (1954) *Adat en Islamietische Plichtenleer in Indonesië.* The Hague.
——— (1973) *Pengaruh Kristen Terhadap Hukum Adat.* Jakarta.
QUARITCH WALES, H. G. (1959) 'The Cosmological Aspect of Indonesian Religion.' *Journal of the Royal Asiatic Society*: 100–139.
RADCLIFFE-BROWN, A. R. (1935) 'Patrilineal and Matrilineal Succession.' *Iowa Law Review* 20: 286–303.
——— (1952) *Structure and Function in Primitive Society.* London.
RAZ, JOSEPH (1970) *The Concept of a Legal System.* Oxford.
——— (1971) 'The Identity of Legal Systems.' *California Law Review* 59: 795–815.
REDFIELD, R. (1964) 'Primitive Law.' *University of Cincinnati Law Review* 33: 1–22.
RESINK, GERTRUDES J. (1968) *Indonesia's History between the Myths: Essays in Legal History & Historical Theory.* The Hague.
ROSS, ALF (1968) *Directives & Norms.* London.
SALEEBY, N. (1905) *Studies in Moro History, Law, and Religion.* Manila.
SALMOND, JOHN (1957) *Jurisprudence* (11th ed.) London.
SAMSON, ALAN A. (1968) 'Islam in Indonesian Politics.' *Asian Survey* 8: 1001–1017.
SCHÄRER, H. (1963) *Ngaju Religion. The Conception of God among a South Borneo People.* The Hague.
SCHILLER, A. A. (1936) 'Native Customary Law in the Netherlands East Indies.' *Pacific Affairs* 9: 254–263.
——— (1942–43) 'Conflict of Laws in Indonesia.' *Far Eastern Quarterly* 2: 31–47.
——— (1955) *The Formation of Federal Indonesia.* The Hague.
——— (1956) 'Indonesian Law' in *Studies in the Law of the Far East and Southeast Asia*: 90–104. Washington.
SCHLEGEL, STUART A. (1970) *Tiruray Justice.* Berkeley.
SCHRIEKE, B. (1957) *Indonesian Sociological Studies, Part II: Ruler & Realm in Early Java.* The Hague, Bandung.
SELOSOEMARDJAN (1962) *Social Changes in Jogjakarta.* Ithaca.
SERI, MUSTOPA HUSIN (1970) 'Pasirah dan Pamong desa adalah Peleksana Hukum Adat dan Kepala Adat Pengadilan Perdamaian

tetap ada, jang dihapuskan Pengadilan Adat.' *Hukum Nasional* 8: 76–84.
SERIE, MUSTOPA HUSIN (1969) 'Tindjaun Mengenai Hukum pidana dalam K.U.H.P. dan Hukum Pidana Adat.' *Hukum Nasional* 5: 58–69.
SINGARIMBUN, MASRI (1965) 'Kinship and Affinal Relations among the Karo of North Sumatra.' Canberra: dissertation, Australian National University.
SLAMET, INA E. (1963) *Pokok-pokok Pembangunan Masjarakat Desa.* Djakarta.
SLAMET, M. (1939) 'De beteekenis van den term Adatrecht in de Wetgeving.' *Indisch Tijdschrift van het Recht* (supplemental volume) 151: 63–111.
SLAMETMULJANA (1967) *Per-Undang2-an Madjapahit.* Djakarta.
SMITH, J. C. (1968) 'The Unique Nature of the Concepts of Western Law.' *Canadian Bar Review* 46: 191–225.
SNOUCK HURGRONJE, C. (1893) *De Atjehers* (2 vols.) Leiden.
——— (1924) *Verspreide Geschriften* (4 vols.) Leipzig.
SOEBEKTI, R. (1970) 'Tata Hukum Nasional'. *Hukum Nasional* 10: 2–16.
SOEKANTO, SOERJONO (1969) 'Garis-garis Besar Hukum Perkawinan Adat Kebuayan Suay Umpu Mego-Pak Lampung Pepadon.' *Hukum Nasional* 5: 13–52.
——— (1972) 'Inheritance Adat Law in Indonesian Peasant Society.' *Malaya Law Review* 14: (2) 244–258.
SOEMARDJAN, SELO (1962) 'Land Reform in Indonesia.' *Asian Survey* 1: (2) 23–30.
SOEPOMO, R. (1952) 'Hukum Adat Dikemudian hari Berhubung Dengan Pembinaan Negara Indonesia.' *Hukum* 4/5: 3–18.
——— (1967) *Hukum Perdata Adat Djawa Barat.* Djakarta.
——— (1972) *Pertautan Peradilan desa Kepada Peradilan Gubernemen.* Djakarta.
SOERIPTO, K. R. M. H. (n.d.) *Hukum Adat dan Pantjasila dalam Undang2 Pokok Kekuasaan Kehakiman.* Universitas Negeri Jember: Fakultas Hukum.
——— (1973) *Hukum Adat dan Pancasila dalam Pembinaan Hukum Nasional Indonesia.* Universitas Negeri Jember: Fakultas Hukum.
——— (1973a) *Beberapa Bab Tentang Hukum Adat Waris Bali.* Universitas Negeri Jember: Fakultas Hukum.
SOETIKNO, IMAM (1971) 'Penjesuaian Hukum Adat Suku Dani Terhadap Hukum Negara Republik Indonesia.' *Hukum Nasional* 14: 20–50.

SOLUS, HENRY (1927) *Traité de la Condition des Indigènes en Droit Privé*. Paris.
STIRLING, PAUL (1965–66) 'Comment on the Legal Situation in Indonesia.' *Comparative Studies in Society and History* 8: 50–55.
STONE, JULIUS (1964) *Legal System and Lawyer's Reasonings*. Sydney.
SUBEKTI, R. & TAMARA, J. (1965) *Kumpulan Putusan Mahkamah Agung Mengenai Hukum Adat*. Djakarta.
SUNY, ISMAIL (1963) 'Legal Education in Indonesia.' *Far Eastern Review* 10: (4) 474–479.
SUPOMO, R. (1947) *Kedudukan Hukum Adat Dikemudian Hari*. Jogjakarta.
—— (1950) *Undang Undang Dasar Sementara Republik Indonesia*. Djakarta.
—— (1952) *Hubungan Individu dan Masjarakat dalam Hukum Adat*. Djakarta.
—— (1953) 'The Future of Adat Law in the Reconstruction of Indonesia' in Thayer (ed.) *Southeast Asia in the Coming World*: 217–235. Baltimore.
—— (1958) 'Adat Law in Indonesia.' *Revista Juridica de Buenos Aires* 1: 96–128.
—— (1965) *Sistim Hukum di Indonesia Sebelum Perang Dunia Ke. II* (7th ed.) Djakarta.
—— (1966) *Bab-bab Tentang Hukum Adat*. Djakarta (re-issue).
SUPRAPTO (1963) *Dasar Pokok, fungsi, Sifat-sifat dan bentuk Hukum Nasional*. (Palembang) *Seriwidjaja* No. IV.
SURYADARMAWAN, LOA (1962) *Himpunan Keputusan-keputusan dari Mahkamah Agung*. Djakarta.
SYED NAGUIB AL-ATTAS (1969) *A General Theory of the Islamization of the Malay-Indonesian Archipelago*. Kuala Lumpur.
TANNER, NANCY (1969) 'Disputing and Dispute Settlement among the Minangkabau of Indonesia.' *Indonesia* 8: 21–62.
TANNER, R. E. S. (1966) 'The Selective Use of Legal Systems in East Africa.' *E. Afr. Soc. Inst. Soc. Res. Conf.*, Jan., E: 966–977.
TASRIF, S. (1971) *Menegakkan Rule of Law dibawah orde baru*. Djakarta.
TAUFIK ABDULLAH (1966) 'Adat and Islam: an examination of conflict in Minangkabau.' *Indonesia* 2: 1–24.
TELUKI, A. (1966) *Perbbandingan Hak Milik Atas Tanah dan Recht van Eigendom*. Bandung.
TER HAAR, B. (1929) 'Western Influence on the Law for the Native Population' in Schrieke (ed.) *The Effect of Western Influence on the Native Civilizations of the Malay Archipelago*: 158–170. Batavia.

―――― (1937) *Het adatprivaatrecht van Nederlandsch Indië in Wetenschap, Practijk en Onderwijs*. Batavia.
―――― (1948) *Adat Law in Indonesia* (trans. Haas & Hordyk) with an introduction by E. A. HOEBEL & A. A. SCHILLER. New York.
UMAR, JUNUS (1966) 'The Payment of Zakat al-Fitrah in a Minangkabau Community.' *Bijdragen tot de Taal-, Land- en Volkenkunde* 122: 447–454.
UTRECHT, E. (1955) 'Resepsi Hukum Belanda.' *Hukum dan Masjarakat* 1: (2) 6–27.
―――― (1957) 'Hukum Pidana jang tidak tertulis.' *Madjalah Hukum dan Masjarakat* 2: (1) 19–26.
―――― (1959) *Pengantar dalam Hukum Indonesia*. Djakarta.
―――― (1969) 'Land Reform.' *Bulletin of Indonesian Economic Studies* 5: (3) 71–88.
VANDENBOSCH, A. (1932) 'Customary Law in the Dutch East Indies.' *Journal of Comparative Legislation and International Law* (3rd ser.) 14: 30–44.
VAN DEN STEENHOVEN, G. (1970) *The Land of Kerenda*. Nijmegen.
―――― (1973) 'Musjawarah in Karo-Land.' *Law & Society Review* 7: 693–718.
VAN DER KROEF, JUSTUS M. (1951) 'Indonesia and the Origins of Dutch Colonial Sovereignty.' *The Far Eastern Quarterly* 10: (2) 151–169.
―――― (1952) 'Society and Culture in Indonesian Nationalism.' *American Journal of Sociology* 58: 11–24.
―――― (1958) 'Religious Organization and Economic Process in Indonesia.' *Southwestern Social Science Quarterly* 39: 187–202.
―――― (1963) 'Peasant and Land Reform in Indonesian Communism.' *Journal of Southeast Asian History* 4: 31–67.
VAN DER MEULEN, J. C. (1924) *Het adatrecht der Inlanders in de Jurisprudentie, 1912–1923*. Leiden.
VAN DIJK, R. (1954) *Pengantar Hukum Adat Indonesia*. Bandung.
VAN HINLOOPEN LABBERTON D. (1933) *Dictionnaire de Termes de Droit Coutumier Indonésien*. Amsterdam.
VAN NIEL, R. (1964) 'The function of land rent under the cultivation system in Java.' *Journal of Asian Studies* 23: 357–376.
VAN VOLLENHOVEN, C. (1909) *Miskenningen van het Adatrecht*. Leiden.
―――― (1918) *Het Adatrecht van Nederlandsch Indië* — vol. I. Leiden.
―――― (1919) 'The Study of Indonesian Customary Law.' *Illinois Law Review* 13: 58–62.

——— (1921) 'Families of Language and Families of Law.' *Illinois Law Review* 15: 417–423.
——— (1931) *Het Adatrecht van Nederlandsch Indië*—Vol. II. Leiden.
——— (1933) *Het Adatrecht van Nederlandsch Indië*—Vol. III. Leiden.
VERGOUWEN, J. C. (1964) *The Social Organization and Customary Law of the Toba-Batak of Northern Sumatra* (trans. Scott-Kemball). The Hague.
VON WRIGHT, G. H. (1963) *Norm and Action*. London.
WAGENER, J. H. (1932) *De Verhouding tusschen het Nederlandsche en het Nederlandsche-Indisch Privaatrecht*. Utrecht.
WEATHERBEE, DONALD E. (1966) 'Traditional Values in Modernizing Ideologies: Indonesian example.' *Journal of Developing Areas* 1: 41–53.
WERTHEIM, W. F. (1964) *Indonesian Society in Transition*. The Hague.
WESTRA, H. (1939) 'Custom and Muslim Law in the Netherlands East Indies.' *Transactions of the Grotius Society* 25: 151–167.
WIDJOJOATMODJO, R. A. (1942–43) 'Islam in the Netherlands East Indies.' *Far Eastern Quarterly* 2: 48–57.
WIGNJODIPURO, SUROJO (1971) *Pengantar dan Azas Azas Hukum Adat*. Bandung.
WILKEN, G. A. (1921) *The Sociology of Malayan Peoples* (trans. Hunt). Kuala Lumpur.
WILLINCK, G. D. (1909) *Het Rechtsleven der Minangkabau Maleiers*. Leiden.
WIRJONO PRODJODIKORO (n.d.) *Hukum Antargolongan di Indonesia*. Bandung.
——— (1957) 'Case Note on Case No. 516/1955 G.' *Hukum* 1/2: 137–142 at 141–142.
——— (1959) 'Agrarian Law in Indonesia.' *Review of Contemporary Law* 6: 64–67.
ZORAB, E. A. (1954) 'De Rechtspraak van de derde Kamer (Adatkamer) van de Raad van Justitie te Batavia.' *Bijdragen tot de Taal-, Land- en Volkenkunde* 110: 132–153.

INDEX

ABENDANON, J. H. (cited), 89.
Acheh (Aceh), North Sumatra, 9, 29, 34, 36, 40.
Acheh law area, 30.
Adat: definitions of, 3–4, 28, 30, 33, 34–41, 52, 56, 66; sultanates and, 9–10; varied meanings of, 50, 51; in indigenous culture, 51–6; oral tradition of, 52–3, 67; and individuals' duties, 54; lack of data on, 113.
Adat courts, 100, 109–10.
Adat Katumanggungan, 38.
Adat law: variety of, 1; Dutch colonial policy towards, 1, 3, 11–20, 95–6; future of, 1–2, 152; applied to majority of population, 3, 20, 23, 25, 134; limited by legislation, 3, 10, 19, 26, 46, 63, 73, 114–15, 117, 119, 122, 128, 138; its place in the legal system, 4; to be proved by experts, 4; in villages, 7, 152; in Republic of Indonesia, 10, 20–9; Dutch scholars' studies in, 15, 16, 19, 21, 34–6, 41, 44, 50–1, 52, 53, 56–62, 66, 103, 110, 135; mainly unwritten, 20, 28, 52, 59, 64, 65, 104, 141; widow's inheritance in, 25–6; socially constructed, 33–48, 51, 53–4, 56, 57–9, 60, 63, 92, 93, 110, 119, 152; must be culturally confined, 35, 41; compromise important in, 42, 63, 105, 129; defined, 42–6; judicial decisions on, 48, 57, 61, 68, 129–35, 142; in legal thought, 50–1, 56–67; when servient to Dutch law, 52; and Islamic law, 59–60, 91–2, 94–5, 96–8, 100–9; produces many lawsuits, 66, 124, 137; in plural law system, 72–87; subject to civil courts, 100; 'living law', 103, 104, 110; and land, 104, 113, 115, 117–21, 136; some Muslims wish to abolish it, 107; Basic Agrarian Law and, 111–24, 131, 132, 139; conversion of rights in, 117; courts a source of, 127.
Adat Law School, 15.
Adat Minangkabau, 38, 50, 87, 92, 98, 104, 109, 149; texts and *perbilangan* of, 53.
Adat Parapatih, 37.
Adatrecht, 28, 30, 59–60, 63, 64, 152.
Adhi, Ida Bagus Ngurah (cited), 152.
Adiwinata, S. (cited), 32, 138.
Adviser on Arabian and Native Affairs, 95.
Agam, Sumatra, 37.
Agrarian Act of 1870 (*Staatsblad* 55 of 1870), 13, 82, 113, 125.
Ahmad Ibrahim (cited), 109.
Air, rights in, 116, 118.
Algemene Bapalingen van Wetgering (*Staatsblad* 23 of 1847), 71, 88.
Alisjahbana, S. Takdir (cited), 69.
Ambon Island, 39, 73, 153.
Ambon Moluccas law area, 30.
Anglo-American law, 62, 150.
Animism, 91.
Anthropology, 34, 108, 150.
Appeals, 17, 96, 100, 101, 127, 128.
Arabs in Indonesia, 71.
Arbitration, 54.
Arminjon, Pierre, 77; (cited), 89.

BADARUZZAMAN, NJ MARIAM DARUS (cited), 138.
Bali and Lombok law area, 30.
Bali Island: sultanate in, 9; *desa* in, 34, 40; texts in, 53; Islam not found in, 91; courts in, 127; adat

168 INDEX

in, 130; conciliation in, 142.
Bangka and Billiton Islands, 41, 127.
Bangka and Billiton law area, 30.
Banjermasin (Bandj-), Borneo, 97, 100, 101.
Banks, 73, 84.
Barkun, Michael (cited), 153.
Bartholomew, G. W. (cited), 89.
Basic Agrarian Law of 1960, 31; and adat, 3, 26, 43–4, 72, 111–24, 130–1, 132, 139; a step towards national law, 22, 26, 70, 82–3, 87, 110, 134; nuclear family in, 32; has abolished choice of law in land matters, 76.
Basic Laws of 1815 and 1855, 94.
Basic Provisions of Judicial Authority (1970), 100, 102.
Bastin, J. (cited), 29.
Batak territory, 34, 109, 132–3; people of, 38, 132–3.
Batavia, Java, 11, 14, 17, 77, 93, 127.
Batin people, 38.
Behaviour, 4; guided by law, 5, 7, 47, 58, 145, 147, 151; adat and, 27, 33, 51–2, 54.
Benda, Harry J. (cited), 29, 95, 109.
Bisschop, W. R. (cited), 30.
Black, Mary and Metzger, Duane (cited), 153.
Bodi-Chaniago adat system, 37.
Boerenbeker, E. A. (cited), 68.
Boland, B. J. (cited), 109.
Borneo (Kalimantan): sultanates in, 9; Dayak peoples of, 39; adat in, 41; religious courts in South Borneo, 97, 103; inheritance in, 101; leases in, 126; jurisdiction of Superior Court over, 127.
Borneo law area, 30.
Boru (*beru*) (clan receiving wives), 38.
Bukit Tinggi, Central Sumatra, 106.
Bureau (Directorate) of Religious Justice, 100.
Burridge, K. O. L. (cited), 153.

CARPENTIER ALTING, J. H. (cited), 49, 110.
'Case', analysis of, 143–5, 152.
Cassation, 20, 100, 128, 136, 137.
Cassutto, I. (cited), 89.
Celebes Islands, 9, 39.
Central and East Java law area, 30.
Ceram Island, Moluccas, 37.
Chairul Anwar (cited), 67.
Children: illegitimate, 76, 86; adopted, 88, 104, 134; as heirs, 104, 134.
Chinese in Indonesia, 16, 21–2, 70, 71, 84, 93; family law of, 23.
Choice of law, 76, 86, 101, 102, 103, 106.
Christianity, 75, 93, 98; Indonesian Christians, 71, 73, 86, 132–3.
Citizenship, 10, 25, 64, 70, 113, 119.
Civil Code, 19, 21, 22, 23, 24, 82, 84, 113, 117, 120; submission to, 85, 102.
Civilization: under French law, 19; served by law, 147.
Civil jurisdiction, 17, 18, 100, 127, 128.
Civil law, 6, 14, 16, 36, 56–7, 72, 81, 119, 129, 134; precedent in, 62.
Clans in adat, 34, 49, 107; non-localized, 34, 36–7; localized, 37, 39; regional communities of mixed, 37–8; patrilocal, 38.
Code of Police and Criminal Procedure (1848), 13.
Code of Procedure (1941), 129.
Codification: of law, 21–2, 23, 29, 31, 78, 87, 134; of adat, 27, 53, 54–5, 56–7, 62, 65, 67.
Colonial law: and adat, 24–5, 27, 63; partly retained after independence, 21–2, 23, 31, 62, 68, 111, 113, 117, 124; village justice under, 141.
colonial system: legal pluralism in, 1, 11, 16, 59, 63, 64, 66, 67; adat under, 1, 3, 9, 11–20, 42, 46–7, 56, 77; law in, 7–8, 57–9; established, 10; administration under, 12–13; Ethical Policy, 14, 95; and Islam, 16; colonialism,

INDEX

22, 23, 95; 'divide and rule', 59, 62, 70; introduces conflict of laws, 80; and modernization in Dutch Indies, 95; adat and Islam in, 106–7; and land, 113.
Commercial Code (1938), 16, 19, 22, 73.
Commercial law, 16, 22, 24, 87.
Commercial matters, 75–6.
Commissioner for Native Affairs, 11.
Common law, 62, 81, 83, 129.
Communities in adat, 52; regional, 34, 37–8, 39; territorialized kinship-based, 39; based on kinship, 39, 118, 141; *Gaukang*, 39–40; territorial, 40, 118, 141; territorially-based, 40–1; genealogical and territorial, 55; and land, 63, 82, 118, 120, 121, 130 (*see also* Clans: *Desa*: Tribes).
Comparative law, 45, 46, 48, 52, 144.
Compensation, 74, 115, 146, 153.
Compromise, 54, 97–8, 105, 106, 108.
Concepts: of law, 42–6, 48, 54, 57; in *fikh*, 92; in sociology, 148, 150, 151; of conflict, 148; of rights and obligations, 150.
Conciliation, 129.
Conflict of jurisdiction between Islam and adat, 100–4, 106.
Conflict of laws, 15, 21, 23, 43, 76–8, 80, 81; adat not to be administered if in conflict with other laws, 17; interracial, 56.
Conflict of principle, 80.
Congress of the Netherlands East Indies Jurists' Association (1877), 77.
Constitutions of Netherlands East Indies (*Indische Staatsregeling*): (1854), 13, 18, 19, 20, 46, 93; (1925), 18, 19–20, 30, 71, 72, 75, 88.
Constitutions of Republik Indonesia, 9, 10, 25, 46, 111; (1945–9), 21, 26, 31, 49, 71, 88, 111–12, 124, 128; Federal (1945–50), 21, 124; Provisional (1950–9), 21, 26, 30, 49, 124; Revived Constitution of 1945, 124.
Constitutions of the Netherlands: (1814), 12; (1848), 13.
Contract: of service, 19; choice of law in, 21, 84–5; sources of law on, 23–4; Djojodigoeno condemns freedom of, 28, 64; adat and, 43; usually governed by European law, 75–6; for sale of goods, 77; of marriage, 77; conflict of laws and, 80; of sale with right of repurchase, 85; under Basic Agrarian Law, 120; for sale of land, 133–4 (*see also* Labour contracts).
Contract of Work, 8.
Contracts Code, 22.
Conversion Provisions of Basic Agrarian Law, 117, 119, 125, 126.
Cooley, Frank L. (cited), 152, 153.
Corporations, 2, 8, 75.
Corruption, 24.
Court of Aldermen, 11.
Courts: may be influenced by social practice, 5; and plural law, 6–7; separate organization of, 17; a source of law, 24, 27, 127; and Supreme Court's decisions, 26; and adat, 44–5, 47, 66, 127–38; and conflict of laws, 82; classification of, 100–1, 127; adat and Islamic law in, 101; and judicial innovation, 134–5.
Cousins, marriage of, 107.
Criminal Code (1918), 30, 56.
Criminal Code for Natives (1872), 16.
Criminal jurisdiction, 12, 13, 17, 18, 100, 127, 128.
Crown Ordinances, 111; Crown Ordinances of 1875 and 1885, 14.
Culture: cross-cultural application of legal terms, 35, 43, 44–5, 49; cultural facts, 46–8; adat and, 50–6; Dutch culture needed for the modernization of Dutch Indies, 95; Western, 148.

INDEX

Custom, 7; adat as, 50, 92; contrasted with law, 146, 147.

DAENDELS, MARSHAL HERMAN W., 11, 94.
Damian, Eddy and Hornick, Robert N. (cited), 31, 109, 124.
Dayak peoples, 39.
Debt(s), 121; imprisonment for, 19; security for, 118, 121, 123; rural indebtedness, 123.
de la Porte, André, 19, 78; (cited), 49, 89, 90.
Departments, 112; of Education, Religion and Industry, 14; of Justice, 14; of Agriculture, 130 (*see also* Ministries).
'Depernas' (cited), 68.
Desa (village in Java, Sunda and Bali), 34, 40, 97.
Descent, 149, 150.
Development: economic, 2, 57, 115; legal, 4; the goal of law, 8; social and economic, 8, 43; of Islamic law, 32.
Diamond, S. (cited), 153.
Direct and indirect government under Dutch, 9, 10, 17–18.
Dispute settlement, 26, 53, 54, 141, 146, 148, 152.
District courts: Supreme Court and, 26, 136–7; jurisdiction of, 100, 101, 128–9; supervised by High Courts, 128; and mediation, 129, 140, 141; cases decided by, 131–2; and village justice, 140, 141–3.
Districts, 12, 13, 17; District Officers, 11–12, 14; District Judge, 17.
Divorce in Islamic law, 87, 92, 94, 96–7, 99, 100, 102–3.
Djakarta, 2, 21, 85.
Djojodigoeno, M. M., 21, 64–5, 66; (cited), 28, 30, 31, 32, 64, 65, 67, 68.
Djojodigoeno, M. M. and Tirtawinata (cited), 68.
Dominance among clans, 38.

Dominant and servient legal systems, 5, 24–5, 52, 57–8, 62, 65.
Dowry (*mahr*), 97, 100.
Draft Civil Code (1920), 16.
Draft Law on Contract, 23, 51.
Dutch, 9; and legal pluralism, 1, 63; create adat law areas, 1; dominate Indonesia, 10; their official attitude to adat, 11–20, 34, 36, 39–40, 56–7, 59, 62, 63; and Islam, 14, 93–4; introduce civil code into Dutch Indies, 23; their scholars' work on adat, 36, 56–62, 63, 67; and colonial law, 57; separate law for, 70; in mixed marriages, 86–7, 132 (*see also* Colonial system).
Dutch law, 11, 14, 36, 52; legal terms in, 49; and commerce, 71.
Duties, 54, 55, 150, 151 (*see* Obligation).

EAST SUMATRA, MALAYA AND WEST BORNEO LAW AREA, 30.
Economic: development, 2, 57, 115; sufficiency, 8; conditions, 17; equality, 66; obligations, 146, 147.
Education, religious, 98–9.
Efficacy of law, 4–5, 7 (*see* Validity of law).
Effluxion of time, 123, 131–2, 135.
Egalitarianism, 8, 25, 66, 115.
Eight Year Plan of 1960, 22, 110.
Emergency Law 1 of 1951, 129, 138, 152.
Enactment of 1874 (*Staatsblad* 94 of 1874), 19.
Enggano Island, off South Sumatra, 37.
English colonial law, 19, 81.
Enthoven, K. L. J. (cited), 68.
Epstein, A. L. (cited), 153.
'Equalization', 75.
Ethical Policy, 14–15, 95.
Ethics, 51, 54.
Ethnography of law, 141, 143–51.
Eurasians, 22.
Euri (regional community), 38.

INDEX

European courts, 127-8.
European land, 82, 117.
European law: adat subject to, 18-19, 46, 73; influences adat, 19, 73-4; submission to, 19, 75-6, 77, 83, 84, 85; usually governs commercial and labour contracts, 19, 21, 73, 76, 84; as source of law, 24; adat translated into legal concepts of, 30; contrasted with adat, 51, 55, 64, 81-2; municipal law in, 52; codification of, 56; may be applied to non-Europeans, 72-3; equal in status with Indonesian, 79; and land, 113 (*see* Civil law: Dutch law).
Europeans: separate laws for, 11, 16, 17, 71; extraterritoriality for, 18; their views on adat, 49, 52, 53, 55 (*see also* Dutch).
Exogamy, 36, 38, 107.
Explanatory Memorandum to Basic Agrarian Law, 114, 115, 116, 125.
Exploitation of land, 121, 130-1, 135.
Extraterritoriality, 18.

FAMILY: nuclear, 32, 49, 106, 107; extended, 49.
Family law: Muslim, 1, 2, 16, 19, 63-4, 75, 87, 103, 107; Chinese, 23.
Family planning, 66.
Farid, Andi Zainal Abidin (cited), 32.
Fatwa (legal opinion), 105.
Federation, 20, 62, 128; Federal Constitution (1945-50), 21, 124.
Fikh (jurisprudence), 53, 92, 108.
Flores Island, Lesser Sundas, 37.
Foreign corporations, 2, 8.
Foreign Orientals, 18, 70, 71.
Fortes, M. (cited), 153.
Fortune-telling, 93.
French colonies, 77, 79.
Furnivall, J. S. (cited), 12, 29.

GAMPONG (village in Acheh), 34.
Gaukang (kalompoan: arajang), 39-40, 49.

Gautama, Sudargo (cited), 31, 32, 69, 89.
Gautama, Sudargo and Harsono, Budi (cited), 31, 49, 88, 89, 125, 126.
Gautama, Sudargo and Hornick, Robert N. (cited), 88, 89.
Gautama, Sudargo and others (cited), 2, 8.
Gayo, Alas and Batak lands law area, 30.
Gayo people, 34, 36-7.
Geertz, Clifford (cited), 67, 109.
General Administrative Regulations, 111.
General Courts, 127.
Gifts, 97, 118, 132, 139.
Goadby (cited), 77.
Good faith, 133.
Gorontal (-alo), Celebes, 41, 136.
Gorontalo law area, 30.
Gouwgioksiong (cited), 31, 90, 138.
Government justice, 127.
Government Regulations, 112; no. 38 of 1960, 132; no. 56 of 1960, 110, 123, 124, 132; no. 10 of 1961, 117, 126; no. 224 of 1961, 124; no. 41 of 1964, 124.
Governor-General, 11; promulgates Regulations, 73, 94, 111.
Gray, John Chipman (cited), 62, 68.
Grotiud, Hugo (cited), 71.
Groves, William C. (cited), 153.
'Guided democracy', 22, 26.
Guyt, H. (cited), 68.

HAKIM, S. A. (cited), 69.
Hak milak (ownership), 118, 120.
Hak ulajat (communal right to dispose of land), 26, 44, 115, 126.
Han Bing Siong (cited), 30.
Harsono, Budi (cited), 118, 125.
Hart, H. L. A. (cited), 153.
Hazairin, 107-8; (cited), 32, 110.
Headman: of village, 12, 13, 136; of sub-clan, 36-7; of *nagari*, 37; in Bali, 40.
Herziene Indonesisch Reglement (*Staatsblad* 44 of 1941), 127, 129, 138.

High Courts: jurisdiction of, 100, 128–9; decisions of, 101, 132, 136, 139; adat cases form main part of work of, 137.
Hinloopen Labberton, D van (cited), 30, 67.
Hofsteede, W. M. F. (cited), 152.
Holleman, F. D. (cited), 68.
Hooker, M. B. (cited), 31, 54, 89, 126.
House of Representatives, 112.
Hukum adat, 63, 64.
Hukum hartabenda, 75–6.
Hula hula (clan providing wives), 38.
Husband and wife, 76, 77, 88.

IHERING (cited), 65.
Imprisonment, 74; for debt, 19.
Indian-derived traditions, 91.
Indians in Indonesia, 71.
Indies Juridical Conference (1939), 68.
Indirectly-governed territories, 127.
Indische Staatsregeling, 1925 (*Staatsblad* 415 of 1925), 18, 19–20, 30, 71, 72, 75, 88.
Individual: adat and, 33, 36, 61, 63, 64, 119; in contemporary Indonesia, 64; in Islam, 92; and conflict between adat and Islam, 98, 103; and land, 118–19; and culture, 152.
Indonesian legal language, 42–4.
Indonesian Marriage Law, No. 1 of 1974, 87.
Indonesians: Djojodigoeno on, 28, 64; like compromise, 105, 106.
Inflation and currency, 123, 133.
Inheemsche Rechtspraak in Rechtstreeks Bestuurd Gebied (*Staatsblad* 80 of 1932), 18, 128, 138.
Inheritance: no submission to European law over, 19, 75; by widow, 25–6, 134, 136; Islamic law modernized on, 32; adat and, 63; European can acquire adat land by, 82; under Islamic law, 94, 96; difference between adat and Islamic law of, 98, 101–2,

103–6, 107; of rights in land, 121, 130, 131–2.
International law, 113.
Inter-personal law, 24, 79.
Interracial and inter-religious marriage, 86–7, 132.
Interracial law, 15, 24, 72, 78–87.
Islam: in North Sumatran sultanates, 9; Dutch and, 14, 16, 93–6; and nationalism, 14, 94, 95–6, 98; influences some adat texts, 53; is a religious and political system, 91; strengthened under Japanese occupation and Republik, 98–9, 107; to be accepted whole or not at all, 104–5.
Islamic law, 20, 25; its law of inheritance modernized, 32; and adat, 59–60, 91–2, 94–5, 96–8, 100, 101–9; and witnesses to marriage, 75; and inter-religious marriages, 86, 87–8; courts and, 100–1; inheritance in, 101–2; proposals for reform of, 107–8.

JAKARTA, 136 (*see* Djakarta).
Jambi, Sumatra, 9, 38, 127.
Japanese occupation of Indonesia, 20, 23, 30, 59, 83, 98, 100, 107, 110.
Jaspan, M. A. (cited), 25, 31, 60, 68, 153.
Java, 71; sultanates in, 9, 35, 116, 125; Dutch administration in, 11, 12–14; under British, 11–12; Superior Court's jurisdiction over, 17, 127; federation and, 20; adat in, 34, 35; adat texts and proverbs in, 53; Christians in, 73; Islam and, 91–2, 97, 99–100, 102, 103; classification of depth of religious belief in, 92; religious courts in, 94, 100, 101; compromise between Islam and adat in, 97–8; transfer of land by will in, 120; sharecropping in, 122; conciliation in, 142.
Java: Central, 40, 64, 125; East, 40.
Jaya Song Decree, 9, 29.

INDEX

Jogjakarta and Surakarta law area, 30.
Jogjakarta principality, Java, 116, 125.
Josselin de Jong, J. P. B. de (cited), 30, 49, 60, 68, 153.
Jual (transfer), 42–3; jual janji, 126.
Judges: may be guided by social practices, 5; as legislators, 6, 19–20, 25, 46, 134, 152; in Native Courts, 17; how far bound by Civil Code, 23; and adat, 25, 60; value of decisions of, 27, 61, 65; as mediators, 42, 61, 129, 140, 141; Muslim, 94, 99; in Republik, 128 (see also Courts).
Judicial decisions: on adat, 3, 44, 48, 61, 68, 129–35, 142; publication of, 61, 66, 68, 108, 137; reference to rules and statutes in, 65, 68; Western law may influence adat through, 74; conflict of laws and, 76, 80; on adat and Islamic law, 108; cases outside administrative records of, 143–4.
Jurisdiction, disputes over, 128; between adat and Islamic law, 100–5.
Jurisprudence: (a) body of law, 33, 61; (b) judicial decisions, 48, 76, 137.
Jurisprudensi Indonesia, 137, 138.
Jurists, 17, 141; and adat, 4, 19, 27, 35, 50–1, 52, 56; and legal language, 42, 46; and precedent, 62; on the need to replace Western with indigenous law, 63, 66; on codification, 67; on the need for legal pluralism, 71; on the effect of European law on adat, 73; on conflict of laws, 77; on consistency of common law, 81; and court system, 136; and 'conflict', 139; and sociology, 151.
Justice: sense of, 23–4, 25, 28–9, 65; principles of, 46; social, 66; socialism and, 115.
Justice and equity, 18, 19; and good conscience, 6.

KABANDJAHE, North Sumatra, 142.
Kadi, 94; Kadi courts, 97.
Kahin, G. M. (cited), 68.
Kampuang (resident sub-clans), 37–8.
Karo-Batak people, 142.
Karo-land, North Sumatra, 142; Karo people, 141; adat in, 142.
Kartohadiprodjo, Soediman (cited), 31.
Kelsen (cited), 8, 45, 81.
Kinship groups in adat, 34, 35–6, 37, 38–9, 41, 42, 54, 82, 104, 149; and administration of justice, 7; and mediation, 140–1; obligations of, 146.
Koentjaraningrat (cited), 49, 67.
Koesnoe, Mohamed (cited), 31, 35, 49, 68, 69, 110, 138, 152, 153.
Kollewijn, R. D., 79; (cited), 78, 81, 88, 89.
Koran, 100, 105, 107, 108, 110.
Korinchi people, 38.
Korn, V. E. (cited), 67.
Kota-Piliang adat system, 37.
Krishnamurthy, S. (cited), 30.
Kuria, 34, 42.
Kusumadi Pudjosewojo (cited), 28, 64, 67, 68.

LABOUR CONTRACTS, 73, 76, 84.
Lampong Islands, South-east Sumatra, 36, 127.
Land: under Dutch rule, 1, 12, 13, 22, 82, 113; Regents' rights in, 11, 13, 34; Raffles and, 11–12; state-owned, 12, 13, 82; under Basic Agrarian Law, 26, 76, 82–3, 87, 112–18, 121, 124; adat rules for, 34, 37, 39, 40, 51, 55, 63, 73, 75, 104, 113, 115, 117–21, 136; maximum and minimum holding of, 112, 113, 116, 119; transfer of, 118–19; allocation of, 118–19.
Landgeracht (police court), 15.
Landgerichte (Native Court), 11.
Land pledging, 121, 122–4, 126, 131, 133.

174 INDEX

Landraad (Native Court), 10, 11, 12, 127, 140.
Land Reform Court, 138.
Land Registry Office, 117, 120, 123.
Law: definitions of, 3, 33, 35, 52, 135, 136, 145, 151, 152; efficacy of, 4–5; guides behaviour, 5, 7, 47, 145, 147, 151; institutional, 5–6, 7; state and, 5–6; whether must be acceptable to majority of nation, 22, 26, 45, 58, 66, 108, 153; oral, 28, 52, 59, 64, 65, 100, 104, 141; absolute, 54; Dutch theories on, 57; positive, 58, 60, 65, 66, 110; choice of, 76, 82–7, 101, 102, 103, 106; reform of, 107–8; uncertainty of contemporary, 113–14, 116, 120; contrasted with custom, 145–7, 148–50; and sociology, 149.
Law on the Abolition of Private Estates (1 of 1958), 125.
Law on the Conversion of Land Lease Regulations in the Principalities (13 of 1948), 125.
Law on the Supreme Court (13 of 1965), 100, 138.
Law Regulation for the Outer Territories, 1927 (*Staatsblad* 227 of 1927), 17, 127, 138.
Law reporting, 61, 66, 68, 108, 137.
Laws: no. 22 of 1946, 75, 99, 102; no. 32 of 1954, 102, 110; no. 45 of 1957, 103; no. 20 of 1964, 122; no. 2 of 1960, 122; no. 13 of 1965, 129; no. 28 of 1956, 130, 138; no. 7 of 1970, 138; no. 1 of 1961, 152.
Leases, 19, 121–2, 125.
Legal administrators, 34, 35, 42.
Legal personality, 8, 61.
Legal pluralism: in Dutch policy, 1, 11, 16, 59, 63, 64, 66, 67; practice is not law till recognized by courts, 5; courts may have to enforce oral law, 6; contemporary views on, 8, 21, 63; criminal law in, 14; relaxation of, 15; civil law in, 16–17; its effect on adat, 19, 56, 59, 72–87; groups based on, 22; defined, 43;

sovereignty of one system in, 62; adat and Islamic law in, 98–106; marriage and, 132–3.
Legal terminology, 43–6; in adat, 26, 34, 35, 36–40, 42–3, 119, 120–1, 122, 126; in Islamic law, 92, 108; sociology and, 143–4, 145, 147, 149.
Legislation, 3, 66; judges may act as legislators, 6, 19–20, 25, 46, 134, 152; modifies adat, 10, 17–20, 26, 46, 59, 73, 114–15, 117, 122, 128; *Volksraad* and, 15; civil law affected by new, 24; whether validates law, 56–8; helps to validate adat, 57; on adat and Islamic law, 108; under Republik, 111–12; to implement Basic Agrarian Law, 114, 117; establishes courts, 127; regulates courts' procedure, 129.
Leiden University, 15.
Lev, Daniel S. (cited), 22, 31, 49, 105, 110.
Levi, Edward H. (cited), 153.
Levy, R. (cited), 109.
Lex fori, 78–9.
Liaw, Yock Fang (cited), 67.
Limapuloh Kota, 37.
Lineage head, 37.
Logemann, J. H. A. (cited), 68.
Lombok Island, 9, 40, 127, 142.

McALEAVY, H. (cited), 126.
Macassar (Makasar), Celebes, 17; High Court of, 101, 133, 136, 139.
MacCormack, Geoffrey (cited), 153.
Madura, Java: Native Courts in, 17; Superior Court's jurisdiction over, 17, 127; Islamic law in, 20, 99, 101, 102, 103; *desa* in, 40; adat and Islamic law in, 94, 100.
Magic, 50, 51.
Maharun Batuah, A. M. and Bagindo Tanameh, D. H. (cited), 67.
Maine, Sir Henry, 33, 48.
Maintenance, wife's claim for, 100, 102.
Majapahit kingdom, Java, 9, 10, 91.

INDEX

Malay lands, 9, 34, 35, 41.
Malaysia, 50, 126.
Malinowski, Bronislaw, 27, 60, 146, 153.
Mare Liberum, 71.
Marga (an adat community), 37, 39, 42.
Marriage: mixed, 19, 77, 82, 86–7, 88, 132–3; in patrilocal clans, 38; adat rules for, 45; with European is a reason for submission to European law, 75; conflict of laws and, 79, 80; inter-religious, 85–6; in Islamic law, 92, 94, 96–7, 99, 100, 102–3, 107.
Marriage Enactment of 1929 (*Staatsblad* 348 of 1929), 96, 109.
Marriage Law, 134.
Marriage Ordinance for Christian Indonesians (*Staatsblad* 84 of 1933), 73, 86, 89, 90, 133, 139.
Mataram kingdom, Java, 9, 10, 29.
Matrilineal adat systems, 32, 34, 37, 38, 106, 107.
Mecca, pilgrimage to, 93.
Medan, North Sumatra, 17, 138, 139.
Mediation in adat, 54, 61, 63, 140.
Mendapo (an adat community), 38.
Mentawei Islands, off West Sumatra, 34.
Metzger, D. G. and Williams, G. E. (cited), 153.
Middle East, 91, 107.
Mieremet (cited), 152, 153.
Milik (ownership), 34, 119.
Military Courts, 138.
Minahasa law area, 30.
Minahasa Peninsula, Celebes, 39, 73.
Minangkabau law area, 30.
Minangkabau people, 86, 106, 148, 153.
Minangkabau territory, 34, 37, 38, 49, 97–8, 106, 108, 109, 119, 120.
Ministers: Regulations of, 112; of Agriculture and Agrarian Affairs, 117; of Internal Affairs, 117, 121.
Ministries: of Religion, 98–100, 102; of Justice, 100.

Mochtar Naim (cited), 49.
Modernization: of law, 1, 4, 80; and adat, 25, 57, 114, 129; Islamic law and, 32; social, 66; Dutch Indies and, 95; and economic and legal development, 134.
Moertono, Soemersaid (cited), 9, 29, 153.
Molucca Islands, 71.
Monogamy, 132.
Moore, Sally F. (cited), 48, 153.
Morality, 54–5, 146.
Mortgages, 73, 114, 117.
Muhammad Hasbi Ash-Shiddieqy (cited), 110.
Musjawarah (conciliation), 44, 141–2.
Muslims: and nationalism, 14, 94, 95–6, 98; jurisdiction over, 102–3; most Indonesians are, 104–5.

NADER, LAURA (cited), 49, 153.
Nagari (a regional community), 34, 37–8, 49.
Nagari Basa, B. (cited), 49.
Napoleonic wars, 11–12, 93.
Nasrun, M. (cited), 49, 109.
National Development Plan, 62.
Nationalism in Indonesia, 14–15, 20, 98.
Nationalization of Dutch businesses, 22.
National law, 1; does not admit social practice, 5; Djojodigoeno on, 21; in National Plans, 22, 62–3; is a possibility, 25; adat as basis of, 27, 124; Islam as, 32; cannot be rejected by followers of adat, 58; place of adat in, 67, 69; and courts, 134; *Jurisprudensi Indonesia* sets standards for, 137.
Native Civil Service, 14.
Native Courts, 12, 17, 94, 96, 127–8, 140.
Native states, 35, 140; Native States Regulation (1938), 30.
Natives, colonial power's duty to ensure welfare of, 12, 14, 95.

Natsir, M. (cited), 109.
Naturalization, 19.
Natural resources, 115.
Nature, adat and, 54, 55.
Nawawi (cited), 110.
Nederburgh, I. A., 19, 57, 59, 62, 78; (cited), 67, 89.
Negori (-ry), 39.
Netherlands, 12, 13, 14, 17, 111.
Netherlands East India Company, 11, 71, 93.
Netherlands East Indies: Japanese occupation of, 20; civil code in, 31; adat in, 36, 39, 56, 61, 94; law in, 57, 63; *adatrecht* in, 60; no rule of precedent in, 62; legal pluralism in, 70, 71; European and Indonesian laws have equal status in, 79; conflict of laws in, 81; Islamization of, 91; adat and Islamic law in, 93-8; land in, 119; courts a source of adat in, 127; village justice in, 140.
Neumeyer, M. H. (cited), 77.
New Guinea law area, 30.
Nias Island, off north west Sumatra, 38.
Noer, Deliar (cited), 109.
Normative systems, 89, 152; efficacy of legal norms, 4–7; adat derived from cultural norms, 28; norms do not exist independently of society, 33, 47; all law is formed into, 35, 47, 58; norms may be *of* or *for* behaviour, 52; individual as a point of normative reference, 54, 55, 61; law related to norms on which state's sovereignty rests, 57; common law and Dutch Indies' law contrasted as, 81; normative propositions in a sociological 'case', 145.
Notopuro, Muhamed Hardjito (cited), 32.
Notosusanto (cited), 110.

OBLIGATION: in adat, 2, 35, 51–2, 54, 55, 92; national law does not demand total change in, 8; obligations from a number of systems should not be mixed, 45; defined in terms of the individual, 61; identified by Dutch in terms of indigenous systems, 62; determined by individual's racial group, 70; rights and obligations of engaged persons, 88; Islamic law and adat contrasted over, 92; and land, 126; sociological theories on, 145–7, 150–1.
Occupation of land, 34, 119, 120.
Ordinances, 18, 111; Ordinance Concerning Registered Marriages (1937), 96; *Ordonnantie op de Dorprechtspraak* (*Staatsblad* 102 of 1935), 140, 152.
Outer Provinces (Territories), 14, 15, 17, 100, 102, 127.
Ownership of land, 42, 82, 117, 118–21, 124; adat and, 34, 113–14, 118–20; maximum and minimum limits of, 113, 116, 125; absentee landlords, 113, 116; owner must cultivate his land, 116, 122.

PADANG, Central Sumatra, 17, 106.
Palembang, South Sumatra, 9, 127.
Palewali, 131.
Pandjar (agreement for sale of land), 133–4, 139.
Pantjasila (Five Principles), 23, 27, 31, 49, 66.
Patrilineal adat systems, 25, 32, 34, 36, 38, 39, 105–6.
Penal Code: (1872), 14; (1918), 15.
Pencharian, 34.
Penghulu (Muslim judge), 20, 94–5, 96.
People's Assembly, 111–12.
People's Peace Congress, 49.
Perbilangan (adat sayings), 53.
Personal law, 22, 23, 81.
Pigeaud, Theodore G. Th. (cited), 9, 10, 29.
Poedjosoebroto, R. Santoso (cited), 138.
Police and Procedure Code for Natives and Foreign Orientals

INDEX

of Java and Madura (1848), 16.
Police courts, 15, 21.
Police matters, 12, 13.
Politics: and law, 4, 5, 7–8, 66, 87, 103, 108–9, 137; purpose of, 4; and adat, 9, 24, 26–7, 47–8; and adat terms, 44; Islam and, 99, 101, 106, 110.
Polygamy, 96, 132–3.
Possession of land, 34, 119.
Preanger, 40.
Precedent, 28–9, 61–2, 65, 81, 137, 145.
Pre-colonial era in Dutch Indies, 9–10, 52.
Prescriptions, 52, 53, 57.
Presidents, 111–12; Presidential Decrees, 112.
'Priests', Muslim, 14, 74, 94; *priesterraaden*, 94–5, 96.
Principles: adat as, 50; of adat, 53, 63, 65; of law, 63, 152.
Prins, J. (cited), 90, 100, 106, 109, 110.
Private international law, 77, 78–9, 81.
Private law, 70, 81, 85, 89, 147–8.
Priyayi, 11, 95.
Property, 2; adat rules on, 16, 22, 25, 26, 34, 42, 54; widow and, 25; transfer of, 42–3, 132; movable, 92; in Islamic law, 97, 100, 103–4.
Proverbs, adat law contained in, 53.
Provisional People's Congress, 27.
Provisional People's Consultative Assembly, 62.
Provisional People's Deliberative Council, 134.
Pubian clans in Lampong, 36–7.
Public interest, adat may be disregarded in, 18, 20.
Punishment, 146–7.
Pusaka (ancestral land), 119, 142.

RACE: and legal separatism, 1, 11, 12, 70, 71, 82; and land, 1, 12, 82–3, 88, 113.
Radcliffe-Brown, A. R., 60; (cited), 146, 149, 153.

Raffles, Sir Stamford, 11–12, 13.
Raz, Joseph (cited), 8, 48, 153.
Rechtskringen (adat law areas), 1, 10, 16, 30, 34, 49, 62, 79.
Rechtsreglement Buiteengewesten (*Staatsblad* 227 of 1927), 127, 138.
Recognition money, 121, 126.
Reconciliation in marriage, 99, 100, 102–3.
Redfield, R. (cited), 153.
Regeling op de Gemengde Huwelijken (*Staatsblad* 158 of 1898), 76, 77, 85–7, 89, 90.
Regents, 11–14, 96; Regency judges, 17; Regency Courts, 21.
Regeringsreglement: (1815), 12, 94, 109; (1818), 12; (1836), 13; (1854), 13; (1855) (*Staatsblad* 2 of 1855), 71, 88.
Registration: of land, 82, 117, 120, 126; of marriage, 87, 96, 99–100; of divorce, 99–100; and choice of law, 103; of sales, 120; of land pledges, 123; and adat, 138.
Regulation: on Duties of Resident and Regent (1867), 14; of Native Justice in Directly Governed Territory (1932), 17, 30; Governing the Voluntary Acceptance of European Private Law (*Staatsblad* 12 of 1917), 19, 30; for the Administration of Justice in the Outer Territories, 31, 142, 152; on Native Corporations (*Staatsblad* 569 of 1939), 73, 89; on Native Associations (*Staatsblad* 570 and 571 of 1939), 73, 89; on Indonesian mortgages (*Staatsblad* 542 of 1908), 73, 89; for Commissaries-General (1818), 93; on Court Organization and the Administration of Justice (1808), 94; *Hoof voor Islamietische Zaken* (*Staatsblad* 116 of 1937), 96, 109; for Religious Justice outside Java (*Staatsblad* 638 of 1937), 96, 109.
Regulations, 111; of a Minister, 112; of the Minister of Agrarian

178 INDEX

Affairs (no. 14 of 1961), 125, 126, 131, 139; of the Minister of Internal Affairs (no. 1 of 1967), 126.
Religion, 146; adat and, 51–2; freedom of, 93, 95, 98, 99.
Religious Affairs Officers, 98.
Religious (Islamic) Courts, 73, 87–8, 92, 96, 99, 138; law on (*Staatsblad* 53 of 1931), 73, 89; and secular courts, 87, 100–2, 103–5.
Rent for land, 12.
Republik Indonesia: 'New Order' in, 8, 24; adat in, 9, 10, 43–4, 56, 62–7, 75–6; some of its law disregarded by rural population, 22, 26, 45, 66, 108, 153; and test of legal validity, 46; law-population divisions in, 70; adat and Islamic law in, 101; courts a source of adat, 127; courts in, 128–9, 141; village justice in, 140, 141.
Repudiation of marriage, 92, 99, 100.
Repugnancy law, 19.
Residents, 12–13, 14; Residencies, 11, 98, 127; Residency Courts, 17.
Responsibility, individual and collective, 147–8.
Revised Native Regulations (1941) (*Staatsblad* 44 of 1941), 16, 17, 30.
Revolutionary outlook in Indonesia, 44, 47–8, 66.
Rights and duties, 54, 63, 88, 145–6, 149, 150, 151.
Ritual and ceremonial, 50; ritual obligations, 146.
Ross, Alf (cited), 153.
Royal Decrees, 111; of 1917 (*Staatsblad* 12 of 1917), 75, 89; of 1870 (*Staatsblad* 118 of 1870), 82, 90.
Rukunan (compromise), 41, 47.
Rules, in sociology, 150, 151.
Runggun adat (dispute settlement), 141–2.
Rural population: and adat, 2; and law, 103, 153; indebtedness of, 123.

SADAN TORAJA PEOPLE, 39.
Sale: of land, 42–3, 120, 123; of rights in land, 121, 123, 131.
Sanction: and law, 35, 145–6; and adat, 53, 54, 60, 61.
Sapir, Edward (cited), 46.
Sarekat Islam movement, 95–6.
Sasak people, 142, 152.
Sawah (wet rice land), 131, 132, 139.
Scandinavian Realists, 153.
Schiller, A. A. (cited), 1–2, 8, 30, 31, 80, 89, 109, 138.
Scholars: and adat, 1–2, 15, 16, 19, 36, 42, 50, 52, 53, 56–62, 59, 66, 67, 149; Islamic, 95; and sociology, 143–51; and law, 145.
Secular courts, 108; and religious, 101–4.
Security for debt, 2, 118, 121, 123.
Self-governing territories, 10, 21, 116, 127–8; Self Government Regulations (1938), 18.
Selosoemardjan (cited), 31, 125.
Sengkang, 133.
Shafi'i school of Islamic law, 107, 110.
Sharecropping, 122, 126.
Shari'a (Islamic law), 91, 97, 103.
Short Contract, 14.
Singarimbun, Masri (cited), 152.
Slamet, M. (cited), 67, 68.
Slametmuljana (cited), 10, 29.
Smith, J. C. (cited), 49, 153.
Snouck Hurgronje, Christiaan, 95, 96–7; (cited), 29, 59, 67, 68.
Socialism: equivalent to communism, 8; in Netherlands, 14; in Indonesia, 44, 48, 49, 66, 115.
Social needs, 18, 20; social objectives, 3–4, 7–8, 10, 66, 107, 115.
Social practice: and law, 4, 5–6, 7; social function and land, 26, 115.
Social structure: adat based on, 33–48, 51, 53–4, 56, 57–9, 60, 63, 92, 93, 110, 119, 152; Islam and, 91, 107; law based on, 145, 151, 152; sociology and, 149.
Sociology: its terminology applied to adat, 36, 42; important for study of adat, 48; and studies of

(a) adat, 50, 51 (b) adat and Islamic law, 108 (c) village justice, 141; and legal validity, 57; defines (a) law, 59, 151 (b) adat, 60; its concept of conflict, 148–9.
Soebekti, R., 137; (cited), 31.
Soekanto, Soerjono (cited), 49.
Soekarno, President Ahmad, 22, 23, 111, 124.
Soepoemo, R. (cited), 49, 68, 152.
Soeripto, K.R.M.H. (cited), 31, 49, 152.
Soetikno, Imam (cited), 69.
Solus, Henry, 77, 79; (cited), 89.
Sources of law, 6, 7, 24, 47, 57, 65, 92, 97, 152; courts as, 24, 27, 127 (*see also* Legislation).
South Celebes law area, 30.
South-East Asia, 118, 123.
South Sumatra law area, 30.
Sovereignty: of sultans, 10, 57; adat and state sovereignty, 55, 56–9, 62, 67, 115; Islam and state sovereignty, 93.
Srivijaya kingdom, Sumatra, 91.
Staatsblad: 94 of 1874, 19, 30; 152 of 1882, 94, 100, 109; 63 of 1937, 100, 109; 482 of 1932, 109; 53 of 1931, 109.
State: and law, 5–6, 135; and adat, 9–29, 56–9, 63, 66–7, 114–15, 119; and land, 12, 13, 82, 119, 121, 127; sovereignty of, 55, 56–9, 62, 67, 115; can be sued, 83; makes grants of land, 121.
Status, 8, 33, 54.
Statutes: of Dutch Parliament, 111; of Republik, 112, 128, 137.
Stirling, Paul (cited), 31.
Stone, Julius (cited), 153.
Sub-clans, 36, 37.
Subekti, R. and Tamara, J. (cited), 126, 138, 139.
Submission: to European law, 75–6, 102; to religious courts, 105.
Succession to property, 2, 110, 121, 149.
Sufi mystics, 91.
Suharjo, 22.

Suku (kinship group), 37, 38, 42.
Sultanates, 9–10, 53, 57.
Sumatra, 9, 14, 53, 71; North, 9, 36, 91, 142; South-east, 36; Central, 37; South, 39, 102, 126; East, 41.
Sunda Islands, 34.
Sunni schools of law, 107.
Superior Courts, 17, 127; Superior Native Courts, 17, 127.
Supernatural, adat and the, 53.
Supomo, R., 28, 63–4, 107; (cited), 31, 67, 68, 110.
Suprapto (cited), 69.
Supreme Court, in Dutch Indies, 11, 17.
Supreme Court, in Republik: jurisdiction of, 20, 100, 128–9; declares Civil Code abolished, 23; circular letters of, 23, 72, 88, 112, 128, 136; out of touch with popular feeling, 26, 136; and lower courts, 26, 135, 136–7; initiates legal change, 47, 134–6; decisions of, 49, 72, 84, 85–6, 101–2, 103, 120, 123, 126, 130–3, 135; Supreme Court Law (1 of 1950), 129, 138; publishes law reports, 137, 139.
Surakarta principality, Java, 116, 125.
Suryadarmawan, Loa (cited), 138.

TANAH DATAR, West Sumatra, 37.
Tanner, Nancy (cited), 110, 153.
Tanner, R. E. S. (cited), 153.
Tasrif, S. (cited), 3, 8.
Taufik Abdullah (cited), 19, 110, 153.
Taxation, 9, 12, 29.
Ter Haar, B.: and administration of justice, 18, 127, 140; recognizes importance of adat law, 21, 47, 61; opposes unification of adat law, 27–8; on adat communities, 34, 36–41; on legal terminology, 42–3, 44, 144; defines adat, 61–2, 66; believes adat to be based in social structure, 65; on Islamic and adat law, 107; on

adat land tenure, 104, 113, 118, 119, 125; (cited), 30, 36–41, 48, 49, 67, 68, 73–4, 89, 110, 125, 126, 138, 139, 153.
Ternate Archipelago law area, 30.
Ternate Island, Moluccas, 9.
Territorial communities in adat, 34, 35–6, 39–41, 42, 55.
Texts, 10, 52–3.
Tidore Island, Moluccas, 9.
Timor Archipelago law area, 30.
Timor Islands, 9, 20.
Toba-Batak people, 53, 105, 110, 146, 152.
To Mori people, 39.
Toraja Territory law area, 30.
Tradition, 82; in adat, 1, 2, 26, 53, 59, 62, 63, 106; Indonesians respect, 28, 64; traditional legal systems, 80; Indian-derived, 91; and land, 118, 119–20; basis of customary sanctions, 146–7.
Transfer of property, 42–3, 132.
Tribes: localized, 38–9; territorially based, 39.
Tribunals, 47; in villages, 7, 140, 141, 142; indigenous, 11; classification of, 17; religious, 94 (*see* Courts).

ULIASER ISLANDS, 39.
Umpama, 53.
Unification: of law, 16–17, 20, 21–2, 23, 70, 80, 87, 88; unified law, 8, 29; of judicial administration, 20; of adat, 27–8; rejected by Dutch, 57; of Islamic inheritance law, 104, 110.
Unitary state, 10, 20; unitary law, 16, 20, 27.
'Unlawful acts', 83–4.
Urban population, 1–2, 95, 103, 106.
Usage, 45, 53, 64; adat as, 50, 92.
Usufruct, 119, 120, 126.
Utrecht, E. (cited), 90, 124.

VALIDITY: of marriage, 75, 86, 87; of status, 100; of sociological concepts descriptively, 149; of village justice, 152.
Validity of law, 5, 56–7, 108; of adat, 3, 42, 61, 106; prescriptive and descriptive, 3, 7–8, 57–60, 80, 106, 108; social practice and, 5; can be tested in courts, 46; state and, 135.
van den Berg, L. W. C., 77–8.
Vandenbosch, A. (cited), 30.
van den Steenhoven, G., 31; (cited), 49, 141–2, 152, 153.
van der Kroef, Justus M. (cited), 29, 30.
van der Meulen, J. C. (cited), 68.
van Dijk, R. (cited), 67.
van Niel, R. (cited), 29.
van Vollenhoven, C.: recognizes importance of adat law, 15, 21, 47; opposes Westernization of law, 16, 19, 78; opposes unification of adat law, 27; defines adat, 27, 63, 66; and sanction in adat law, 35; on legal terminology, 44, 144; on validity of law, 57–61, 65; on Islamic and adat law, 107; on adat land tenure, 118–19; and legal administration, 104; (cited), 29, 48, 49, 67, 68, 110, 126, 152, 153.
Vergouwen, J. C. (cited), 49, 110, 146, 152, 153.
Villages: justice in, 7, 18, 21, 97, 140–3, 145–6, 150, 152; basic unit of administration, 12, 13, 49; cultivation in, 15; and adat, 34, 65, 97.
Vital spirits, 39.
Volksraad (Parliament), 15.
von Wright, G. H. (cited), 81, 89.

WAGENER, J. H. (cited), 89.
Wagering, 73.
Waqaf (religious trust), 99.
Water, rights in, 115, 116, 118.
Wattensoppeng, Celebes, 132, 139.
Weatherbee, Donald E. (cited), 30.
Weber, Max (cited), 149.
Wertheim, W. F. (cited), 49, 94, 109.

INDEX

Westernization, 15, 16, 19, 78.
Western legal systems: as models, 1–2, 8, 15, 18, 22, 28, 65, 66–7; municipal law in, 6, 44, 52, 58, 150; codification in, 15, 22, 29, 65, 67; their influence on adat, 19, 57, 73–4; individuals in, 28, 33, 48; compared with adat, 33, 63, 64; legal terminology of, 35; language theory in, 45; precedent in, 65; and conflict of laws, 98; Islamic law and, 107; its jurisprudence and ethnography, 151 (*see also* Colonial law: Dutch law: European law).
West Java law area, 30.
Westra, H. (cited), 96, 109, 110.

Widjojoatmodjo, R. A. (cited), 88, 93, 109.
Widow, and inheritance, 25–6, 134, 136.
Wignjodipuro, Surojo (cited), 69.
Willinck, G. D. (cited), 31.
Wirjono Prodjodikoro, 23, 31; (cited), 25, 67, 90, 125.
Witnesses: expert, 4; to marriage, 75, 133.
Women: equal rights for, 25; and division of property after divorce, 103; in patrilineal communities, 105–6.

Zelfbestuursregelen (*Staatsblad* 529 of 1938), 128, 129, 130, 142, 152.